The
Principal's
BOOK OF LISTS

◆ ◆ ◆ ◆ ◆

Robert D. Ramsey, Ed. D.

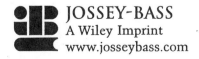
JOSSEY-BASS
A Wiley Imprint
www.josseybass.com

Published by Jossey-Bass
A Wiley Imprint
989 Market Street, San Francisco, CA 94103-1741   www.josseybass.com

Library of Congress Cataloging-in-Publication Data

Ramsey, Robert D.
    The principal's book of lists / Robert D. Ramsey.
      p. cm.
    ISBN 0-13-447749-9
    ISBN 0-7879-6661-4 (layflat)
    1. School management and organization—United States—Handbooks,
manuals, etc.   2. School principals—United States—Handbooks,
manuals, etc.   3. School principals—United States—Miscellanea.
I. Title.
LB2801.A2R35   1996   96-28871
371.1'012—dc20

FIRST EDITION
Copyright 10 9 8 7 6 5 4 3 2 1

Section III. Curriculum, Evaluation, and Staff Development 97

Section IV. Athletics and Activities 175

Section V. Discipline 205

Section VIII. Legal Matters *315*

Section IX. Parent/Community Relations and Communications *327*

Section X. Personal and Professional Wellness _355_

Section XI. Miscellany 391

Section One

ADMINISTRATION AND LEADERSHIP

1. 6 RULES FOR PRINCIPALS

Rule 1. Listen to parents; they're the kids' first teachers.

Rule 2. If it's good for kids, it's good.

Rule 3. If there's no fun, there's not much lasting learning either.

Rule 4. Kids are more important than teachers.

Rule 5. Teachers are more important than principals.

Rule 6. Principals are only important if they help kids and teachers.

2. ELEMENTARY PRINCIPAL — LIST OF DUTIES AND RESPONSIBILITIES (SAMPLE)

1. Provide key leadership in establishing the vision and mission of the school and in formulating strategic plans to support school goals.

2. Provide strong instructional leadership for the development and implementation of a well-balanced curriculum that meets the needs of all pupils.

3. Be familiar with current understandings of child development and learning theory.

4. Assume primary responsibility for creating a positive school climate where all children can learn and succeed.

5. Assume ultimate responsibility for student discipline and safety.

6. Work with district administrators in the recruitment, selection, and assignment of all school personnel.

7. Assume ultimate responsibility for the supervision and evaluation of all personnel in the school.

8. Implement appropriate building-level staff development programs as needed.

9. Work with staff and parents to develop appropriate and meaningful school policies, procedures, and regulations.

10. Oversee the proper maintenance and use of school facilities and equipment.

11. Assume responsibility for developing and monitoring an annual school budget and for implementing appropriate systems of internal control and recordkeeping.

12. Communicate fully with parents on all matters affecting the education and welfare of their children.

13. Provide leadership and support for parent groups such as the PTA, PTO, PAC (Parent Advisory Council), or Site Management Council.

14. Establish procedures to assure continuous evaluation and improvement of all school programs and services.

15. Perform other duties as assigned by designated supervisor(s) or the Superintendent.

3. SECONDARY PRINCIPAL — LIST OF DUTIES AND RESPONSIBILITIES (SAMPLE)

1. Provide key leadership in establishing the vision and mission of the school and in formulating appropriate strategic plans to support school goals.

2. Provide strong instructional leadership in the development, implementation, coordination, and evaluation of a balanced curricular and cocurricular program to meet the needs of all students.

3. Assume primary responsibility for creating a positive schoolwide climate that promotes effective teaching and learning.

4. Work with district administrators in the recruitment, selection, and assignment of all personnel.

5. Assume overall responsibility for the supervision and evaluation of all school personnel.

6. Initiate and implement appropriate staff development programs for all categories of employees as needed.

7. Assume responsibility for the formulation, implementation, enforcement, and review of appropriate school procedures, rules, and regulations.

8. Assume ultimate responsibility for student discipline.

9. Oversee proper maintenance and improvement of all school buildings, grounds, and equipment.

10. Assume responsibility for developing and monitoring an annual school budget and for implementing appropriate systems of internal control and recordkeeping.

11. Foster a climate of positive school-community relations, provide full and complete information to the community about school programs, and involve the community and its resources in the educational program.

12. Perform other duties as assigned by designated supervisor(s) or the Superintendent.

4. ASSISTANT PRINCIPAL — LIST OF DUTIES AND RESPONSIBILITIES (SAMPLE)

1. Serve as advisor to the Principal.

2. Assume primary responsibility for the discipline and attendance of designated students.

3. Provide leadership and supervision for the student activity program (secondary).

4. Assist with the selection, supervision, and evaluation of school personnel with special responsibility for clerical, custodial, security, and food service staff members.

5. Serve as office manager for the Principal's office.

6. Serve as liaison to designated departments (secondary).

7. Assist in the formulation of school policies, rules, and regulations.

8. Supervise the preparation and distribution of all school handbooks and policy manuals.

9. Assume fiscal responsibility for the school's activity and auxiliary funds (secondary).

10. Represent the school at designated events and functions.

11. Act as Principal in the absence of the Principal.

12. Perform such other duties as assigned by the Principal.

5. WHAT DOES A PRINCIPAL DO? (CHILD'S VIEW)

(Student comments reprinted from the October 1980 issue of *Know Your Schools*, St. Louis Park, MN, Public Schools' community newsletter.)

"The Principal is the owner of the school."

"(The Principal) tells the children to go home."

"If you're lost, (the Principal) shows you the way."

"(The Principal) talks to bad kids and asks them why they did it."

"(The Principal) makes the school tidy and stops fights."

"(The Principal) does very hard work and works hard at it."

"(The Principal) makes sure no one climbs the walls."

6. SOME NEW ROLES FOR SCHOOL PRINCIPALS

Changing times and a changing youth agenda make new demands on school leaders. In addition to the traditional caretaking roles as managers of budgets, buildings, and buses—and keepers of discipline— today's elementary and secondary principals are being called on to assume new responsibilities as identified below:

Champion of Children First. Children and youth aren't doing very well in American society. Look at the record: high infant mortality rate, child abuse, missing children, teenage crime and violence, teen pregnancy, runaways, adolescent drug use. With the disintegration of parenting, dysfunctional families, loss of sense of community, and poor public policy, children and teenagers are at risk more than ever before. We must focus again on producing leaders and contributing citizens. Society needs someone to champion the cause of strengthening families and putting children first if we are to have a better tomorrow. If school leaders don't do it, who will?

Dream Catcher. Through visioning and strategic planning, today's principals are expected to help shape a dream of the school's future. More than ever before, effective principals have to be able to instruct and inspire pupils, parents, and the public about the possibilities of what their school can become.

Prospector. Principals in the 1990s need a radar for resources. Because of continuing downsizing, budget cuts, and fiscal constraints, educational leaders now have to scratch and claw for sufficient resources to maintain and improve school programs. Through nontraditional fund raising, creative reallocation of resources, and aggressive "partnering" with businesses and other organizations, principals have to find new ways to supplement normal funding sources. Being "resourceful" has taken on new meaning for today's elementary and secondary principals.

Counselor Without Portfolio. Principals don't have to be lawyers, but they do have to be aware of the labyrinth of legal pitfalls confronting school personnel and other professionals. School leaders must know how to buffer staffs from potential litigation and to operate the school within constantly shifting legal parameters. Matters of curriculum, instruction, and student discipline shouldn't have to be settled in the courts. Savvy principals will keep educational decision-making within the educational community.

Mosaic Maker. Schools are more diverse and inclusive than ever before. It's up to the principal to help staff and community members accept today's classroom—one that is multicultural and accessible to students with disabilities—and to make diversity a strength, rather than an excuse. Differing individuals and groups within the school can remain fragmented, or they can be blended into a meaningful human mosaic. Principals and teachers have to be mosaic makers today.

7. QUALITIES OF SUCCESSFUL ELEMENTARY AND SECONDARY SCHOOL PRINCIPALS*

1. Genuine compassion for kids, and passion for teaching and learning.

2. A clearly defined vision for the school.

3. Ability to inspire and instruct.

4. Planning, prioritizing, and organizing skills.

5. The goal-setting habit.

6. Communication skills (written, verbal, nonverbal, and listening).

7. Commitment to excellence.

8. A philosophy of empowerment.

9. Ambiguity tolerance (capacity to live with partial fulfillment and unsolved problems).

10. Comfort with chaos (ability to face and manage change).

11. An antenna for anticipating problems.

12. "Street smarts" and political savvy.

13. Ability to remain in touch with reality.

14. Capacity to release the abilities of others.

15. Ability to manage and move beyond disappointment.

16. Confidence tempered with humility.

17. Self-discipline and self-control.

18. Energy and enthusiasm.

19. Determination to maintain a balanced life.

20. Commitment to lifelong learning.

21. Optimistic view of the future.

22. Courage to be authentic.

23. A preference for proaction.

24. Motivational and "selling" skills.

25. Willingness to take risks and make mistakes.

26. A "people first" attitude.

27. Capacity to work with diverse individuals and groups.

28. Empathy for the challenges and frustrations of parenthood.

29. Negotiating skills.

30. Comfort with ever-changing technology.

7. QUALITIES OF SUCCESSFUL ELEMENTARY AND SECONDARY SCHOOL PRINCIPALS*,
CONTINUED

31. An open leadership style and a capacity for self-disclosure.

32. Skill in problem-solving and conflict resolution.

33. Flexibility and adaptability.

34. Willingness to take responsibility, give credit, and accept blame.

35. Team-building capabilities.

36. Imaging and rehearsal skills.

37. Impatience with second-rate efforts and commitment to continuous improvement.

38. Greater interest in getting results than in controlling.

39. Resiliency (an ability to bounce back and to remember the good times in the bad times).

40. Absolute integrity (a fierce commitment to honesty and truthfulness in all dealings).

41. Exuberance for life and the principalship!

*Note: No priority is intended or implied.

8. RECURRING MONTHLY ACTIVITIES FOR PRINCIPALS

A typical Principal's monthly activities include:

- Identification of Goals and Setting of Priorities for the Month.
- Classroom Visitations and Follow-up Conferences with Teachers.
- Staff Reminders (Discipline Policy, Attendance and Tardy Procedures, Substitute Teacher Plans, etc.).
- Review of Monthly Check List and Tickler Files.
- Reservation of Time for Brainstorming and Future Planning.
- Implementation of One "Crazy Idea" to Improve the School.
- Weekly Bulletins for Staff.
- Fire Drill.
- Student Assemblies, Pep Fests, etc.
- Walk-through of Facilities with Head Custodian to Identify Physical Plant Needs.
- Faculty Meeting.
- PTA/PTO, Parent Advisory Council (PAC) and/or Site Council Meeting(s).
- Department/Grade Level Meetings.
- Student Council Meeting.
- Mentoring Meeting with Probationary Staff.
- District Administrators' Meeting.
- School Board Meetings.
- Dissemination of Parent Newsletter.
- Publication of Student Newspaper.
- Press Releases for Local Newspaper.
- Review and Follow-up on Bus Violations.
- Review of Eligibility Lists (secondary).
- Attendance at Athletic Contests (secondary).
- Spot-check of Expenditure Budget Accounts and Response to "Red Flag" Items.
- Compilation and Submission of Monthly Attendance Report.
- Hosting of Parent Coffee Hours.
- Saturday Open-door Public Office Hours (once each month).
- Publication of Monthly Lunch Menus.
- Review of Progress Toward Annual Building Goals.
- Checkup of Status of Ongoing and Ad Hoc Committees.
- Update of Office Bulletin Board.
- Posting of Upcoming Events on Outdoor Display Board.
- Recognition of "Student of the Month."

9. (PRINCIPAL'S MONTH-BY-MONTH CHECKLIST) *JULY*

(The following check list reflects a typical Principal's schedule. Precise calendars will vary from school to school.)

_____ Important dates/events.

   • Independence Day (4)

_____ Complete staffing, scheduling, and assignment of students for coming year.

_____ Finalize School Calendar for coming year.

_____ Finalize building goals for coming year.

_____ Review/revise school policies.

_____ Complete and submit State Reports.

_____ Review changes in Master Contracts for all employee groups.

_____ Analyze past year's discipline referrals.

_____ Prepare new staff packets.

_____ Develop field trip schedule for coming year.

_____ Summer Curriculum Writing.

10. (PRINCIPAL'S MONTH-BY-MONTH CHECKLIST) *AUGUST*

(The following check list reflects a typical Principal's schedule. Precise calendars will vary from school to school.)

_____ Important dates/events.

• National Night Out Against Crime (in participating communities)

_____ Complete Summer Curriculum Writing.

_____ Summer school ends.

_____ Prepare back-to-school communications (students, staff, and parents).

_____ Prepare school opening press release for media.

_____ Publicize bus schedule.

_____ Check birth and vaccination certificates (school nurse or health aide).

_____ Finish back-to-school workshop plans.

_____ Meet with new PTA officers to plan year.

_____ Schedule year's social activities for students.

_____ Athletic practices begin (secondary).

_____ Check/test bell signal system.

_____ Establish fire drill schedule (minimum of 9 per year).

_____ Recruit parent volunteers.

_____ Identify room mothers.

_____ Compile directory information.

_____ Organize student groups (i.e., bus patrol, student council, etc.).

_____ Make locker assignments.

_____ Make homeroom assignments.

_____ Assign lunchroom periods.

_____ New staff orientation.

10. (PRINCIPAL'S MONTH-BY-MONTH CHECKLIST) *AUGUST,* CONTINUED

_____ Orientation for reserve teachers (substitutes).

_____ Back-to-school workshop for teachers.

_____ Final check of buildings and grounds.

_____ New student orientation.

_____ School begins (in some states).

11. (PRINCIPAL'S MONTH-BY-MONTH CHECKLIST) *SEPTEMBER*

(The following check list reflects a typical Principal's schedule. Precise calendars will vary from school to school.)

_____ Important dates/events.

- Labor Day (first Monday)
- Rosh Hashanah (Jewish holiday—dates vary)
- Yom Kippur (Jewish holiday—dates vary)
- Citizenship Day (17)

_____ Badges to new staff.

_____ Make schedule and class adjustments as needed.

_____ Set up classroom visitation schedule.

_____ Schedule faculty, department, grade level, and other regular meeting dates.

_____ Bus safety training for students.

_____ Establish emergency calling tree.

_____ Meet with Social Committee to plan year's activities for staff.

_____ Reestablish Business-Education Partnerships.

_____ Collect premiums for optional student accident insurance.

_____ PTA-PTO membership drive.

_____ Report first week's daily attendance to District Office.

12. (PRINCIPAL'S MONTH-BY-MONTH CHECKLIST) *OCTOBER*

(The following check list reflects a typical Principal's schedule. Precise calendars will vary from school to school.)

_____ Important dates/events.

- Columbus Day (second Monday—Monday Holiday Bill)
- United Nations Day (24)
- Halloween (31)
- State Teachers Convention (in many states)
- Fire Prevention Week
- Return to Standard Time (Turn clocks back one hour)

_____ School pictures.

_____ Annual Fund-raising Event (e.g., magazine sales drive).

_____ Parent Open House.

_____ Student Council elections.

_____ Homecoming (secondary).

_____ Capital budget requests due.

_____ Prepare for National Education Week.

_____ PSAT Testing (secondary).

13. (PRINCIPAL'S MONTH-BY-MONTH CHECKLIST) *NOVEMBER*

(The following check list reflects a typical Principal's schedule. Precise calendars will vary from school to school.)

_____ Important dates/events.

- Veterans Day (11)
- Election Day (first Tuesday after the first Monday)
- Thanksgiving (fourth Thursday)
- National Education Week (celebrated in many districts)
- Chemical Health Week (celebrated in some districts)

_____ Last chance to drop classes with no failure (secondary).

_____ End of quarter.

_____ Honor Roll.

_____ Report Cards.

_____ Parent-Teacher Conferences.

_____ Winter sports begin (secondary).

14. (PRINCIPAL'S MONTH-BY-MONTH CHECKLIST) *DECEMBER*

(The following check list reflects a typical Principal's schedule. Precise calendars will vary from school to school.)

_____ Important dates/events.

- Christmas (25)
- Hanukkah (Jewish holiday—dates vary)

_____ Complete first semester teacher evaluation conferences and reports.

_____ Solicit input in preparation for next fiscal year's budget.

_____ Conduct midyear assessment of physical plant and capital equipment needs.

_____ Locker checks and clean-out.

_____ Holiday staff party.

_____ Make appointment for annual physical examination.

_____ Winter break.

15. (PRINCIPAL'S MONTH-BY-MONTH CHECKLIST) *JANUARY*

(The following check list reflects a typical Principal's schedule. Precise calendars will vary from school to school.)

_____ Important dates/events.

   • New Year's Day (1)
   • Martin Luther King, Jr., Birthday Observance (Monday Holiday Bill)

_____ Initiate goal-setting for the following year.

_____ Initiate follow-up study of previous students.

_____ Finalize midyear changes (new hires, class or schedule adjustments, etc.).

_____ Make plans for kindergarten round-up and preschool screening (elementary).

_____ Career Day (secondary).

_____ College Financial Aid meeting (secondary).

_____ Standardized Testing Program.

_____ Orientation for new staff members.

_____ End of semester.

_____ Honor Roll.

_____ Report cards.

16. (PRINCIPAL'S MONTH-BY-MONTH CHECKLIST) *FEBRUARY*

(The following check list reflects a typical Principal's schedule. Precise calendars will vary from school to school.)

_____ Important dates/events.

- Valentine's Day (14)
- Susan B. Anthony Birthday (15)
- President's Day (Monday Holiday Bill)
- Black History Month
- Chinese New Year
- Purim (Jewish holiday—dates vary)

_____ Begin plans for graduation (secondary).

_____ Student/Parent Information Meetings on registration for coming year (secondary).

_____ Complete registration and enrollment for coming year (secondary).

_____ Pride Week (Spirit Week) activities.

17. (PRINCIPAL'S MONTH-BY-MONTH CHECKLIST) *MARCH*

(The following check list reflects a typical Principal's schedule. Precise calendars will vary from school to school.)

_____ Important dates/events.

- St. Patrick's Day (17)
- Women's History Month
- Easter (varies between March and April)

_____ Vision, hearing, and scoliosis screening.

_____ Spelling Bee.

_____ Student Science Fair.

_____ Initiate preparation of building orders and requisitions for coming year.

_____ End of quarter.

_____ Honor Roll.

_____ Report cards.

_____ Spring Parent-Teacher Conferences.

18. (PRINCIPAL'S MONTH-BY-MONTH CHECKLIST) *APRIL*

(The following check list reflects a typical Principal's schedule. Precise calendars will vary from school to school.)

_____ Important dates/events.

- Easter (varies between March and April)
- Return to Daylight Savings Time (set clocks ahead one hour)
- National Volunteer Recognition Week
- Arbor Day

_____ Immunization clinic (elementary).

_____ Build Master Schedule for coming year (secondary).

_____ Complete Graduation arrangements (secondary).

_____ Standardized Testing Program.

_____ Spring sports begin (secondary).

_____ Tornado drill (where applicable).

_____ Finalize Summer School plans.

_____ Recommend any terminations or nonrenewal of probationary personnel.

19. (PRINCIPAL'S MONTH-BY-MONTH CHECKLIST) *MAY*

(The following check list reflects a typical Principal's schedule. Precise calendars will vary from school to school.)

_____ Important dates/events.

- May Day (1)
- Cinco de Mayo (5—Hispanic Celebration)
- Mother's Day
- Memorial Day

_____ Parent visitations to identify teacher preferences for coming year (elementary).

_____ Set Final Examination schedule.

_____ Check status of probationary students and inform parents of possible failures.

_____ Solicit dates for next year's school calendar.

_____ Conduct awards programs/assemblies (athletic, academic, fine arts, etc.).

_____ Initiate parent opinion survey for school improvement.

_____ Finalize Graduation plans, including all-night senior party (secondary).

_____ Call for final reports from all ongoing and ad hoc committees.

_____ Locker clean-out.

_____ Get teachers' summer addresses.

_____ Prepare building year-end report.

20. (PRINCIPAL'S MONTH-BY-MONTH CHECKLIST) *JUNE*

(The following check list reflects a typical Principal's schedule. Precise calendars will vary from school to school.)

_____ Important dates/events.

- Anne Frank Day (12)
- Flag Day (14)

_____ Final examinations.

_____ Honor retirees.

_____ Recognize (celebrate) volunteers and reserve teachers (substitutes).

_____ SAT Testing (secondary).

_____ Sign diplomas (secondary).

_____ End-of-school picnic.

_____ Confer with students who will not graduate (secondary).

_____ Baccalaureate Service (secondary—where allowed).

_____ Graduation (secondary).

_____ School out for students.

_____ Collect teacher job targets for coming year.

_____ Closing staff workshop.

_____ Check in teacher materials/supplies.

- Record books
- Permanent record cards
- Dental and health cards
- Keys
- Lists of failures

_____ Honor Roll.

_____ Mail year-end report cards.

_____ Summer School begins.

_____ Conduct year-end inventory of textbooks, supplies, and equipment.

20. (PRINCIPAL'S MONTH-BY-MONTH CHECKLIST) *JUNE,* CONTINUED

_____ Complete book orders and supply requisitions for coming year.

_____ Close out and audit financial records.

_____ Review summer maintenance, repair, remodeling, and groundskeeping schedules.

_____ Summer curriculum writing begins.

_____ Review/revise student and parent handbooks.

21. BACK-TO-SCHOOL STAFF INFORMATION CHECKLIST

(Schools are among the few institutions in society that start fresh every year. Principals must remind both veteran staff and newcomers of important policies, procedures, and other routine information AT THE BEGINNING OF EVERY SCHOOL YEAR! The following is a typical list of topics that should be reviewed annually.)

Staff Information Check List

_____ Building emergency procedures

_____ Blue Alert Team procedures

_____ Suicide Prevention/Intervention Guidelines (if applicable)

_____ Fire drill information for students

_____ Medical information on selected students (from nurse or health aide)

_____ Insurance options for students at parents' cost

_____ Directory information guidelines for parents and right to exclude names

_____ Guardian/Parent procedures for picking up children during school

_____ Substitute teacher procedures

_____ Sexual harassment policy, definitions, and reporting procedures

_____ Policies on alcohol, tobacco, and drugs

_____ Student rights and responsibilities

_____ Staff Handbook (if applicable)

_____ Student Handbook (if applicable)

_____ Parent Handbook (if applicable)

_____ Building telephone calling tree

_____ Important school calendar dates

_____ Required communication with parents

_____ PTA/PTO information

_____ Grading and reporting policy and guidelines

21. BACK-TO-SCHOOL STAFF INFORMATION CHECKLIST, CONTINUED

_____ Curriculum and scope/sequence guides (if applicable)

_____ School discipline plan

_____ Attendance and absence procedures

_____ Master Contract requirements

_____ Reminder of employee forms/information to be submitted to Personnel
(e.g., insurance)

22. THE PRINCIPAL'S AUDIENCES

Principals deal with a broader range of the public than most leaders in other fields. Success depends largely on how skillfully school leaders can play to these diverse audiences and orchestrate the dynamic interaction among these forces in and outside of the school. The primary audiences that must be addressed by every Principal include:

Students
Parents
Faculty/Employees
District Administrators
Local School Board
City Leaders
Taxpayers
Family
Friends
Feeder Schools
Alumni
Preschool Parents (elementary)
Accrediting Associations
State Departments/Boards
Labor Unions
Athletic Boosters (secondary)
Legislatures
General Public
Media
Federal Government
Professional Organizations
Universities/Colleges
Social Service Agencies
Businesses/Employers
Athletic League/Conferences (secondary)
Health Department
Contractors
Chamber of Commerce
Fire Marshals
Code Inspectors
Realtors
Police
Neighbors Around the School

23. SUCCESS SECRETS FOR WORKING WITH THE SUPERINTENDENT

- Get reports in on time.
- Admit mistakes promptly. (Don't pass the buck.)
- Alert the Superintendent to problems-in-the-making. (Superintendents don't like surprises.)
- Make friends with the Superintendent's Executive Assistant or Secretary. (This is one of the most valuable allies a Principal can have.)
- Don't "bad-mouth" the Superintendent behind his or her back. (It may come back to haunt you.)
- Give the Superintendent some credit for your school's successes.
- Handle problems at the building level.
- Don't bypass the Superintendent to deal directly with School Board members.
- Don't make promises you can't deliver.
- Keep the Superintendent fully informed of developments (good and bad) in your building.
- Don't seek favors or preferential treatment.
- Stay on budget.
- Limit comments to the media. Let the Superintendent be the spokesperson for the school district.
- Be informal when appropriate—but be professional at all times.
- Be a team player.
- Be honest and tell the truth.
- Be upbeat. (Winners refuse to be negative.)
- Don't exceed the bounds of your authority or level of responsibility. (Never take unauthorized actions.)
- Give your Superintendent something to laugh about once in a while.
- Remember, the boss isn't always right; but the boss is always the boss.
- Do your job right—every time!

24. DO'S AND DON'TS FOR GETTING ALONG WITH OTHER PRINCIPALS AND ADMINISTRATORS

1. Don't try to play "one-upmanship" with other administrators.

2. Share ideas and programs freely.

3. Stay away from cliques and factions.

4. Praise other principals and schools freely.

5. Avoid use of gossip, rumor, or innuendo.

6. Use humor to defuse tense situations.

7. Don't make a habit of complaining about the District Office.

8. Admit mistakes and be willing to show your vulnerability.

9. Don't abandon a colleague in trouble. (The tables may be turned someday.)

10. Be passionate about kids!

25. WHY THE SCHOOL'S CULTURE MUST BE A PRIORITY FOR ALL PRINCIPALS

Cultivating the culture of the organization is a major function of effective school leaders. Following are ten reasons why the culture of the school must be at the top of every Principal's agenda:

1. The culture sets standards of performance, productivity, and expectancy.

2. The culture defines what "quality" means in the organization.

3. The culture provides meaning and fosters fulfillment.

4. The culture transforms a random group (or a mob) into a smoothly functioning team.

5. The culture can make effort and commitment a cultural imperative.

6. The culture transforms the whole into something greater than its individual parts.

7. The culture defines how people treat each other in the organization.

8. The culture sends a message about the place and the people in it.

9. The culture provides support and rewards.

10. The culture is guardian of the organization's values.

26. 25 ELEMENTS OF AN EFFECTIVE SCHOOL CULTURE

Part of being a Principal is nurturing the culture of the organization. No school can out-perform its own beliefs, expectations, and mores. Here's what an effective school culture looks like:

1. People are there because they want to be.

2. Students and teachers think what they're doing is important.

3. Strangers can feel the excitement in the building.

4. Students and teachers share high standards and a commitment to excellence.

5. The atmosphere is encouraging and supportive.

6. Individuals and groups are productive—not just busy.

7. People care about each other and are nice to each other.

8. There is freedom from fear.

9. People are free to make mistakes.

10. Everyone is a cheerleader for everyone else.

11. People get second chances.

12. People know about the history and heroes of the organization.

13. The school has clear goals and everyone knows what they are.

14. There are lots of celebrations. (People celebrate mistakes, as well as successes.)

15. Most people are upbeat and optimistic.

16. Students and adults are fiercely loyal to the organization.

17. There aren't many rules.

18. Collaboration is more important than competition.

19. People radiate a "modicum of cockiness."

20. Honesty is a priority.

21. People don't have to be alike to be liked.

22. Students and teachers have fun—every day!

23. Change and creativity are valued.

24. Risk-taking is not only allowed, but encouraged.

25. Students and teachers feel they have latitude in achieving goals.

27. SIGNS OF A NEGATIVE SCHOOL CLIMATE

- Absenteeism (student and staff) is high.

- Above-average discipline referrals, suspensions, and expulsions.

- Boredom is a habit.

- Teacher transfer requests are common.

- Labeling students is a common practice.

- "Lounge talk" is bitter and pessimistic.

- Adult concerns take precedence over student needs.

- Punishment is a frequent topic of conversation.

- Fear is a strategy.

- Both students and staff members use words such as "tension" and "impersonal" to describe the school's atmosphere.

- Favoritism is blatant.

- Tracking is the preferred way of doing business.

- Property damage and destruction are common.

- Laughter is a rare occurrence.

- Sleeping students and sleepy teachers are common sights.

- Teachers use the curriculum as a weapon (e.g., extra homework, lower grades, etc.).

- Few parents ever show up at school unless summoned.

28. AN INFORMAL MORALE AUDIT
(SYMPTOMS OF A NEGATIVE SCHOOL CULTURE)

Scoring: Even one check mark is too many.

_____ The rule book is thicker than the curriculum guide.

_____ Teachers don't know students' names.

_____ Buildings and grounds are littered and unkempt (and nobody cares.)

_____ Sexist and racist graffiti are commonplace.

_____ Lots of students are failing.

_____ Everyone complains about paperwork.

_____ There are lots of closed doors.

_____ Disrespect is commonplace.

_____ Students and teachers admit they are afraid.

_____ There is little or no socializing among staff members.

_____ Union reps are frequent visitors.

_____ It's hard to find anyone reading for fun.

_____ Profanity has become accepted.

_____ Violence is increasing.

_____ Participation in athletics and other activities is declining.

_____ It is common knowledge that there are weapons on the campus—every day.

29. SCHOOL VISION STATEMENT
(A SAMPLE STATEMENT OF VISION, VALUES, AND BELIEFS)

We believe in the following fundamentals:

- SUCCESS—All people can learn and learning should be lifelong. Everyone should experience success and be duly recognized. Such success is essential to self-actualization and development of a positive self-concept. Our goal is a program and environment that yield "zero rejects."

- EXCELLENCE—We believe that our school has achieved excellence and can achieve eminence. Our goal is to be the best we can be.

- SERVICE—The whole community is our customer and our sole purpose is to serve; thus, we value parental and community involvement. Getting along with people is the single most important talent we bring to our profession.

- EMPOWERMENT—We believe in empowering people, decentralizing decision making and fostering opportunities for growth for all students and staff.

- CULTURE—The culture of the organization is an important and powerful variable that should be nurtured and celebrated in order for our schools to be healthy, happy, and productive places to live and learn.

- TEAMWORK—We are one another's greatest strength and all are accountable for organizational outcomes. Collaboration, congeniality, open communication, caring, listening, and loyalty are essential to the success of our schools.

- EVALUATION—Evaluation should drive instruction to meet individual student needs and maximize mastery learning. Effective evaluation and the proper use of results can enable us to reallocate limited resources to accomplish desired goals.

- THE FUTURE—We have a positive view of the future and believe we can create such a future. It is our job to model this belief for our students, our community, and ourselves.

(The above visioning statement has been adopted by the St. Louis Park, MN, Public Schools.)

30. BUDGET DEVELOPMENT CALENDAR
(EXAMPLE)

January—Principal and staff identify building goals and priorities for coming year.

February–March—Individual grade level teams and/or departments develop budget requests to support building goals.

April—Principal reviews individual requests in light of building goals and previous budget allocations and formulates overall school budget for submission to district office.

May—District administration reviews proposed building budgets and formulates districtwide budget for recommendation to School Board.

June—School Board approves budget.

A.S.A.P.—Principals and staffs are informed of final budget allocations.

Ongoing—Individual budgets are monitored and adjusted according to changing needs.

31. TIME LINE FOR LAYOFFS (SAMPLE)
(UNREQUESTED LEAVE PLACEMENT/ PROBATIONARY
TEACHER NONRENEWAL)

When budget reductions and enrollment declines necessitate teacher layoffs, attention must be paid to all applicable statutes and contract provisions (seniority clauses). Principals are advised to seek legal counsel as laws vary by state. The following sample calendar illustrates due process procedures required in many states.

February—School Board sets staffing level for coming year.

March—Secondary Principals identify specific staffing needs based on student registrations for coming year. Elementary Principals verify enrollment projections.

— Principals issue *informal notice* of *proposed* unrequested leave placement/probationary nonrenewal.
— School Board acts to *propose* unrequested leave placement/probationary nonrenewal.
— Principals hand-deliver notice of Board action.
— Question-and-answer session for affected teachers.

April—Termination Hearings (if requested by affected teachers).

May—FINAL BOARD ACTION on unrequested leave placement.

— Principals hand-deliver final notice of unrequested leave placement.
— District personnel provide outplacement counseling and assistance.

32. TIME LINE FOR REGISTERING AND SCHEDULING SECONDARY STUDENTS
(EXAMPLE)

Parents and students (junior and senior high) frequently complain about having to sign up for classes months in advance. Nevertheless, early registration is essential to effective and timely scheduling of secondary students. The calendar below is typical of the process in many secondary schools across the country.

January—Provide registration orientation to all students, emphasizing course requirements and curriculum changes (new courses).

— Provide orientation to incoming students from feeder schools.

February—Conduct parent meetings to inform and answer questions regarding registration for the coming year.

— Students make course selections for coming year.

March–April—Tally student course selections.

May—Develop Master Schedule based on preliminary tally of student course selections.

June—Schedule all secondary students.

July—Make any necessary changes in Master Schedule and individual student schedules.

August—Distribute individual student schedules.

— Last opportunity for students to make course changes.
— Make any final adjustments or schedule changes.

September—Classes start.

33. STEPS IN STRATEGIC PLANNING (SAMPLE)

(Specific strategic planning models vary from district to district. The planning cycle outlined below can serve as a prototype.)

Step 1—The School Board, working with stakeholders and others, conducts an internal and external scanning process to identify "what is" and "what could be."

Step 2—The School Board uses the results of the scanning process to create the "vision of a preferable future" and to craft a mission statement for the schools.

Step 3—The School Board sets priorities for the coming school year designed to fulfill the mission and advance the organization toward the vision.

Step 4—Principals and staffs develop building goals for the year in accord with the district priorities. Each building goal should be accompanied by a Learner Impact Statement (similar to an Environmental Impact Statement) spelling out how students will be positively affected.

Step 5—Administrators and teachers define specific departmental/grade level strategies and individual job targets to achieve building goals.

Step 6—Building staffs implement planned strategies.

Step 7—Building staffs evaluate progress and measure achievement of goals.

Step 8—District administration reports to the School Board on progress toward priorities, and on existing gaps between the desired future and the current status of implementation.

Step 9—The School Board makes any necessary midcourse corrections and redefines priorities for the next year.

Step 10—The cycle is repeated (Steps 4–10).

34. REQUISITION CALENDAR (EXAMPLE)

(Making sure that every classroom has necessary materials and supplies requires an orderly process for purchasing and ordering these items. The time line below is representative of such a system.)

March 15—A standard list of general supplies will be distributed for consideration of quantities.

March 25—A list of last year's periodicals and newspapers will be distributed to assist in determining selections.

April 1—A standard list of elementary and secondary art supplies will be distributed for consideration of quantities.

— Industrial art supply needs should be submitted on proper requisition form.

April 15—Submit classroom and office furniture needs on designated requisition form. Please indicate color preference. (Capital items will be ordered pending approval of the capital expenditure budget by the School Board.)

— Supplemental art supplies not included on standard art supply list (e.g., clay, craft items, drafting items) should be submitted on requisition form.

— A standard list of science supplies will be distributed for consideration of quantities.

— Recommended cut-off date for orders from current-year budget. Requisitions received after this date will be applied to next year's budget.

April 30—Submit elementary and secondary physical education supply needs on requisition form.

— Submit home economics supply needs on requisition form.

— Submit secondary textbook orders on requisition form.

— A standard list of health supplies will be distributed for consideration of quantities.

— *All other categories of elementary and secondary orders should be submitted on requisition form. (April 30 is the recommended cut-off date for next-year orders. Receipt will not be guaranteed for beginning of the coming school year on requisitions received after this date.*

Notes—Standard lists will be distributed only to people who have received them in the past. If there is a category you have not received but feel you should, please contact the business office.

— Items submitted on requisitions will be combined with other orders when possible to get the best price for the District. For this reason, you may see a change in vendor or brand.

35. CONSIDERATIONS AND CRITERIA FOR MAKING SCHOOL COST REDUCTIONS

Budget reduction is always a painful process. Having a plan can help. The following suggestions have guided many school leaders in making tough budget cuts:

- Start early. Have a time line and stick to it.

- The school's vision, mission, belief statements, and goals should determine budget priorities.

- Involve all stakeholders in the process, but leave the final decisions to those who can be held accountable.

- Be open, honest, and upfront throughout the process. (Don't make promises you may not be able to keep.)

- Avoid simplistic across-the-board reductions. (Not all programs are equal.)

- Cut first as far away from instruction (the classroom) as possible.

- Cut things before people; but don't kid yourself. Education is a labor-intensive industry. Significant savings always require layoffs.

- Allow no "sacred cows." All areas and programs should be subject to scrutiny, with survival depending on merit.

- Begin by eliminating programs and services that are offered or available elsewhere (i.e., from city recreation programs, YMCA, etc.).

- Consider long-term as well as short-term impacts of cuts under consideration.

- Follow negotiated contracts meticulously. Seniority provisions often dictate the order of layoffs.

- Accept reality; increasing class size is the *only* way to save big bucks in most school districts.

- Consider revenue-raising measures, along with budget reductions.

- Look for efficiencies before effecting more drastic economies.

- Ask if programs or services can be scaled back, rather than eliminated entirely.

- Don't be fooled into thinking that cuts in curriculum development and staff development are "painless." Every retrenchment has impact. These may be among the last areas you want to cut.

- Consider offering programs on alternating years, rather than eliminating them completely.

- Realize that the administrator will be everybody's "whipping boy." Administration should be cut; but always retain sufficient leadership to carry on business with surviving programs and services.

- Preserve enough communication staff to tell the school's story throughout the reduction process and beyond.

- Identify more cuts than you need. If things get worse, you don't want to have to start all over.

36. 5 TESTS OF AN EFFECTIVE MASTER SCHEDULE (SECONDARY)

In many secondary schools, the master schedule drives much of what happens to and with students every day of the year. The following tests can help determine whether or not you have a user-friendly and workable schedule of classes:

1. Required courses are spread evenly throughout the day.

2. Conflicts among singletons (courses offered only once a day) are kept to a minimum.

3. Either-or choices are reduced by minimizing conflicts between competing elective courses.

4. Time of day has been considered. (Don't put all of the most difficult courses at the end of the day.)

5. Space usage and traffic patterns have been considered. (Don't overschedule one part of the building while other areas remain relatively empty.)

37. CRITERIA FOR ASSIGNING ELEMENTARY PUPILS TO CLASS SECTIONS

The following factors should be considered in assigning elementary pupils to specific teachers and classes:

Parent preference (if any)
Student preference (if any)
Previous teacher recommendations
Compatibility of teaching and learning styles
Friendships
Separation of twins and siblings
Family history with a given teacher
Balance of ability levels
Racial and gender balance
Equity in assigning behavior problems
Distribution of leadership
Student and teacher interests/talents
Feuds
Rivalries
Prejudices
Personality clashes
Receiving teacher's feelings and preferences
Hunches and "gut feelings"

38. EASY WAYS FOR PRINCIPALS TO PRACTICE "MWWA"
(MANAGEMENT WHILE WALKING AROUND)

Good principals don't lead from behind the desk or at the end of the intercom. They go where the action is.

In the corporate world, respected CEOs have practiced "management while walking around" (MWWA) for some time. They make it a point to be out and about maintaining close contact with staff and customers.

In the complex structure of today's schools, MWWA has also become an element of effective administration. Being visible isn't easy. It requires time and takes saying "no" to lots of other tasks and activities that can get between the leader and the "real world" of the school. It's worth the effort.

Even the busiest principal can find ways to practice MWWA; the following examples may be helpful:

- Schedule daily "visibility time" to spend in the halls before and after school.

- Eat lunch with students and teachers.

- Supervise study hall occasionally.

- Hang out in the teacher's lounge.

- Load buses.

- Help serve lunch.

- Chaperone parties.

- Go on student field trips.

- Visit game practices and rehearsals.

- Use walk-by and drop-in classroom observations.

- Help a teacher grade one class's papers.

- Shoot hoops with the kids after school.

- Read to students in the classroom.

- Take teachers to coffee during their prep period.

- Substitute-teach once in a while.

- Ride the activity bus.

- Try your hand at a physical education activity along with the students.

- Supervise the playground for a week.

- Sit in on departmental/grade level meetings.

- Spend a few minutes reading in the school library each day.

- Shadow your head custodian for a day.

- Sit on the bench during a game.

- Take a class along with the students.

- Take a turn at supervisory duty.

38. EASY WAYS FOR PRINCIPALS TO PRACTICE "MWWA"
(MANAGEMENT WHILE WALKING AROUND), CONTINUED

- Help out with a classroom party.
- Teach a class for one semester.
- Talk with students at a bus stop.
- Walk the parking lot with security personnel.
- Act as prompter for a school play rehearsal.
- Go outside with the students during a fire drill.
- Relieve the crossing guard some morning.
- Help the office secretaries duplicate and collate a major project.
- Try taking a math test along with the students.
- Be guest conductor of your school orchestra for a couple of numbers.
- Play a practice round with the golf team.
- Sit in on a parent-teacher conference.

39. THE PRINCIPAL'S RESPONSIBILITY FOR PLANT MANAGEMENT

Principals aren't maintenance engineers or grounds keepers. Nevertheless, they are ultimately responsible for respecting and protecting the physical plant of the school. As chief steward of all of the school's buildings, grounds, and facilities, the Principal has the following specific responsibilities:

1. Ensuring the safety of all facilities.

2. Preserving and maintaining the infrastructure of the school.

3. Meeting the standards and requirements of all applicable building codes.

4. Establishing a systematic program of preventive maintenance.

5. Employing an adequate staff of properly trained and licensed custodial/maintenance personnel.

6. Maintaining a regular schedule for monitoring and inspecting all facilities, equipment and mechanical systems.

7. Providing adequate security throughout the school plant.

8. Assuring appropriate accessibility for those with disabilities.

9. Adapting facilities to meet changing needs.

10. Promoting energy efficiency wherever possible.

11. Recommending necessary and desirable capital improvements.

12. Upgrading facilities as new and better products become available.

13. Maintaining and enhancing (where possible) the aesthetic appearance of the physical plant.

14. Engendering a sense of pride and ownership in the school's physical facilities on the part of students and the community.

15. Using facilities efficiently to achieve educational goals and to accommodate both school and community needs.

40. GUIDELINES FOR COMMUNITY USE OF SCHOOL FACILITIES

Schools belong to the community. Public use of elementary and secondary school buildings and grounds should be encouraged within reasonable bounds. As steward of all school facilities, the Principal must make facilities available for community use, protect school property, and limit liability risks. The generic guidelines below can help govern reasonable public use of the school plant:

1. All district policies, local ordinances, and zoning requirements must be followed in any community use of school facilities.

2. Usage fees may be charged when necessary to cover utility and custodial costs.

3. School, parent, and district use of facilities takes priority over other community uses.

4. A school representative (often a custodian) must be present in the building during any community activity or event.

5. Food preparation equipment and facilities may be used only under supervision of authorized food service personnel.

6. Community users may be required to furnish a certificate of liability insurance.

7. Adult supervision must be provided during any community use of school facilities.

8. The use of alcohol, drugs, and tobacco is prohibited on all school property (including buses and other school-owned vehicles).

9. All school property, furniture, and equipment should be left as it was found.

10. All accidents requiring medical attention that occur during community use of school facilities must be reported to school authorities.

11. The school is not responsible for loss or damage to personal property.

12. Use of school facilities may be denied to groups that may be damaging or prejudicial to the best interests of the school or the school district.

41. PRINCIPAL'S ROLE IN NEGOTIATIONS

A principal is often caught in the middle during contract negotiations. As an administrator, he or she is an arm of management. At the same time, the principal must retain effective working relationships with all parties in order to get the job done when a settlement is reached.

The guidelines below identify the tricky professional role elementary and secondary principals must play throughout the collective bargaining process:

- Serve as a conduit of information between parties.

- Protect the name of the school and all school property, no matter how heated or ugly bargaining may become.

- Put negotiations in perspective. No matter how emotional things may get at the bargaining table, student welfare must always come first.

- Help identify and clarify issues and suggest solutions to problem areas.

- Keep day-to-day operations running as smoothly as possible despite the distractions generated by collective bargaining.

- Maintain good faith (credibility) with all parties.

- Do not permit students to be used as pawns in the negotiating process.

- Talk about issues—not personalities.

- Get the job done, no matter what is happening with negotiations.

- Understand the bargaining process (i.e., rhetoric and posturing are normal, perception is sometimes more important than reality, all sides must "win" something, etc.).

- Don't "bad-mouth" either side.

- Avoid rumors.

- Don't leak confidential information.

- Let others talk to the media about the progress of negotiations.

- Don't bend any rules out of loyalty to one side or the other.

- Don't try to be a hero and settle things all by yourself.

- Act as a calming influence.

- Practice patience.

- Remain hopeful. (There will be a settlement.)

- Avoid use of militaristic metaphors such as "battle lines," "trenches," etc. They only heat up emotions.

- Keep a sense of humor.

- Depersonalize negotiations. (People don't always mean what they say in the heat of emotion.)

- Serve as a bridge between factions.

- Act as point person to lead things back to normalcy when settlement is reached.

- Practice amnesty. (Don't hold grudges.)

- Interpret and manage the new contract fairly and consistently.

42. CHECK LIST FOR DELEGATING AUTHORITY

Effective leaders have to get results by working through other people. One of the secrets of working smarter is to delegate authority. The trick is to know what to delegate, when to delegate, and how to delegate. The check list below can help:

_____ Delegate only tasks that are commensurate with the abilities of the person receiving the assignment. (Don't set up a person to fail.)

_____ Delegate for the right reasons (e.g., you don't have time, someone else can do it better, a fresh approach is needed). Never delegate duties as punishment!

_____ Don't always delegate "dirty work." Sometimes, delegate the fun stuff.

_____ It's O.K. to delegate tasks that stretch and challenge the delegate.

_____ Don't wait too long to delegate. Be sure there is enough time to meet expectations.

_____ Consider the work load of the other person before delegating duties.

_____ Delegate duties to the person who can get the job done—not just to the person who may want it most.

_____ Define the task (project) clearly and completely and spell out expected results in detail.

_____ Answer all questions regarding the delegated task.

_____ Provide adequate resources to complete the task.

_____ Allow latitude in how expected outcomes are achieved.

_____ Inform others of delegated authority.

_____ GET OUT OF THE WAY!

_____ Be available for consultation, but don't keep looking over the delegate's shoulder.

_____ Do not take back delegated tasks except in extreme emergency.

_____ Give feedback when task is completed. (Give credit if task is satisfactorily accomplished. Share blame if something goes awry.)

_____ Celebrate successes.

43. DO'S AND DON'TS FOR BETTER REPORT WRITING

In any report-writing or other writing project, it is important for Principals to pay attention to the following suggestions and precautions:

DO

- Accumulate data A.S.A.P.
- Take time in selecting a title.
- Strive for an attention-getting first paragraph.
- Personalize your writing.
- Use plain words.
- Simplify data.
- Put back-up details in appendices.
- Proofread carefully (Reading out loud helps.)

DON'T

- Use fancy type or font styles.
- Overuse slang.
- Employ sexist terms.
- Use abbreviations.
- Use acronyms.
- Include irrelevant data.
- Fall back on clichés.
- Try to be cute.
- Do anything that will confuse your readers.

44. 20 WAYS TO IMPROVE FACULTY MEETINGS

1. Announce regularly scheduled meetings early on.

2. Hold no more meetings than necessary.

3. Start on time and end on time.

4. Change the setting periodically. (Try holding meetings in different classrooms.)

5. Avoid top-down meetings whenever possible. (Participation is imperative.)

6. Encourage humor.

7. Be a facilitator, not a lecturer.

8. Radiate enthusiasm. (If you're not excited about the meeting, don't expect others to be.)

9. Arrange seating so participants can see one anothers' faces.

10. Involve staff members in planning meetings.

11. Distribute agendas in advance.

12. Use meetings to solve problems, not just dispense information.

13. Use a workshop format and hands-on activities when appropriate.

14. Encourage idea sharing between departments and grade levels.

15. Allow time for new ideas, discussion, questions, feedback, etc.

16. Always summarize and distribute minutes.

17. Develop follow-up activities.

18. Encourage teachers to share interesting projects.

19. Always include some upbeat topics or activities.

20. End on a positive note.

45. WAYS TO WORK SMARTER

When you can't work any longer, harder, or faster, the only recourse is to work smarter. Working smarter is an attitude and a way of life. The following tips can help achieve both:

- Adopt a "work smarter attitude." Question routines and look for ways to streamline bureaucracy.
- Do the right thing first.
- Do things right the first time.
- Don't get sucked into thinking that more is always better.
- Realize that not every task deserves A+ treatment.
- Have a reason for what you do.
- Simplify rules.
- Make prioritizing a priority.
- Have a written plan for the day—every day!
- Break big jobs into bite-size, manageable tasks and get started.
- Do the most important things first.
- Dare to delegate. (Point people in the right direction and get out of their way.)
- Don't make other people's problems your problems.
- Don't *always* be accessible. There's a reason that doors are made to close.
- If something doesn't "feel right," don't do it. Back off for awhile.
- Block out time to think. (This is a "must" for all leaders.)
- Use downtime (wait time) for constructive purposes.
- Don't write memos that don't need writing or hold meetings that don't need to happen.
- Make modern office technology work for you and your staff—not vice versa.
- Anticipate problems. Have contingency plans.
- Work ahead. There's no law that says you can't do tomorrow's work today.
- Use form letters, stock memos, etc. You don't have to create everything anew every time.
- Remember that no deadline is absolutely absolute.
- Schedule yourself to work when other people (interrupters and distracters) are not around (i.e., early morning, during lunch hour, after school hours, etc.).
- If you feel overwhelmed, stop; take stock; and start again one step at a time.
- If you don't have the data, trust your "gut feeling."
- Do what you can do and move on. Don't fret. Guilt is one of the worst time wasters of all.
- If an idea isn't working, dump it.
- You don't bring your family to work; so don't take your work home to your family every night.
- Take care of yourself, so you can take care of business.

46. LISTENING TECHNIQUES THAT CAN MAKE YOU A BETTER PRINCIPAL

1. Give the speaker your full attention. It's the only way to ensure you won't miss or misinterpret important points.

2. Maintain eye contact with the speaker.

3. Position yourself so you can hear easily.

4. Listen with your eyes. Notice gestures, facial expressions, body language, etc.

5. Ask questions for clarification.

6. Take notes when necessary.

7. Quiz yourself on meaning as you listen.

8. Listen to the whole message. (Don't form premature conclusions or start formulating your response before the speaker is finished.)

9. Work with what you hear (i.e., mentally organize it, categorize it, analyze it). It helps retention.

10. Summarize what you think you've heard by paraphrasing it back to the speaker.

47. BODY LANGUAGE TIPS FOR PRINCIPALS

Principals may not be celebrities, but they are highly visible public officials. From small conferences to large convocations, they are in the public eye. Their image often becomes the school's image as well.

It pays for Principals to pay attention to body language that sometimes sends a different message from what is being said. Here are some of the body messages to watch out for:

- Touching the nose, rubbing the eyes, or excessive blinking can convey the impression of lying.

- Leaning forward indicates interest.

- Adjusting your collar sends a message of discomfort.

- Legs crossed at the ankles convey insecurity.

- Open arms and open hands indicate an openness to listening and to paying attention to another person.

- A lowered head or lowered eyes suggest unapproachability.

Being aware of these signals can help Principals speak effectively with their body language as well as with their words.

48. TIPS ON WORKING WITH COMMITTEES

Committees have a bad name in many schools because there are too many of them that do too little. It doesn't have to be that way. Committees can be useful tools for planning and problem solving. The following advice will help you make better use of both ad hoc and standing committees:

- Have a good reason for the existence of every committee. (Every committee should have a defined purpose.)

- Limit the size of each committee. (The group should be only as large as needed to get the job done. Anything over 20 isn't a committee; it's a mob.)

- Have only the right people on a committee. (Everyone should have a reason for being there and have something to contribute.)

- Balance membership. (If everyone thinks alike, the committee is useless.)

- Set limits (what the committee can and can't do).

- Give each committee access to the information, resources, and authority needed to get the job done.

- Don't prescribe how a committee will function.

- Never try to manipulate committee outcomes.

- Establish a time frame for ad hoc committees.

- Set term limits or rotate membership on standing committees where appropriate.

- Committees should meet only when there's something to do.

- Hold all committees accountable. (If a committee doesn't make things happen or make things better, you don't need it.)

- Document all committee work.

- Establish watchdog mechanisms to prevent overlap or duplication of committee work.

- Keep reminding committee members why they are there.

- Celebrate benchmark achievements.

- Give committees full credit for what they do.

- Let committees die natural deaths. (When the work's done, the committee's done.)

49. TIPS ON HANDLING VISITORS AND INTERRUPTIONS

- Don't make your office too comfortable or appealing. It's supposed to be a workspace, not a lounge.

- Set aside specific times each day to answer phone calls and receive visitors.

- If you're busy, say so. (People respect busy people. Don't be afraid to say, "This is a bad time. Can we get together later?")

- Arrange your office so that your desk faces away from people passing by.

- If someone interrupts you, don't lay your pen or papers down. As long as you keep holding them, they signal that you still have work to complete.

- Remain standing. Visitors will get the hint.

- Don't offer coffee unless you intend to socialize for a while.

- Indicate upfront how much time you can spend with a visitor.

- Make a definite time to continue the conversation.

- Don't always leave your door open. Sometimes, a "door ajar policy" is best.

- Get out of your office and find some other out-of-the-way place to work if you need an uninterrupted block of time.

- Go to the other person's classroom or office instead of having that person come to you. That way, you control the length of the visit.

- Ask uninvited visitors to help with the work you're doing. (Most visitors don't want a job. They're just trying to get away from their own work.)

- Have a prearranged plan with your secretary to interrupt if a visitor stays too long.

50. TIPS ON HANDLING PAPERWORK

- Eliminate excess paperwork. Always ask, "Is this form (letter, memo, report, record, etc.) really necessary?"

- Remember that the wastebasket is a time-saving device.

- Don't just shuffle paper; do something with it.

- Strive to handle every piece of paper only once.

- Model clear, concise writing. You may educate your staff to write economically.

- Learn to skim and scan when you read.

- Read only what you need to read. Skip unnecessary details. (Sometimes, the introduction and conclusion are enough.)

- "Junk" junk mail. (Don't waste time on irrelevant ads, etc.).

- Delegate your paperload. (Have someone else screen your mail.)

- Dictate when possible (if you're comfortable with the technology.)

- Develop a battery of form letters.

- Use old reports as models for new ones.

- Write quick answers and responses on letters and memos, rather than drafting a new document.

- Have someone "ghost-write" or "ghost-read" for you when necessary.

- Use quick and easy E-mail messages, rather than paper memos.

51. TIPS FOR WORKING WITH POLITICAL LEADERS

- Expect political leaders to have a hidden agenda. (Their agenda doesn't have to be your agenda.)

- Understand that, in politics, people don't always say what they mean and things are not always what they seem to be.

- Do your job right every day—no matter which way the political winds are blowing.

- Don't tie your star to any political figure; shine in your own right.

- Be authentic. Tell the truth and stick to your principles.

- Always put loyalty to kids and to the organization over politics.

- Don't be dazzled by rhetoric.

- Don't cut deals or make promises you can't keep.

- Never take unfair advantage.

- Remember, political figures come and go. The kids show up every day.

- Don't take sides with any political faction.

- Fight for principles—not for political gain.

- Avoid playing one-upmanship or trying to manipulate other people.

- Give credit where credit is due and accept your share of blame.

- Keep a low profile during political infighting. (When everything hits the fan, it's not distributed equally. You don't want to be in the line of fire.)

- Don't expect or seek favors.

- If it helps kids, let political leaders take some credit for your results.

- Compromise lots of things—but not your ethics or your dignity.

- Be patient. If today's politics aren't working in your favor, wait for tomorrow's.

52. WHAT PRINCIPALS SHOULD KNOW ABOUT COMPUTERS

Principals don't need to know how to perform complicated computer functions. They do, however, need to know how to tap computer wizardry to work smarter in today's complex school environment. All elementary and secondary Principals should at least know the following basics of computer applications:

1. Simple computer functions (i.e., how to start up the computer and initialize a disk; how to use the keyboard, the mouse, programs, files, and the printer, etc.).

2. What the computer can do for you and your school.

3. What computers can't do.

4. What software and networks are available for school use.

5. Where to go for training, information, and help.

6. Who can "troubleshoot" computer problems in your school.

7. Fundamentals of "ergonomics" (How to choose, arrange, and use furniture, equipment, space, lighting and other working conditions to avoid such health-related risks as muscle damage, eye fatigue, carpal tunnel syndrome, injuries, etc.).

8. Everyday language of the computer including the terms below:

    a. Backup—copying a disk or file to avoid loss.

    b. Balloons—small boxes holding information about objects on the screen.

    c. Bit—the smallest unit of information a computer can hold.

    d. Byte—a unit of information made up of a fixed number (usually 8) of bits.

    e. Command—an instruction that makes the computer perform some function.

    f. Cursor—pointer.

    g. Eject—removal of a disk from a disk drive.

    h. File—an identified collection of information on a disk.

    i. Floppy Disk—a plastic disk that stores information.

    j. Font—a unique typographic design (letters, numbers, symbols, etc.)

    k. Format—initialize (see definition).

    l. Hard Disk—a metal disk sealed in a disk drive or cartridge.

    m. Icon—a small picture of a file, disk, menu, etc.

    n. Initialize—prepare a disk to receive information.

    o. Input—information "put" into a computer from an external source.

    p. Interface—how a computer communicates with a printer or other external device.

    q. Memory—the hardware component of a computer system that can store information.

    r. Menu—a listing of computer items from which you can order (choose).

    s. Modem—a device that links computers.

52. WHAT PRINCIPALS SHOULD KNOW ABOUT COMPUTERS, CONTINUED

t. Monitor—a display device.

u. Mouse—a device that controls the pointer on a computer screen.

v. Open—to make available.

w. System Extension—a program that extends system capabilities.

x. Trash—an icon that discards programs, files, etc.

y. Virus—a program designed to damage files; it can be spread through networks or bulletin board services, or on a disk.

z. Window—rectangular box that displays information on a computer.

53. 101 WAYS TO BE A BETTER PRINCIPAL TOMORROW

Following are specific traits and actions that characterize the best school leaders. Adopting their practices can make you a better Principal overnight.

1. Be on time for every appointment.
2. Put off procrastinating.
3. Have written goals for every day and every year.
4. Use plain talk—all the time.
5. Praise more than you criticize.
6. Be physically rested and ready every day.
7. Don't hide behind the telephone.
8. Treat everyone alike—fairly.
9. Don't live with lies.
10. Never take sole credit for anything.
11. Look for successes, not mistakes.
12. Admit it when you don't know what you're doing.
13. Be sincere. Phonies are quickly identified.
14. Shut up when it's appropriate.
15. Write clearly (and legibly).
16. Go out of your way to help people.
17. Learn to say "No" and "I don't know."
18. Leave your prejudices in the parking lot.
19. Don't gossip or feed the rumor mill.
20. Have fun at work (and let others have fun also).
21. Always keep trying to think of better ways to do things.
22. Reward people. Promote from within whenever you can.
23. Respect confidential information.
24. Be loyal to your school and school district—or leave it.
25. Admit it if you make mistakes.
26. Don't whine.
27. Work hard—every day.
28. Let other adults call you by your first name.
29. Never sabotage another person's or school's program.

53. 101 WAYS TO BE A BETTER PRINCIPAL
TOMORROW, CONTINUED

30. Don't make decisions in anger.

31. Be willing to work beyond your contract occasionally.

32. Get your own coffee.

33. Forget about sarcasm.

34. Obey laws and follow district policy.

35. Get back to people promptly.

36. Keep promises and remember commitments.

37. Don't chew gum on the job.

38. Pay attention at meetings and act interested.

39. Finish what you start.

40. Laugh every day.

41. Learn something new every day.

42. Remember your school's mission (why you're doing what you do).

43. Don't be embarrassed to volunteer.

44. Don't brag.

45. Don't nag.

46. Treat visitors like guests.

47. Remember, your "customers" aren't always right—but they're always your "customers."

48. Don't let anyone think he or she has asked a dumb question.

49. Apologize when you should.

50. Be patient with beginners.

51. Push for higher standards.

52. Be confident—not arrogant.

53. Don't work when you're sick.

54. Be a cheerleader for others.

55. Organize your day—every day.

56. Never make anyone a public laughingstock.

57. Evaluate yourself (and be tough on yourself).

58. Clean up your own mess.

59. Try to leave things better than you find them.

53. 101 WAYS TO BE A BETTER PRINCIPAL TOMORROW, CONTINUED

60. Use your wastebasket more than your file cabinet.

61. Associate with winners. Distance yourself from malcontents.

62. Look for answers, not excuses.

63. Be upbeat!

64. Do at least one thing you really like to do each day.

65. Be loyal to vendors and service providers (if they deserve it).

66. Care about what happens to your school and the people in it.

67. Keep memos short and to the point.

68. Use your school district's services.

69. Don't sulk or pout when things don't go your way.

70. If someone else has a better idea, use it and give that person credit.

71. Do what's right.

72. Don't settle for sloppy.

73. Be above petty office politics.

74. Save some time to think, plan, and dream each day.

75. Don't take work home every night. You deserve a life of your own.

76. Try to work smarter, not harder.

77. Be willing to compromise (except when it comes to ethics).

78. Don't cheat or steal.

79. Take your vacations and encourage others to do the same.

80. Don't waste time or materials.

81. Criticize in private; praise in public.

82. Keep everyone informed of important matters that affect them directly.

83. Walk your talk.

84. Don't make someone else do your dirty work.

85. Know what's going on in other schools.

86. Pay attention to the culture of your school.

87. Make personal contact regularly with everyone you supervise.

88. Don't have too many rules.

89. Don't cover for incompetents.

90. Remember birthdays and other important things about people you supervise.

53. 101 WAYS TO BE A BETTER PRINCIPAL TOMORROW, CONTINUED

91. Be a teacher.

92. Be a friend as well as a supervisor.

93. Visualize success for yourself and your organization.

94. Do your best, and then don't worry about it.

95. Keep up with new technologies.

96. Don't be afraid to ask for help.

97. Work hard to get your staff the best tools and supplies.

98. Give up on bad ideas.

99. Don't take people or things for granted.

100. Be straightforward in reporting bad news (no sugar-coating).

101. Be enthusiastic!

Being an effective Principal is mostly the result of doing lots of little things right. Winners pay attention to details. Success is a matter of nuance.

You can be a better Principal tomorrow by starting to do what the best school leaders do. What it takes to succeed is laid out in the actions of others. Getting better at what you do is a choice. Just do it!

54. YOU MAY BE TOO OLD FOR THE JOB WHEN . . .

(The principalship isn't just for the young. Seasoning is sometimes an important qualification. Nevertheless, you might want to consider retirement when you spot these signs that you may be getting too old for the job.)

1. You have to turn down your hearing aid at pep rallies.

2. You have trouble remembering the Superintendent's name.

3. You doze off at your own meeting.

4. You have trouble telling the difference between the older students and the newer teachers.

5. Your school loses a championship game and you really don't care.

6. Your suits are coming back in style—for the third time.

7. You always have to go to the bathroom in the middle of assembly programs.

8. School lunch gives you heartburn.

9. You have personal memories of most of what they teach in second semester American history.

10. You can't remember why you called this meeting.

11. Students complain about your dentures clicking when you talk over the intercom.

12. It's hard to stay awake until the PTA meeting is over.

13. You remember when chewing gum was a major discipline problem.

14. Your great-grandchildren are about to enroll in your school.

15. You say, "We've already tried that," a lot.

16. You've matriculated in graduate school in five different decades.

17. Nothing excites you anymore.

18. The other Principals call you "Sir" or "Ma'am."

55. 6 THEORIES OF LEADERSHIP

1. Trait Leadership

   —Leadership is a set of inherited skills.

2. Situational Leadership

   —Leaders use multiple skills to deal with variable situations.

3. Organizational Leadership

   —Leadership is positional. (It goes with the job.)

4. Political Leadership

   —Leadership is based on Machiavellian manipulation.

5. Visionary Leadership

   —The person with the greatest vision gets to be leader.

6. Ethical Leadership

   —The best leadership is built on integrity, moral behavior, and ethical standards.

56. DEMING'S 14 POINTS OF TOTAL QUALITY MANAGEMENT*

Following are the widely acclaimed 14 points of Total Quality Management (TQM) as identified by W. Edwards Deming:

1. Create a constancy of purpose.

2. Adopt a new philosophy (negativism is unacceptable).

3. Cease dependence on mass inspection.

4. End the practice of awarding business on price tag alone.

5. Improve constantly and forever.

6. Institute training.

7. Institute leadership (helping people do a better job).

8. Drive out fear.

9. Break down barriers between staff areas (departments).

10. Eliminate slogans, exhortations, and targets for workers.

11. Eliminate numerical quotas.

12. Remove barriers to pride in work.

13. Institute a vigorous program of education.

14. Take action to accomplish transformation.

*Deming is a management guru credited with turning around the economy of Japan following World War II.

57. SOME CURRENT CUTTING-EDGE ISSUES FOR LEADERSHIP

Visioning

- No quality of instructional leadership is more significant than the vision of the principal, and the ability to translate that vision and have others support it.
- Nothing happens until there is a vision, but a vision with no sense of purpose is just a good idea.
- "Without a vision, the people will perish." (King Solomon)
- It's not what the vision is, but what the vision does.
- When there is a genuine vision, people excel and learn because they want to.

Customer Satisfaction

- The organization should have an obsession with the customer.
- Customer satisfaction is not enough; "customer delight" should be the goal.
- Listen to the *voice of the customer*.

Systems Thinking

- Processes (not people) cause problems.
- Learning organizations have a shift of mind from seeing problems as caused by something "out there" to seeing how our own actions create our problems.
- Systems thinking shows that there is no "outside" to blame; you and your problems are part of a single system.
- Today's problems come from yesterday's solutions.
- Critics fix blame . . . not the process.
- Somebody has to work on the system. Everybody else is working in it.

Continuous Improvement (Total Quality Management)

- Continuous improvement is a way of life.
- Avoid the myth, "If it ain't broke, don't fix it." This leads to crisis management, waiting for things to break. You should "fix it" all the time.
- The objective is to meet expectations consistently—100% of the time.
- Quality is obtained through prevention-oriented improvement projects.

58. HOW DO ETHICAL LEADERS BEHAVE?

Effective leadership requires that decisions be based on moral values. Ethical leaders hold strong beliefs and act on them consistently. They function with a high level of moral courage and integrity.

You can spot Principals who adhere to high ethics and practice value-based decision making. They do the following:

1. Tell the truth.

2. Keep promises.

3. Accept blame.

4. Obey rules.

5. Use self-discipline.

6. Respect confidences.

7. Avoid half-truths.

8. Reward merit.

9. Remain impartial.

10. Avoid stereotypes.

11. Give second chances.

12. Promote health and safety.

13. Conserve resources.

14. Avoid stealing.

15. Respect privacy.

16. Show loyalty.

17. Strive to get better.

18. Respect others' privacy.

19. Give credit.

20. Avoid politics.

21. Don't cut corners.

22. Protect the environment.

23. Promote the greatest good for the greatest number.

59. CHARACTERISTICS OF "INTUITIVE LEADERS"

- Intuitive leaders have heightened awareness of surroundings, circumstances, events, and other people's ideas.

- Intuitive leaders dare to trust their hunches.

- Intuitive leaders allow serendipity to work for them.

- Intuitive leaders use holistic thinking.

- Intuitive leaders are most successful in dealing with the unexpected and the unpredictable.

- "Does it feel right?" is an important question for intuitive leaders.

- Intuitive leaders understand that intuition is natural and learnable. (Watch children. They use intuition a lot.)

60. NEW YEAR'S RESOLUTIONS FOR PRINCIPALS

Making New Year's resolutions is just another name for goal setting. Your school can operate better this year if you make (*and keep*) one or more of the resolutions below:

1. Upgrade your professionalism. Read professional journals regularly. Become active in your local, state, and national associations. Find out what books are "hot" in the profession and read them. Multiply your contacts by being more visible at professional meetings. All of these efforts will make you feel more "connected." They're guaranteed to make you feel better about yourself and your principalship.

2. Network with other Principals. An extended network of contacts opens up new sources of energy and ideas and can serve as a career support group. You don't have to try to run your school all by yourself anymore.

3. Memorize your school's Mission Statement and recite it frequently. Things go better when you keep in mind why you're doing what you do. Keep your eye on your goal. It's the only way to keep moving in the right direction.

4. Beef up your technological skills. In too many schools, the Principal is the last person to become technologically literate. Technology is more than a fad. It's a way of life and it's the wave of the future—now!

5. Learn students' names. It will expand your presence and influence in the school and enhance your image at the same time. Most Principals want the kind of school where people know one another's names. Make it happen in yours.

6. Put balance in your life. You work to live, not live to work. Insist on having time for family, friends, church, community, and yourself, as well as school. You'll be a better, happier person (and Principal) for it.

7. Spend more time with winners than with losers. Associate with the best and brightest in and out of your school. Distance yourself from whiners; we reflect our associations.

8. Do one specific thing each month to make your school a kinder, gentler place to teach and learn. Winning schools boast an environment where all people feel they belong and are supported.

9. Hire people better than yourself. It's the only way your school can grow, change, and improve.

10. Get fit. You need energy to be an effective Principal. It comes from healthy living. Make it a point to start exercising every week and eating a healthier diet. Fitness is a gift you owe yourself now. Health isn't something you can put off.

61. A PRINCIPAL'S PRAYER

Eternal Spirit,
Please grant me:

compassion to care for all students and families;
insight to know what's right for students;
courage to do what's right for students;
energy to get the job done;
persistence to work through obstacles and disappointments;
commitment to never give up or back off;
humility to know I don't know it all; and
common sense to take care of myself so I can work effectively for all students!

Amen.

62. LEADERS TALK ABOUT LEADERSHIP
(QUOTES)

"Leadership is action, not position." —*Donald H. McGannon*

"Not to decide is to decide." —*Harvey Coy*

"Leaders have a significant role in creating the state of mind that is society." —*John Gardner*

"Leaders are the custodians of a nation's ideals . . . of its permanent hope . . . " —*Walter Lippman*

"Reason and judgment are the qualities of a leader." —*Tacitus*

"The best executive is the one who has sense enough to pick good men to do what he wants done, and self-restraint enough to keep from meddling while they do it." —*Teddy Roosevelt*

"It's not whether you get knocked down, it's whether you get up." —*Vince Lombardi*

"If I felt it was the right thing to do, I was for it regardless of the possible outcome." —*Golda Meir*

"I will prepare and someday my chance will come." —*Abraham Lincoln*

"Plan your work for today and every day, then work your plan." —*Norman Vincent Peale*

"You're only as good as the people you hire." —*Ray Kroc*

"Example is not the main thing in influencing others. It is the only thing." —*Albert Schweitzer*

"The most valuable of all talents is that of never using two words if one will do." —*Thomas Jefferson*

"Love your enemies, for they tell you your faults." —*Ben Franklin*

"Security is mostly a superstition." —*Helen Keller*

"If you can't stand the heat, get out of the kitchen." —*Harry S Truman*

"Well begun is half done." —*Aristotle*

"There is no indispensable man." —*Franklin D. Roosevelt*

"Being powerful is like being a lady. If you have to tell people you are, you aren't." —*Margaret Thatcher*

"One man of courage makes a majority." —*Andrew Jackson*

"The only tyrant I accept in this world is the still voice within." —*Mohandas Gandhi*

"In the middle of difficulty lies opportunity." —*Albert Einstein*

"The sure-thing boat never gets far from the shore." —*Dale Carnegie*

"There is no security in life, only opportunity." —*Douglas MacArthur*

"Failure to prepare is preparing to fail." —*John Wooden*

"Whether you think you can or think you can't — you are right." —*Henry Ford*

"Always do more than is required of you." —*George S. Patton*

Section Two

STUDENTS

63. TODAY'S AGENDA FOR AMERICAN YOUTH

The fears, dreams, and concerns of today's children and youth differ from those of previous generations. There is a whole new agenda of youth issues that students bring into the classroom every day. Helping students handle this agenda is an important role of the school. Today's youth issues now include the following:

Family Issues

Single Parents
Working Parents
Divorced Parents
Blended Families
Reduced Family Time
Deteriorating Parenting Skills

Social Issues

Economic Instability
Threats of War
Environmental Concerns
Racial Tensions
Job Scarcity
Higher Education Costs

Health and Safety Issues

AIDS
Gangs
Violence—Weapons
Addiction and Dependency
Teen Pregnancy

Personal Issues

Insecurity
Lack of Trust
Pessimism About the Future
Peer Pressure
Sexual Identity

64. THE QUESTIONS STUDENTS ASK—
YESTERDAY AND TODAY

Yesterday

In safer, simpler times, the worries children had were reflected in questions like the following:

- Will people like me?
- Where will I go to college?
- What will I major in?
- What kind of job will I have?
- How much money will I make?
- When will I be out on my own?
- Whom will I marry?
- How many children will I have?
- Where will I live?
- What kind of home/car will I have?
- Will I be happy?

Today

The questions asked by today's children and youth are far more critical and troubling:

- Will I be safe?
- Will I be raped?
- Will I get AIDS?
- Will I be murdered?
- Will my parents stay together?
- Will our planet survive?
- Will I be able to afford college?
- Will I make a living?
- Will I be worse off than my parents?
- Will anyone care?

65. NEW POPULATIONS OF CHILDREN AND TEENS

The group of today's children and teenagers in America includes growing populations previously unknown, unnoticed, or negligible in numbers like the following:

1. Crack Babies

2. Fetal Alcohol Syndrome Children

3. Latchkey Kids

4. Home-alone Kids

5. Throw-away Kids

6. Runaways

7. Drop-outs

8. Teen Parents (Single Mothers)

9. Junkies (Alcohol, Drugs)

10. Gang Members

11. Youth Prostitutes

12. Abuse Victims

66. STUDENT RIGHTS AND RESPONSIBILITIES

Students are the only reason schools exist. They are not the property of the school. All students are worthy human beings deserving of respect and the best efforts of the school staff. Student rights must be vigorously respected and protected at all times.

In turn, all students have certain obligations to be contributing participants in the learning process and to be good citizens within the school community.

The basic rights and responsibilities of students at all levels include the following:

All Students Have These

RIGHTS

To be safe.

To be respected as individuals.

To be treated fairly and without prejudice.

To learn without disturbance or distraction.

To have personal property respected and protected.

To express views and to be heard.

To be exposed to competent teachers and positive adult role models.

To be challenged with materials and instructional techniques commensurate with their abilities and learning styles.

To be free from harassment.

To learn in a drug-free, smoke-free, and violence-free environment.

To be called what they choose (i.e., African American, Hispanic, Asian American, etc.).

To have access to appropriate grievance procedures.

All Students Have These

RESPONSIBILITIES

To treat others fairly and without prejudice.

To obey laws and comply with reasonable school rules.

To respect other people's rights, property, and reputations.

To contribute to a positive and safe school environment.

To participate in their own learning (i.e., to strive to learn to the best of their abilities).

To respect and maintain school property.

66. STUDENT RIGHTS AND RESPONSIBILITIES, CONTINUED

To attend regularly.

To avoid violent behavior.

To take education seriously.

To dress and use language appropriate to a businesslike learning environment.

To practice civility and to show respect in all dealings with peers and adults in the school.

67. RIGHTS OF STUDENTS WITH DISABILITIES

Students with disabilities are entitled to all of the same rights as other students and to certain additional safeguards and due process provisions prescribed by law as follows:

All students with disabilities have a right to:

- an appropriate public education;
- an education in the least restrictive environment (i.e., inclusion in the mainstream wherever possible);
- parent and student input into the development of an appropriate Individual Educational Plan (IEP);
- a periodic review of the appropriateness of the IEP and applicable special education programs and services;
- have all changes in placement only in accord with prescribed procedures;
- remain in existing placement until any special education complaint is resolved;
- a hearing (public or private) and/or mediation services to resolve disputes about placement or programming;
- physical access to all appropriate programs, services, and facilities; and
- exemption from regular disciplinary measures (including suspension and expulsion) for behavior or actions caused by the student's disabling condition.

68. MAJOR STRESSORS FOR ADOLESCENTS

being in an automobile accident

beginning a part-time job

birth of a brother or sister

break-up of a relationship

change in dating habits

conflict with a teacher

death of a loved one

divorce of parents

excessively high expectations

failing a test

failing a course

family financial difficulties

fight

being fired from a job

illness of family member

illness or injury of a friend

low grades

moving

peer pressure

personal injury

pregnancy

rejection by a peer

major illness

separation of parents

taking a vacation

traffic ticket

transferring to a new school

69. RITES OF PASSAGE FOR AMERICAN YOUTH

As in many societies, American culture embodies a number of rites of passage that serve as lines of demarcation between various stages of childhood and adult status. The most common rites of passage in American society include:

circumcision

baptism

first communion

bar mitzvah or bat mitzvah

graduation

debutante balls

sweet 16 parties

initiations

70. ESSENTIAL RELATIONSHIPS FOR ALL STUDENTS

To develop (physically, mentally, emotionally, and spiritually), all children and teenagers need a web of affirming relationships including:

- the nurturance of loving parents;
- the sounding board of close friends;
- the support of caring teachers and religious leaders;
- the companionship of supervised youth groups; and
- the sympathetic ear of relatives and mentors.

71. CORE VALUES FOR TODAY'S STUDENTS

Despite enormous diversity within society, it is still possible for most people to agree on certain common moral and ethical belief statements to pass on to children and youth. Following is a list of one community's agreed-upon core values for children:

- To show respect for a higher power.
- To treat the environment gently and reverently and to show concern for the long-term good of the world and the universe.
- To be kind to all creatures.
- To be actively seeking a relationship with a higher power.
- To recognize that corporate worship (whatever faith or denomination) has a positive contribution to make.
- To hold all men, women, and children as being of equal value and worth.
- To do to others as we would wish them to do to us.
- To love, honor, and help our parents and families.
- To honor those who lead us, to work cooperatively with them, to meet their just demands, and to respect those structures designed to allow people to live together in fairness and harmony.
- To show a basic, courteous respect for the dignity of every human person.
- To acknowledge and respect the religious values that have been foundational in the development of this country.
- To reject violence as a solution for community or personal difficulties.
- To seek peace, justice, freedom, and the necessities of life for all people.
- To bear no malice, prejudice, or hatred in our hearts.
- To be honest and fair in our dealings with others.
- To speak the truth and not mislead others by our silence.
- To seek the betterment of our community by personal involvement.
- To understand the importance to society of having work available for all to do.
- To see ourselves and all others as having value and worth in just "being."
- To resist the temptation to envy, greed, and jealousy.
- To recognize, develop, and use our individual and unique combination of talents and abilities.
- To use our possessions wisely and unselfishly.
- To express our sexuality in life-affirming ways.
- To avoid the abuse of our bodies by what we put into them or do with them.

Source: Statement of Core Values for the Children of St. Louis Park, MN. Developed by an interfaith group of clergy and ratified by a majority of churches and synagogues within the community.

72. STUDENT LEARNING STYLES

Good teachers have always known that students learn differently. What works with one learner may flop with another. There may be as many learning styles as there are pupils. Educational researchers have identified a number of discrete learning styles or modalities in learners, including the following:

Visual Learners

Auditory Learners

Kinesthetic (Physical) Learners

Concrete Learners

Abstract Learners

Sequential Learners

Random Learners

Analytical Learners

Flexible Learners

Constricted (Focused) Learners

"Masculine" Behavior Learners

"Feminine" Behavior Learners

Conceptual Learners

Perceptual Learners

Morning Learners

Afternoon Learners

Left-Brain Learners

Right-Brain Learners

Most students have a dominant learning modality, but actually apply a variety of styles (mix and match) in comprehending and mastering new information and knowledge. The best teachers strive to accommodate all learning styles by employing a broad array of instructional materials and techniques.

73. LEFT-BRAIN AND RIGHT-BRAIN FUNCTIONS IN STUDENTS

The two hemispheres of the human brain control different functions and exhibit different characteristics. Some students have right-brain dominance and some have left-brain dominance. Others are fairly balanced between the two hemispheres. Characteristic left- and right-brain functions are outlined below:

Left-Brain Functions

Cognition
Rationality
Logic
Analysis
Sequencing
Objectivity
Factual Orientation
Time Focused
Auditory Learning
Controlled
Math Ability
Linear Thinking

Right-Brain Functions

Intuition
Fantasy
Creativity
Spontaneity
Imagination
Holistic Thinking
Subjectivity
Spatially Focused
Kinesthetic Learning
Emotional
Music Ability
Simultaneous Thinking

74. BLOOM'S TAXONOMY OF HIGHER-LEVEL THINKING SKILLS FOR STUDENTS

Dr. Benjamin Bloom's taxonomy is a widely accepted hierarchy of thinking skills (cognitive development). Effective Principals encourage instruction designed to move students up the scale as their ability and maturity allow. (Surprisingly, even low-ability pupils can master many higher-level thinking skills.)

Bloom's six levels of cognitive development (from simplest to most complex) are:

I.   Knowledge Level—Students learn information by recall and recognition.

II. Comprehension Level—Students are able to translate, interpret, or do something extra with the material.

III. Application Level—Students use information in a new context.

IV. Analysis Level—Students can break down information in order to read between the lines — discern subtle implications, and so on.

V.   Synthesis Level—Students integrate ideas in new and different ways.

VI. Evaluation Level—Students can judge information by considering alternatives, establishing criteria, and defending choices.

75. ALTERNATIVE TYPES OF STUDENT INTELLIGENCE

Student potential cannot be defined by a single IQ score. All students (and adults) have multiple intelligences. The seven different types of intelligence below have been identified by Dr. Howard Gardner, Harvard researcher. (There may be more.)

1. Linguistic Intelligence (a "way with words").

- Reading
- Vocabulary
- Creative Writing
- Impromptu Speaking
- Storytelling

2. Logical/Mathematical Intelligence (ability to use numbers, data, and logic).

- Abstract Formulas
- Outlining
- Deciphering Codes
- Syllogisms
- Problem Solving

3. Visual/Spatial Intelligence (ability to visualize, solve puzzles, and work with spatial relationships).

- Guided Imagery
- Color Schemes
- Patterns
- Mind-mapping
- Pretending

4. Body/Kinesthetic Intelligence (ability in physical activities).

- Body Language
- Exercise
- Mime
- Inventing
- Sports

5. Musical/Rhythmic Intelligence (musical talent).

- Rhythmic Patterns
- Vocal Sounds
- Music Composition
- Instrumental Sounds

75. ALTERNATIVE TYPES OF STUDENT INTELLIGENCE, CONTINUED

- Tonal Patterns

6. Interpersonal Intelligence (relationship ability).

- Giving Feedback
- Intuiting Feelings
- Collaborative Skills
- Sensing Motives
- Group Projects

7. Intrapersonal Intelligence (ability to function independently).

- Silent Reflection
- Metacognition Techniques
- Concentration
- Reasoning
- "Centering" Practices

76. DUE PROCESS STEPS FOR STUDENTS

Democracy doesn't stop at the school entrance. Students are entitled to procedural safeguards, equal protection, and unequivocal application of fair standards and consistent consequences. In our society, school leaders must be champions of due process for all students. The essential elements of due process for students (as for adults) include the following steps:

1. Adoption of reasonable policies, rules, and regulations.

2. Proper notification (complete and accurate information) about all applicable policies, rules, etc.

3. Notice of any accusation or charge of violation or infraction.

4. Full and complete investigation of all allegations or charges.

5. Right to counsel (if needed).

6. Opportunity to confront accusers and cross-examine witnesses (if appropriate).

7. Proper protection from self-incrimination.

8. Right to a full and complete hearing.

9. Documentation of all phases and findings of the investigation.

10. Disciplinary measures in compliance with existing policy, commensurate with the seriousness of the offense, and consistent with action in similar situations.

11. Access to appropriate grievance procedures.

12. Opportunity for appeal.

77. STUDENT GRIEVANCE PROCEDURE
(EXAMPLE)

Every elementary and secondary school should have in place a well-defined grievance procedure that ensures the systematic and consistent handling of all instances where students feel they have received unfair or inappropriate treatment. A typical grievance process includes these steps:

1. The student and/or parent should discuss the issue and seek resolution with the teacher or other staff member involved.

2. If the matter remains unresolved, the issue should be referred to the Assistant Principal or Dean (where applicable) for disposition.

3. If still unresolved, the matter should be directed to the Principal for disposition.

4. If the dispute continues to be unsatisfactorily resolved, it may be referred to the Superintendent of Schools and/or the School Board. (In most cases, the School Board may choose to hear or not to hear the case.) Any decision of the Superintendent or School Board shall be final and binding. (In some circumstances, aggrieved parties may also have recourse to legal remedies.)

78. STUDENT DRESS

Concern for freedom of individual expression has caused formal school dress codes to fall into disfavor. Most schools now permit great latitude and flexibility in student dress. Nevertheless, some limits, like the model guidelines below, still exist.

Appropriate school dress

- does not create a disturbance;
- is not sexually explicit;
- is not pornographic;
- is not drug-related;
- does not contain obscenities;
- does not contain gang symbols;
- is not offensive or inflammatory to other groups or individuals;
- does not create a safety hazard; and
- does not damage school property.

79. A PROBLEM-SOLVING PROCESS FOR ALL STUDENTS

Problem solving is a survival skill that effective schools both teach and model. It is a lifelong legacy that the school can give to every pupil. The process below can be taught to students of any age:

- Recognize that a problem exists. (Own the problem.)
- Define the limits of the problem. (Gather data.)
- Clarify the issues. (Sort out cause and effect; name the parts of the problem.)
- Brainstorm (search) for solutions. Develop a pool of possible remedies.
- Choose the preferable solution.
- Take action.
- Evaluate results.
- Maintain the workable solution or repeat the process until another satisfactory resolution is achieved.

80. HEALTH EXPECTATIONS FOR STUDENTS

The following minimal student health expectations are common in most schools throughout the country:

1. Students should receive a complete physical examination, including a dental check-up, prior to entering kindergarten and annually thereafter.

2. Physical examinations are required for participation in extracurricular sports activities.

3. Students are expected (often required by law) to have certain immunizations before entering school. These most frequently include:

   a. measles;

   b. mumps;

   c. rubella;

   d. diphtheria;

   e. pertussis;

   f. tetanus; and

   g. polio.

4. In many states, students will receive periodic vision, hearing, and scoliosis screenings in school.

5. Students are assumed to be healthy enough to participate in regular physical education activities unless excused by a written note from the parents. Usually, a doctor's excuse is required for nonparticipation beyond three days.

6. Students should be kept out of school if they are ill (i.e., having vomited or had a fever during the previous 24 hours).

7. Students who have had a throat culture should be kept out of school until the results are reported.

8. Students who have had strep throat should be kept out of school for 24 hours after antibiotic treatment has been started and they have been without fever for 24 hours.

81. VIOLENCE IN STUDENTS' LIVES

School officials must be sensitive to the wide exposure to various forms of violence that many students experience in our culture today, including:

Child Abuse

Domestic Abuse

Emotional Abuse

Elder Abuse

Sexual Assault/Misconduct

Sexual Harassment

Rape

Violence Against Women

Hate Crimes

Gang Violence

Violence in the Workplace

Violence in School

Street Violence (Drive-bys, etc.)

Violent Crimes, including Murder

Drug Violence

Violence in Sports (Condoned Violence)

Violence in the Media

Violence in Music

Pornography

Bullying

Threats/Extortion

Today's schools have to accept some responsibility for keeping students safe from violence and for teaching students ways to settle disputes without violence.

82. DANGER SPOTS FOR STUDENTS

Physical attacks, assaults, rapes, and other acts of violence against students on school property have risen dramatically in recent years. Below are areas of the school where students may be most vulnerable if they are not accompanied by others:

- darkened and/or isolated hallways, stairways, or classrooms
- locker rooms
- bathrooms
- swimming pools
- running tracks
- parking lots
- unlit bus stops
- gymnasiums
- practice rooms
- backstage areas (theaters)
- auditoriums
- nurse's office

83. SELF-DEFENSE STRATEGIES FOR STUDENTS

In an increasingly violent society, students must learn how to protect themselves from physical harm wherever they may be. Experts suggest the following strategies for effective self-defense against physical attacks or harassment:

- Be aware of surroundings and avoid risky areas or circumstances.
- Exhibit a demeanor of confidence.
- Carry, and be ready to use, keys as a weapon.
- Know elementary martial arts maneuvers.
- Carry a personal noise alarm.
- Carry mace or a pepper spray.
- Wear a whistle.
- Be armed with a stun gun (where allowed).
- Use a remote unlocking mechanism for your car.
- Check the back seat before entering a car.
- Be prepared to scream or yell at the first sign of any threat.
- Don't be afraid to bite, claw, scratch, and kick if attacked.

It is not recommended that students carry guns or other weapons for defense. The best protection is the company of other trustworthy students or adults.

84. STATISTICS ON TEENAGE COMPULSIVE GAMBLING

Pathological (addictive) gambling is a growing problem among teenagers, spurred on by expanded opportunities and a proliferation of adult gaming activities. Before scheduling the next "Casino Night" at your school, consider the following statistics:

- Teenagers are twice as apt to become "hooked" on gambling as adults.
- Age 14–15 is the most vulnerable period for teenage gambling problems.
- Compulsive gambling is a problem for 1.3 million teens.
- Teens spend $500 million to $1 billion annually on gambling.

Source: Minnesota Council on Compulsive Gambling, 1995.

85. WHO AND WHAT STUDENTS READ IN SCHOOL

Student exposure to literature hasn't really changed much in today's technological era. Following are the authors and books most frequently read in school by high school and first-year college students in the United States:

Most Read Authors

Mark Twain

Nathaniel Hawthorne

Ernest Hemingway

Charles Dickens

William Shakespeare

John Steinbeck

F. Scott Fitzgerald

Most Read Books

The Scarlet Letter

Huckleberry Finn

The Great Gatsby

Lord of the Flies

To Kill a Mockingbird

The Grapes of Wrath

The Odyssey

Source: C.E.E.B. (College Board) report on vocabulary and reading materials used by students, 1994.

86. AWARD-WINNING BOOKS FOR STUDENTS

Newbery Medal Books, 1990–1994*

1990	*Number the Stars*	Lois Lowry
1991	*Maniac Magee*	Jerry Spinelli
1992	*Shiloh*	Phyllis Reynolds Naylor
1993	*Missing May*	Cynthia Ryland
1994	*The Giver*	Lois Lowry

*The Newbery Medal is awarded annually by the Association for Library Services to Children to the author of the most distinguished contribution to American literature for children.

Source: *World Almanac*, 1995.

87. STUDENT HEROES, 1980–1991

1980	Burt Reynolds
1981	Burt Reynolds
1982	Alan Alda
1983	Sylvester Stallone
1984	Michael Jackson
1985	Eddie Murphy
1986	Bill Cosby
1987	Tom Cruise
1988	Eddie Murphy
1989	Michael Jordan
1990	Paula Abdul
1991	H. Norman Schwartzkopf

Source: *World Almanac*, Heroes of Young America: Twelfth Annual Poll, 1992.

88. STUDENT MARKING SYSTEM—GRADE POINT EQUIVALENTS (EXAMPLE)

Most schools (particularly secondary schools) continue to have some form of grading system for marking and reporting student progress. Such systems often play an important role in determining grade point averages and rank in class, which can affect college admissions or job placement. Until a better way of evaluation and communication is developed, it is important that the school's grading system be well defined, clearly explained, and consistently applied. Below is a workable marking and grade point system that can be adapted in most school settings:

Grade Point Equivalents

A = 4.0

A– = 3.67

B+ = 3.33

B = 3.0

B– = 2.67

C+ = 2.33

C = 2.0

C– = 1.67

D+ = 1.33

D = 1.0

D– = .67

E = .33

F = 0

NG (No Grade) = 0

P/F (Pass/Fail) = Not used in GPA

A student's grade point average and class rank will be based on the marking system above. A grade of A+ is viewed as an intrinsic reward and given a grade point average equal to an A.

89. STUDENT DIRECTORY INFORMATION

Not all data regarding students is private or protected. Some student information gathered by the school may be designated as Directory Information (public information), and may be disclosed unless prior written denial of disclosure has been received from the student's parent or guardian. In many places, local policy designates the following student data as Directory Information:

Student Name

Student Address

Student Phone Number

Date and Place of Birth

School of Attendance

Most Recent Previous School Attended

Current Grade or Grade(s) Completed

Dates of Attendance

Degrees and Awards Received

Participation in Officially Recognized Activities/Sports

Weight and Height (if member of an athletic team)

Picture for School-approved Publications, Newspapers, and Videos

Any question about student directory information should be referred to the Principal's Office.

90. STUDENT STUDY HABITS SELF-EVALUATION CONTINUUM

Ultimately, student success in school depends on effective study habits. This chart provides a way for students and parents to evaluate existing study habits, skills, and attitudes, and to identify areas needing improvement.

STUDY HABITS, ATTITUDES, AND SKILLS CONTINUUM

	WEAK		STRONG
Effort.	I	I	I
Concentration	I	I	I
Accuracy	I	I	I
Listening Skill	I	I	I
Following Directions	I	I	I
Organization.	I	I	I
Prioritization	I	I	I
Planning Ability	I	I	I
Efficiency.	I	I	I
Persistence	I	I	I
Neatness	I	I	I
Completeness	I	I	I
Reading Skills	I	I	I
Writing Skills	I	I	I
Math Skills	I	I	I
Problem-Solving Ability.	I	I	I
Willingness to Tackle			
Tough Assignments	I	I	I

91. STUDENT SUPPORT ORGANIZATIONS

Effective schools have a number of built-in organizations designed to support and assist individuals with a variety of problems inside and outside of the school. A representative list of such organizations appears below:

AFDA—Athletes for Drug Awareness

Student Diversity Committee

Save Our Surroundings (SOS)

Senior Advisory Board

SADD—Students Against Drunk Driving

Student Council

Welcome Committee

Youth Development Council

Peer Counselors Organization

Conflict Resolution Managers Group

ALANON (and other 12-Step Support Groups)

92. YOUTH-SERVING AGENCIES

Principals and schools don't operate in a vacuum. Many organizations and groups serve as allies in helping to mold and motivate children and youth to become positive, contributing adults. A partial list of youth-serving agencies available in many communities includes:

YMCA

YWCA

Jewish Community Centers

Boy Scouts of America

Girl Scouts of America

Campfire Girls

4-H Clubs

Indian Guides

Young Pioneers

Boys and Girls Clubs of America

Little League

Big Brothers

Key Clubs

Demolay

American Field Services (AFS)

Amateur Athletic Union (AAU)

Job's Daughters

Civil Air Patrol

Junior Achievement

Babe Ruth League

Big Sisters

93. ORGANIZATIONS FOR STUDENTS WITH DISABILITIES

Following is a partial list of agencies and organizations outside the school that are available to assist students with disabilities:

African American Lupus Foundation, Inc.

Alliance for Mentally Ill

Alternatives for People with Autism, Inc.

American Civil Liberties Union

American Council of the Blind

American Diabetes Association

American Heart Association

American Cancer Society

American Lung Association

Association for Retarded Citizens (ARC)

Boy Scouting for People with Special Needs

Children's Heart Fund

Cystic Fibrosis Foundation

Deafness Education and Advancement Foundation

Division of Rehabilitation Services

Down's Syndrome Association of America

Emotions Anonymous

Goodwill Industries/Easter Seal

HEAL (Human Ecology Action League)

Learning Disability Association

Legal Advocacy for Persons with Developmental Disabilities

Legal Aid Society

Little People of America

Lupus Foundation of America

Mental Illness Anonymous

American Association of Deaf Citizens, Inc.

Depressive and Manic Depressive Association

Multiple Sclerosis Society

Muscular Dystrophy Association

93. ORGANIZATIONS FOR STUDENTS WITH DISABILITIES, CONTINUED

National Center for Youth with Disabilities

National Ataxia Foundation

National Spinal Cord Injuries Association

Opportunity Workshop, Inc.

PACER (organization of parents of Special Education students)

Spina Bifida Association of America

National Sjogren's Syndrome Association

United Cerebral Palsy Foundation of America

United Fund

94. TOP 10 EXCUSES STUDENTS GIVE FOR NOT HANDING IN HOMEWORK— THEN AND NOW

Excuses Then

1. HOMEWORK??!
2. It's in my dog.
3. It's at home.
4. It's in my locker.
5. I lost it.
6. I forgot to take my book home.
7. I didn't know how to do it.
8. I thought it was optional.
9. I didn't understand the assignment.
10. I didn't hear the assignment.

Excuses Now

1. My computer has a virus.
2. I faxed it to you. Didn't you get it?
3. That was one of my other multiple personalities in class yesterday.
4. The assignment discriminates against girls (boys, blacks, etc.).
5. The assignment isn't politically correct.
6. It violates my religious freedom.
7. Are you harassing me?
8. I want to plea bargain.
9. My psychic advised me not to do it.
10. I have Attention Deficit Disorder.

95. THINGS STUDENTS KNOW THAT MANY PRINCIPALS, TEACHERS, AND PARENTS DON'T KNOW

- How to sleep until noon
- How to set a VCR
- Names of the hottest rock stars
- "Teenageese" (their own special language)
- Whose parents are out of town
- What "grunge" was all about
- What gang symbols mean
- How to surf the Internet
- Who's having sex with whom
- How to use a coat hanger to open a locked car
- The words to popular songs
- Where to get drugs
- Who the easy teachers are
- How to win at video games
- Where to get the best and most french fries for your money
- The most popular beers
- How to study with both the radio and the TV blaring
- How to dance to today's music
- The best places to meet girls (or boys) at the mall
- Who sells cigarettes to minors
- What "sucks" and what doesn't
- What the artist formerly known as Prince is all about
- The best (and most expensive) sneakers
- Which adults you can trust
- What loyalty to a friend really means
- Why kids are a whole lot brighter and better than most grown-ups think they are

96. SIGNS OF AN UNDER-ACHIEVING STUDENT

- Resists homework
- Argumentative and defensive (short fuse)
- Forgetful
- Careless
- Frequently daydreams
- Is always bored
- Associates with other nonachievers
- Plays teachers and parents against each other.

97. NOTABLE QUOTABLES ABOUT STUDENTS
(CHILDREN AND YOUTH)

"You can learn many things from children. How much patience you have for instance."
—*Franklin P. Jones*

"The modern child will answer you back before you've said anything."
—*Laurence J. Peter*

"You know children are growing up when they start asking questions that have answers."—*John J. Plomp*

"We must have . . . a place where children can have a whole group of adults they can trust."—*Margaret Mead*

"Children need love, especially when they do not deserve it."—*Harold S. Hulbert*

"Children are our most valuable resource."—*Herbert Hoover*

"Youth is the trustee of posterity."—*Disraeli*

"Young men have a passion for regarding their elders as senile."—*Henry Adams*

"Children are unpredictable. You never know what inconsistency they're going to catch you in next."—*Franklin P. Jones*

"At every step, the child should be allowed to meet the real experience of life; the thorns should never be plucked from the roses."—*Ellen Key*

Section Three

CURRICULUM, EVALUATION, AND STAFF DEVELOPMENT

98. THE PRINCIPAL'S ROLE IN CURRICULUM DEVELOPMENT

Principals don't have to be experts in curriculum or achieve mastery of all subject areas. Nevertheless, as instructional leaders, Principals must understand the essentials of a sound, balanced curriculum and be accountable for ensuring an effective instructional program throughout the school. The Principal's specific responsibilities for the curriculum include the following:

1. Know what the existing curriculum is.

2. Acknowledge limitations of background, knowledge, and expertise in certain areas. Let curriculum experts and specialists do what they do best.

3. Analyze data before implementing curriculum initiatives.

4. Insist that everything taught be important and relevant, and make sense to learners.

5. Block out quality time for curriculum planning and design. (The curriculum of the school is too important to just let it happen.)

6. Implement a systematic cycle and process of curriculum review.

7. Get the right people involved in curriculum development, including teachers, parents, and students.

8. Provide leadership in defining what a good curriculum looks like.

9. Encourage experimentation and innovation.

10. Tolerate and celebrate mistakes.

11. Bend the rules to free up promising, nontraditional practices.

12. Demand that evaluation drive instruction. All programs should be able to show results and prove that they work.

13. Build a "nuts and bolts" staff development program to help teachers understand and implement new curricular approaches.

14. Provide adequate resources to design, implement, and support a healthy curriculum.

15. Demonstrate energy and enthusiasm for curriculum reform.

16. Challenge the status quo. Don't be afraid to ask the tough questions.

17. Inform the public about the curriculum.

18. Market the curriculum.

99. ALL THE PRINCIPAL REALLY NEEDS TO KNOW ABOUT CURRICULUM

Principals don't have to know everything about the instructional program, but they do need to know some things well. Principals should be generalists, not specialists. Here's what every Principal really needs to know about the school's overall curriculum:

- It's important to be on top of what's happening, what's important, what's needed, and what's possible.
- The best curriculum is a balanced curriculum.
- Subject matter must be logically organized.
- A good curriculum is a series of opportunities, not an obstacle course.
- The curriculum should be built around what students need, not what teachers like.
- If the curriculum isn't learnable, it doesn't belong in a public school.
- The course of studies should be adaptable to all ability levels.
- The curriculum should grow out of the school's vision and mission.
- Parents, students, business leaders, and community members should have a say in the curriculum.
- Effective curriculum features hands-on, real-world learning experiences.
- The curriculum should be inclusive, gender-fair, multicultural, and globally oriented.
- A good curriculum is a compass, not a fence. It should permit flexibility in teaching and learning.
- The curriculum should be more about possibilities than about requirements.
- The curriculum should be future-oriented.
- An information society requires a curriculum that is resource-based and emphasizes thinking skills.
- Process is more important than product in teaching and learning.
- The curriculum should be as interdisciplinary as resources and teacher talent permit.
- There is some politics in every curriculum decision.
- The Principal should guard against provincialism in the curriculum.
- Learning should reach beyond the classroom.
- Curriculum review must be continuous and unrelenting.
- The curriculum is only as good as the staff development program that supports it.
- Fun should be part of every school's curriculum. There is joy in learning and it ought to show.

100. CURRICULUM INFLUENCES

Principals and teachers don't build the curriculum in a vacuum. In every school, the instructional program has roots in, and is shaped by, a variety of such influences at the building, district, community, state, and national levels as:

- History and Tradition
- Social Issues
- Legal Requirements
- Economics
- Student Interests and Needs
- School Reform Movements
- Collective Bargaining
- Accrediting Agencies
- Textbook Publishers
- National Emergencies
- Parent Organizations
- Research
- Political Agendas
- Accountability Demands
- Public Pressure
- Court Decisions
- Foreign Competitions
- Teacher Specialties
- Special Interest Groups
- Test Makers
- Availability of Materials
- Religious Groups

101. TYPES OF CURRICULUM COMMITTEES

Curriculum is seldom the product of a single individual's work. Most curriculum is developed and designed by one or more of the following types of committees or task forces at the building or district levels:

Scope/Sequence Committees

Summer Curriculum Writing Teams

Ad Hoc Task Forces

Advisory Committees or Councils

School Effectiveness Teams

Department Chairs

Think Tanks (educational focus groups)

Teacher Assistance Teams

Interdisciplinary Teams

Blue Ribbon Committees

102. CURRICULUM ADVISORY COUNCIL GUIDELINES

More and more schools and school districts are forming Curriculum Advisory Councils (CACs) made up of faculty, parent, student, and public members. Although exact functions and features vary, the guidelines below are representative of most such committees:

Role

- Serve in an advisory (not rule-making) capacity.
- Study and analyze specific curriculum issues.
- Provide feedback on the overall curriculum.

Membership

- 12 parent and community members.
- 12 student reps (one from each grade level).
- 12 staff members (representing all major departments).
- Terms to run two to three years, based on the interest or discretion of the individual.

Qualifications for Membership

- Special interest or experience in curriculum issues.
- Availability for meetings.
- No "axes to grind."
- Relationship skills.
- Analytical skills.
- Communication skills.
- Commitment to public education

103. 5-YEAR CURRICULUM REVIEW CYCLE
(SAMPLE)

This sample process provides for continuous curriculum review, evaluation, validation, and revision by all subject areas in a self-repeating, 5-year cycle. Each of the five phases identified below is intended to last approximately one year:

Mission Phase—Define purposes and goals

Evaluation Phase—Assess present program

Development Phase—Specific curriculum writing/design

Implementation Phase—Trying it out

Refinement Phase—Fleshing out and fine-tuning

Year One

Mission Phase—Language Arts

Evaluation Phase—Math—Foreign Language

Development Phase—Science—Music

Implementation Phase—Social Studies—Physical Education—Vocational Education

Refinement Phase—Health—Art

Year Two

Mission Phase—Health—Art

Evaluation Phase—Language Arts

Development Phase—Math—Foreign Language

Implementation Phase—Science—Music

Refinement Phase—Social Studies—Physical Education—Vocational Education

Year Three

Mission Phase—Social Studies—Physical Education—Vocational Education

Evaluation Phase—Health—Art

Development Phase—Language Arts

Implementation Phase—Math—Foreign Language

Refinement Phase—Science—Music

103. 5-YEAR CURRICULUM REVIEW CYCLE
(SAMPLE), CONTINUED

Year Four

Mission Phase—Science—Music

Evaluation Phase—Social Studies—Physical Education—Vocational Education

Development Phase—Health—Art

Implementation Phase—Language Arts

Refinement Phase—Math—Foreign Language

Year Five

Mission Phase—Math—Foreign Language

Evaluation Phase—Science—Music

Development Phase—Social Studies—Physical Education—Vocational Education

Implementation Phase—Health—Art

Refinement Phase—Language Arts

104–112. K-6 LEARNER OUTCOMES (SAMPLES)

Learner outcomes are an important tool in building a sound instructional program. They answer these questions: What should students know? What should they be able to do? What attitudes should they demonstrate?

The sample K-6 learner outcomes make up a learning blueprint by grade level and subject. They identify the learnings most students will accomplish by the end of each grade level in the following subject areas:

Art

Health

Language Arts-Reading

Mathematics

Media and Technology

Music

Physical Education

Science

Social Studies

104. ART — K-6 LEARNER OUTCOMES
(SAMPLES)

Grades K-3: Students will . . .

- Begin to understand and get ideas from the world around them.
- Work with a variety of materials.
- Make decisions and modify ideas as they work.
- Judge when their work is finished.
- Understand that art works have been produced for many years.
- Examine art works produced around the world.
- Understand that artists' lives affect their work.
- Realize that art reflects culture.
- Make careful and clear distinctions in comparing art.
- Make some general conclusions about art works.
- Study art works to improve their own creativity.
- Understand the following processes involved in perceiving art by focusing on subject matter, technical features, sensory elements, formal structure, and expressive qualities.

Grades 4-6: Students will . . .

- Understand how and where artists get ideas.
- Understand that artists make technical and aesthetic decisions.
- Use ideas from the world around them.
- Recognize process as basic to production.
- Consider various standards to determine whether their work is finished.
- Identify how art mirrors change within their own lifetime.
- Find and describe visual artifacts from the past.
- Compare and contrast qualities as a basis for identifying age of artifacts.
- Appreciate the effect of cultural and temporal context on the appearance of art works.
- Understand that culture plays an important role in defining what art is.
- Understand that art works have distinct characteristics from other objects.
- Make fundamental distinctions when comparing and appreciating art.
- Appreciate issues involved in defining "great art."
- Compare and contrast qualities within various art works.
- Distinguish judgments from preferences.
- Learn to analyze art from several points of view.
- Demonstrate that response to art can be objective or subjective.
- Communicate and defend their conclusions to others.

105. HEALTH — K-6 LEARNER OUTCOMES
(SAMPLES)

Kindergarten: Students will . . .

- Have a basic understanding of four food groups.
- Explain why a good breakfast is important.
- List a variety of foods in each of four food groups.
- Name healthy snacks.
- Explain how enjoying a variety of foods improves health.
- Understand potential dangers in the home.
- Tell ways to prevent accidents.
- Understand that rules help keep us safe.
- Understand why seat belts must be fastened.
- Know how to call 911 for help in an emergency.
- Help make an emergency escape plan for their family.
- Understand the difference between sickness and wellness.
- Describe ways to prevent the spread of disease.
- Demonstrate self-care practices.
- Identify ways to exercise and explain why exercise is important.
- Understand how doctors and nurses help us stay healthy.
- Dress to fit the weather.
- Understand that everyone is unique and worthy.
- Discuss good ways to express feelings.
- Demonstrate acts of kindness.
- Identify appropriate uses of some chemicals.

Grade 1: Students will . . .

- Explain why the body needs food.
- Understand what a nutritious breakfast is.
- Help to plan and fix a nutritious breakfast.
- Try new health foods and snacks.
- Understand how families influence food choices.
- Learn how to evaluate food commercials.
- Understand safety decisions children make.
- Study alternatives for behavior toward strangers.
- Explain safety rules.
- Understand why we need teeth.

105. HEALTH — K-6 LEARNER OUTCOMES
(SAMPLES), CONTINUED

- Explain how sweet foods cause cavities.
- Learn that teeth should be brushed and flossed daily.
- Explain why we need sleep.
- Recognize that coughs and sneezes spread germs.
- Explain that washing hands halts the spread of germs.
- Recognize that each of us is special and unique.
- Understand that people experience different feelings.
- Identify good and bad ways to deal with feelings.
- Understand that we are responsible for our choices.
- Know that the word "drugs" describes both medicines and such substances as alcohol, tobacco, and so forth.
- Understand that children should take medicine only from a trusted adult.

Grade 2: Students will . . .

- Identify meals and snacks from the four groups that promote health.
- Recognize that food is necessary for energy.
- Know we need servings from the four food groups daily.
- Understand that foods in each group have special nutrients.
- Recognize that junk foods are inadequate sources of nutrients.
- Appreciate that individual nutrient needs vary.
- Analyze varied growth patterns depending on heredity and life style.
- Recognize that we need teeth to chew and help us talk.
- Understand that permanent teeth replace primary teeth.
- Know the four types of teeth and their functions.
- Be aware that proper tooth care involves brushing, flossing, and regular dental checkups.
- Understand that brushing removes food and plaque.
- Recognize that dentists clean away decay before filling cavities.
- Analyze healthy foods that develop strong teeth.
- Appreciate that medical and sanitation workers promote community health.
- Understand that serious accidents and illnesses are treated in hospitals.
- Analyze how different workers promote community health.
- Demonstrate responsibility for cooperating with good sanitation practices.
- Understand there are universal emotions.
- Understand their own and others' feelings.

105. HEALTH — K-6 LEARNER OUTCOMES
(SAMPLES), CONTINUED

- Know how to express kind feelings.
- Realize that everyone makes and learns from mistakes.
- Know to avoid taking medicine without supervision.
- List safety practices regarding taking medicine.
- Evaluate the hazards of smoking and using caffeine.

Grade 3: Students will . . .

- Be responsible for choosing and eating healthy foods.
- Identify the four basic food groups.
- Understand proper care and handling of food.
- Demonstrate how to be a wise food consumer.
- Evaluate snacks for nutritional value.
- Understand how basic body parts work.
- Appreciate the complexity and interdependence of human systems.
- Learn how the circulatory, respiratory, and digestive systems function.
- Explain how tobacco harms the body.
- Recognize how exercise, diet, and stress management help the body.
- Describe eye functions, care, and protection.
- Identify the anatomy of the ear.
- Explain the structure of the tongue and nose.
- Understand the function of skin.
- Demonstrate sensitivity for persons with disabilities.
- Realize the value of feelings.
- Be sensitive to ways people show feelings.
- Learn ways to deal with positive and negative feelings.
- Learn to say "no" to unwanted pressures.
- Learn how to get help when needed.

Grade 4: Students will . . .

- Describe a heartbeat.
- List benefits of a healthy circulatory system.
- Understand how breathing works.
- Understand the muscle system.
- Design a personal fitness program.

105. HEALTH — K-6 LEARNER OUTCOMES
(SAMPLES), CONTINUED

- Explain the causes and spread of communicable diseases.
- Classify noncommunicable diseases.
- Discuss the AIDS virus, emphasizing that it is not transmitted by casual contact.
- Demonstrate ways to avoid spreading germs.
- Evaluate ways to maintain personal health.
- Understand that lack of information can lead to anxiety or fear.
- Demonstrate how feelings affect the body.
- Learn constructive ways to handle anger.
- Know how caffeine, tobacco, alcohol, and marijuana affect the body.
- Appreciate individual differences and abilities.
- Recognize the importance of medicine safety.
- Understand the dangers of drug abuse.
- Understand the concept of abuse and neglect.
- Distinguish between good and bad touch.
- Understand ways to protect themselves against abuse.
- Understand the importance of getting help when needed.

Grade 5: Students will . . .

- Be aware of the need to eat different kinds of food.
- Evaluate personal eating habits.
- Recognize the role of feelings in influencing people.
- Understand the causes and effects of eating disorders.
- Appreciate how people grow at different rates.
- Exhibit an interest in fitness and healthy life choices.
- Understand how bones and muscles work together to cause movement.
- Begin to understand the reproductive system.
- Investigate how body changes affect the skin.
- Explain the function of the skin.
- Apply concepts of good hygiene to daily living.
- Understand how to handle difficulties constructively.
- Understand the dangers of drug abuse.
- Evaluate peer pressure regarding drug abuse.

105. HEALTH — K-6 LEARNER OUTCOMES
(SAMPLES), CONTINUED

Grade 6: Students will . . .

- Describe how endocrine glands affect growth.
- Explain how heredity affects growth.
- Understand how health decisions affect growth.
- Show how emotions and relationships change during growth.
- Discuss ways to be wise health consumers.
- Evaluate health-related advertisements.
- Show awareness of prices, labels, and fads in choosing health products.
- Recognize the importance of regular health checkups.
- Identify characteristics of a positive self-image.
- Investigate the causes and effects of stress.
- Explore how to deal with stress positively.
- Analyze defenses against communicable diseases.
- Know the causes, symptoms, and treatment of common respiratory diseases.
- Identify causes and prevention of heart disease and cancer.
- Describe the causes and effects of allergies.
- Demonstrate how healthy life styles prevent and contain diseases.
- Describe effects of the AIDS virus.
- Discuss sources (including parents) for information about AIDS-related issues.
- List guidelines for using medicines safely.
- Express harmful effects of abuse of each major drug type.
- Describe short- and long-term effects of alcohol abuse.
- Understand the disease concept of alcoholism.
- Evaluate how tobacco affects users and nonusers.
- Demonstrate ways to resist peer pressure concerning drug use and abuse.

106. LANGUAGE ARTS-READING — K-6
LEARNER OUTCOMES (SAMPLES)

K-6: Language Arts-Reading outcomes are different from other outcomes because they are not specific to grade levels. Language Arts-Reading represents an "emerging expert" model, rather than an assembly-line acquisition model. This results in horizontal, rather than vertical, development. Students will use the strategies below at progressively more difficult levels. The same outcomes, therefore, apply to all grade levels with varying levels of sophistication and success.

Students will . . .

- Develop appreciation and excitement for reading, writing, speaking, and listening.
- Develop confidence as effective producers and consumers of language.
- Read quality materials in a variety of styles and formats.
- Read grade-appropriate materials with fluency and comprehension.
- Use context to identify word meanings.
- Engage in self-questioning about what is read.
- Be able to summarize key ideas.
- Interpret materials using higher-level thinking skills.
- Recognize relationships in reading.
- Be able to identify such story elements as character, setting, plot, and theme.
- Spend time writing and develop a personal writing style.
- Write clearly and fluently in a variety of formats.
- Use grade-appropriate correct mechanics and spelling in written work.
- Learn to use multimedia as an integral part of language experience.

107. MATHEMATICS — K-6 LEARNER OUTCOMES (SAMPLES)

Kindergarten: Students will . . .

- Count orally forward and backward to figure sums.
- Add and subtract with tens.
- Label sets of objects.
- Determine "less than," "greater than," and "equal to" based on counts.
- Read numbers from number line 0-180.
- Write two-digit numbers.
- Count orally by 1's, 2's, 5's, 10's.
- Count forward and backward from any number by 1's.
- Identify ordinal numbers.
- Demonstrate basic calculator operations.
- Collect data.
- Recognize relationships in graphs.
- Recognize shapes.
- Compare sizes.
- Tell time to the hour.
- Identify coins.
- Count coins for totals less than a dollar.
- Complete patterns for sets of two and three patterns.
- Classify by common attributes.
- Identify which of two sets has more or fewer objects.
- Extend patterns.
- Be aware of estimation.
- Become familiar with simple computer programs.

Grade 1: Students will . . .

- State oral fact drills: sums and differences.
- Use mental arithmetic to add and subtract two-digit numbers.
- Perform written addition and subtraction fact drills.
- Add and subtract with tens from any number.
- Find missing numbers in a sequence.
- Read three-digit numbers.
- Perform rote counts beyond 100 by 1's, 2's, 5's, 10's forward and backward.
- Tally counts to 100.

107. MATHEMATICS — K-6 LEARNER
OUTCOMES (SAMPLES), CONTINUED

- Identify the 1's, 10's, and 100's place.
- Identify even and odd numbers.
- Be able to fold paper in half and in quarters.
- Use the calculator to count by a given number.
- State addition and subtraction fact families.
- Make basic inferences from data.
- Collect data and informally graph the data.
- Graph growth vs. time data.
- Identify points and segments.
- Identify plane figures.
- Name geometric solids.
- Identify tools for measurement.
- Use a ruler to measure centimeters and inches.
- Use a tape measure to measure centimeters and inches.
- Identify the hour hand.
- Use the calendar for identifying dates.
- Use a thermometer to read temperatures.
- Count by pennies, nickels, dimes, and quarters.
- Write total money values less than $5.
- Choose the correct operation to solve word problems in addition or subtraction.
- Apply estimation to solve problems.
- Use a calculator to check addition and subtraction problems.

Grade 2: Students will . . .

- State fact extensions to two-digit numbers.
- Use the calculator memory key correctly.
- Use mental arithmetic to solve two- and three-digit addition and subtraction problems.
- Add and subtract tens and hundreds.
- Identify and write number models for story problems.
- Identify equivalent fractions.
- Write fractions as decimals.
- Find sums of multidigit addends.
- Read, write, and compare four-digit numbers.
- Use tallies and frequency distribution tables.

107. MATHEMATICS — K-6 LEARNER OUTCOMES (SAMPLES), CONTINUED

- Be able to compare fractions.
- Use a number grid for demonstration of place value.
- Compare graphs.
- Find median and mode in a number series.
- Interpret graphed data.
- Identify plane and solid shapes.
- Identify polygons by sides and angles.
- Find perimeter.
- Classify polygons and estimate area.
- Weigh objects with a scale.
- Compare metric and English units.
- Tell time to five-minute intervals.
- Find temperature differences.
- Find sums and differences less than $1.
- Write total money values less than $100.
- Record money, using dollar and cent notation.
- Convert money and make money exchanges.
- Identify relevant data in solving word problems.
- Solve quantitative real-life problems.
- Understand estimation skills.
- Develop competency in use of a calculator to check problems.

Grade 3: Students will . . .

- Add, subtract algorithms.
- Multiply, divide powers of 10.
- Use calculator percent key correctly.
- Understand multiplication and division as inverse operations.
- Know multiplication and division fact families.
- Use formal division procedures.
- Be able to find perimeter and area.
- Read, write, compare numbers beyond five digits.
- Determine intervals from a table.
- Define decimals and fraction relationships.
- Compare fractions.

107. MATHEMATICS — K-6 LEARNER
OUTCOMES (SAMPLES), CONTINUED

- Use addition, subtraction, multiplication, and division algorithms.
- Evaluate two-axis data.
- Predict trends.
- Understand and compute mean, median, and mode.
- Define relationships of geometric shapes.
- Determine relationships of perimeter to area.
- Classify triangles and quadrilaterals.
- Construct polygons using a compass and straight-edge.
- Identify tools in conventional and metric systems.
- Measure to the nearest 1/8 inch.
- Use appropriate units of measure.
- Use equivalencies in measurement.
- Tell digital time to the minute.
- Determine time elapsed.
- Solve two-step money problems.
- Create algorithmic procedures to solve problems.
- Apply information from a recipe, schedule, etc., to solve a problem.
- Use several strategies to solve an open-ended problem.
- Estimate reasonableness of problem solutions.
- Determine relevancy of data for problem solving.

Grade 4: Students will . . .

- Write standard numerals for word norms.
- Develop skill in rounding off numbers.
- Exhibit the ability to compare and order whole numbers through five digits.
- Demonstrate understanding of adding three to four, four-digit whole numbers.
- Develop skill in subtracting four- and five-digit numbers.
- Exhibit the ability to multiply and divide through 9's.
- Multiply and divide three-digit whole number by a one-digit number.
- Multiply and divide three-digit numbers by a two-digit number using a calculator.
- Practice adding and subtracting fractions with like denominators.
- Have awareness of parts of a whole or set.
- Develop skill in interpreting circle and line graphs.
- Interpret a bar graph and a pictograph.

107. MATHEMATICS — K-6 LEARNER OUTCOMES (SAMPLES), CONTINUED

- Express as a fraction the probability of a simple event.
- Compare, write, order, add, and subtract decimals through hundredths.
- Estimate sums of differences of decimals.
- Demonstrate how to tell time accurately.
- Choose appropriate metric and/or customary units of length, weight, mass, and capacity.
- Measure length to the nearest inch.
- Exhibit ability to count, write, and compare money amounts and make change up to $10.
- Identify symmetric and congruent figures.
- Identify intersecting and parallel lines.
- Identify solid figures.
- Investigate finding the perimeter of a polygon.
- Name and locate ordered pairs.
- Name basic geometric shapes.
- Interpret use of vertical bar and line graphs.
- Apply estimation in problem solving.
- Develop skill in solving two-step problems and introduce three-step problems.
- Identify extraneous information in a problem.
- Find an average.
- Interpret remainders.
- Demonstrate giving multiple solutions to an open-ended problem.
- Exhibit ability to read a thermometer.
- Investigate making a tree diagram.
- Understand comparing and ordering.
- Explain and apply ratios.

Grade 5: Students will . . .

- Read and write numbers to billions.
- Compare and order whole numbers.
- Interpret data from a table.
- Locate ordered pairs on a coordinate grid.
- Use a model to illustrate the structure of numbers.
- Compare and contrast different types of numbers.
- Create objects that satisfy certain conditions.

107. MATHEMATICS — K-6 LEARNER OUTCOMES (SAMPLES), CONTINUED

- Explain why a construction is unique.
- Create new problems by changing the conditions.
- Choose the best solution to a construction and defend it.
- Apply previous knowledge to reconstruct missing information in a problem.

Grade 6: Students will . . .

- Read and write whole numbers and decimals.
- Compare whole numbers and decimals.
- Round whole numbers and decimals.
- Solve problems that involve conducting an experiment.
- Estimate sums and differences.
- Add, subtract, and solve equations.
- Measure length to the nearest millimeter.
- Solve problems using estimation and drawing a diagram.
- Estimate the product of whole numbers and decimals.
- Multiply whole numbers and decimals.
- Use the properties of exponents in multiplication.
- Find the area of rectangular figures.
- Solve problems with multistep solutions and identify those with not enough or too much information.
- Estimate quotients of whole numbers.
- Divide whole numbers.
- Solve equations involving multiplication and division.
- Convert units of time and determine elapsed time.
- Use order of operations in simplifying numerical expressions.
- Estimate decimal quotients.
- Divide decimals by whole numbers.
- Estimate and measure capacity and mass using metric measures.
- Solve problems involving estimation and checking.
- Find the greatest common factor (GCF) of a set of numbers.
- Identify prime numbers.
- Find multiples and the least common multiple (LCM).
- Find and compare equivalent fractions and mixed numbers.
- Express numbers as fractions, decimals, and whole numbers.
- Estimate and measure length to the nearest 1/16 inch.

107. MATHEMATICS — K-6 LEARNER OUTCOMES (SAMPLES), CONTINUED

- Measure capacity and weight.
- Add or subtract fractions and mixed numbers.
- Solve problems involving number sense and checking reasonableness of answers.
- Estimate products.
- Divide fractions by fractions.
- Convert customary units of measure.
- Find the areas of triangles and parallelograms.
- Identify and measure angles.
- Classify polygons.
- Identify transformation of geometric figures.
- Write a ratio to compare two quantities.
- Write and solve a proportion.
- Use scale drawings.
- Express percents as decimals and fractions.
- Find circumference and area of a circle.
- Find volume of prisms and cylinders.
- Find probabilities of independent events.
- Express a probability as a fraction, ratio, decimal, or percent.
- Predict outcomes using probabilities and statistics.
- Distinguish between useful and misleading statistics.
- Solve problems involving a simulation.
- Use number lines to represent integers.
- Compare and order integers up to two digits.
- Graph ordered pairs on a grid.
- Solve problems using different strategies.

108. MEDIA AND TECHNOLOGY — K-6 LEARNER OUTCOMES (SAMPLES)

Kindergarten: Students will . . .

- Use simple graphic tools.
- Discuss digital camera pictures on a monitor.
- Suggest ways to manipulate data in a simulation.
- Suggest ways to sort information in a database.
- Participate in demonstration of creating and saving a desktop.
- Identify when to use a desktop publishing program.
- Participate in demonstrations of entering information into a desktop publishing program.
- Identify how to access information through a multimedia document.
- Explain that a computer can control devices connected to it.
- Participate in activities using software-produced music.
- Receive a class message via telecommunications.
- Help decide content to be sent via telecommunications.
- Discuss how people communicate via telecommunications.
- Help create a video.
- Suggest changes in the video (editing).
- Participate in an I-Net activity.
- Use a word processing program to share ideas.
- Observe information-gathering, using various tools.

Grade 1: Students will . . .

- Use computer graphics to share ideas.
- Suggest solutions to problems based on simulation information.
- Suggest solutions to problems based on database information.
- Participate in demonstrations of creating, opening, and saving a desktop presentation.
- Enter information into a desktop publishing program.
- Place a graphic with text.
- Use hypermedia to share ideas.
- Suggest appropriate topics for a hypermedia document.
- Identify how to access information from a multimedia document.
- Compare music compositions on a computer vs. other means.
- Identify the terms *modem* and *telecommunications*.
- Participate in activities using a videodisc.

108. MEDIA AND TECHNOLOGY — K-6 LEARNER OUTCOMES (SAMPLES), CONTINUED

- Participate in a video.
- Participate in an activity using I-Net.
- Use word processing to share ideas.
- Identify when to use a word processing program.
- Search beyond the classroom for information.
- Look at many sources having boldface and italics.
- Experience the idea of webbing.
- Discuss differences between facts and opinions.
- Compare and contrast inferred ideas and factual statements.
- Discuss drawing conclusions from data.

Grade 2: Students will . . .

- Use a digital camera to display pictures on a monitor.
- Participate in demonstrations of inputting, sorting, and selecting information on a database.
- Enter information and graphics into a desktop publishing program with guidance.
- Use a hypermedia program to share ideas.
- Discuss the design of a hypermedia document to present solutions to problems.
- Identify the way to access information from a multimedia document.
- Explain that a computer can control other devices (i.e., CD-ROM, scanner, etc.).
- Demonstrate music composition software.
- Send and receive a telecommunications message.
- Determine when to use telecommunications for information gathering.
- State proper care and handling of basic video and audio equipment.
- Identify the basic parts of a camera.
- Use CD-ROM's and videodiscs to access information.
- Use basic formatting.
- Choose when to use a word processing program.
- Use more than one print and nonprint resource.
- Do a simple search online in a database.
- Demonstrate understanding of uses of indexes and tables of contents.
- Make use of graphic clues and cross references when gathering information.
- Be able to web and sort.

108. MEDIA AND TECHNOLOGY — K-6
LEARNER OUTCOMES (SAMPLES), CONTINUED

Grade 3: Students will . . .

- Design a desktop presenting document.
- Manipulate information using desktop presenting.
- Use basic design rules of desktop publishing (fonts, positioning, etc.).
- Design a hypermedia document to present solutions to problems.
- Demonstrate creation of multimedia resources.
- Discuss when to use multimedia.
- Demonstrate use of music composition software.
- Send telecommunications information as a group project.
- Use the terms *modem, telecommunications, upload*, and *download*.
- Use CD-ROM's and videodisks to access information.
- Use basic formatting.
- Use information from an electronic database when appropriate.
- Regularly use tables of contents and indexes to locate information.
- Use boldface and italic clues.
- Obtain resources by cross-referencing.
- Prepare two simple research projects; be able to classify notes on the topic.
- Use a wide variety of resources to identify examples of biased, opinionated statements.

Grade 4: Students will . . .

- Create graphic images to present solutions to problems.
- Manipulate information in a simulation.
- Print information from a database.
- Enter text and graphics into a desktop publishing program.
- Demonstrate entering data into a graph.
- Link the file.
- Design a hypermedia document to present solutions to problems.
- Use a multimedia resource.
- Produce music using computer software.
- Demonstrate entering data into a spreadsheet.
- Access and communicate information using telecommunications.
- Use telecommunications terms.
- Make changes in a video in post production (editing).

108. MEDIA AND TECHNOLOGY — K-6 LEARNER OUTCOMES (SAMPLES), CONTINUED

- Design and create a video production including visuals.
- Use a tape recorder to communicate information.
- Use CD-ROM's and videodiscs to access information.
- Edit a file.
- Use at least one print, one nonprint, and one electronic resource when making reports.
- Identify a personal topic and locate information using user's instructions.
- Identify implied meanings in a variety of resources.
- Use current events publications to make inferences.

Grade 5: Students will . . .

- Create graphics and import into a desktop publishing program.
- Input, sort, and select information from a database.
- Design a desktop presenting document.
- Enter text and graphics into a desktop publishing program.
- Enter data into a graph and select appropriate type of graph for display of information.
- Add information and graphics, save to a hypermedia file.
- Design a hypermedia document.
- Put sound into a multimedia document.
- Enter data into a spreadsheet and do calculations using the data.
- Design an activity that uses I-Net.
- Choose to use a word processing program for curricular projects.
- Use a variety of resources to gather facts and information.
- Use a variety of resources and tools in data collecting.
- Locate information by using subheadings.
- Use instructions to locate specific information.
- Proceed carefully when clues are presented and use a thesaurus regularly.

Grade 6: Students will . . .

- Create graphics through digitizing pictures using a scanner.
- Create graphic images to present solutions.
- Create multicolumn documents.
- Design a document based on the intended audience.
- Suggest solutions to problems using a graph.

108. MEDIA AND TECHNOLOGY — K-6 LEARNER OUTCOMES (SAMPLES), CONTINUED

- Create a multimedia document using sound, graphics, or videodisc connection.
- Do simple calculations using spreadsheet data.
- Use telecommunications for a collaborative project.
- Use I-Net as a vehicle for communication.
- Edit a file (cut and paste, spell check, find and replace).
- Use basic formatting—justification, tabs, styles, margins, pagination, etc.
- Develop topic sentences based on notes.
- Access information through indexes.
- Use instructions and legends.
- Interpret graphic clues and cross-references.

109. MUSIC — K-6 LEARNER OUTCOMES
(SAMPLES)

Kindergarten: Students will . . .

- Sing in a free, light head voice, alone and with others.
- Express musical feelings through movement.
- Demonstrate steady beat with a simple instrument.
- Apply concepts of beat, loud, soft, fast, slow, etc.
- Improvise music.
- Sing songs from memory.
- Participate willingly in musical activities.
- Experience music of diverse style, culture, and times.

Grade 1: Students will . . .

- Demonstrate understanding of appropriate rhythm patterns.
- Understand melodic concepts of up, down, and simple pentatonic scale patterns.
- Demonstrate understanding of musical phrase.
- Recognize various instruments.
- Play pitched and unpitched percussion instruments.
- Apply musical terms such as tempo, beat, and rhythm.
- Recognize the importance of music in everyday life.

Grade 2: Students will . . .

- Demonstrate understanding of rhythmic elements and patterns.
- Demonstrate understanding of melodic concepts, including repeated tones and pentatonic scale patterns.
- Understand musical form including phrase, AB, ABA.
- Apply such musical terms as *introduction* and *accent*.

Grade 3: Students will . . .

- Demonstrate understanding of rhythmic patterns, including two eighth notes, quarter, half, and whole notes and rests and meters of 2s, 3s, and 4s by singing, playing, and moving.
- Understand melodic concepts, including so, la, do, re, me, so, la, do.
- Show understanding of musical form including round, rondo, and ostinato.
- Play pitched and unpitched percussion instruments, including the piano.
- Respond to music and make aesthetic observations.
- Develop attitudes of cooperation, appreciation, and interest in music.

109. MUSIC — K-6 LEARNER OUTCOMES
(SAMPLES), CONTINUED

Grade 4: Students will . . .

- Recognize letter names of lines and spaces in the treble clef.
- Understand theme and variations.
- Recognize major and minor chords by sound.
- Play Orff instruments and the recorder. (Some students may begin formal string orchestra study at this grade level.)

Grade 5: Students will . . .

- Show understanding of concepts of skips, steps, and simple scale patterns.
- Demonstrate aural recognition of major and minor scales.
- Understand I, IV, and V chords by playing chordal instruments.
- Recognize orchestral families and individual instruments by sight and sound.
- Play baritone ukulele.
- Understand dynamics and notation.
- Explore music of various cultures and times. (Some students will continue string orchestra instruction. Some students will begin formal band instruction at this grade level.)

Grade 6: Students will . . .

- Demonstrate understanding of rhythmic elements, including dotted and triplet notation and time signature.
- Recognize names of lines and spaces in bass clef.
- Understand canon, theme, and variations.
- Recognize orchestral and concert band sound, and individual instruments, by sight and sound.
- Play simple pieces on the guitar.
- Use musical terms, symbols, tempo markings, and key signatures. (Certain students will continue formal string orchestra or band instruction at this grade level.)

110. PHYSICAL EDUCATION — K-6 LEARNER OUTCOMES (SAMPLES)

Kindergarten: Students will . . .

- Recognize and move body parts.
- Perform basic body movements (i.e., twisting, stretching, etc.)
- Identify and use fundamental motor skills.
- Exhibit body balance.
- Explore movement through rhythm.
- Use manipulative objects (e.g., lummi sticks) in response to rhythmic patterns.
- Be aware of physical fitness.
- Participate in large muscle developmental motor skills.
- Be introduced to rules of group activities.
- Perform developmental-perceptual and motor skills in low-organization activities.
- Play cooperatively.
- Experience fun and enjoyment.
- Respect individual differences.

Grade 1: Students will . . .

- Demonstrate movement of each body part.
- Move safely and efficiently through space.
- Perform rhythmic patterns, moving and nonmoving.
- Use dance in the development of physical fitness.
- Understand that rhythm and dance are multicultural.
- Take pride in personal freedom of nonverbal expression through dance and rhythmic activities.

Grade 2: Students will . . .

- Organize and use body parts and spatial concepts.
- Perform moving and nonmoving skills to increasingly mature levels.
- Explain the difference between such motor skills as hopping, skipping, and so on.
- Respond to auditory and visual stimuli when performing motor tasks.
- Perform rhythmic patterns in sequence.
- Perform combination rhythmic movements to changing tempos.
- Be introduced to components of total wellness.
- Identify components of physical fitness.
- Learn about injury prevention and safety procedures.

110. PHYSICAL EDUCATION — K-6 LEARNER OUTCOMES (SAMPLES), CONTINUED

- Measure personal fitness and wellness using the President's Challenge Physical Fitness Program.
- Measure fitness through skinfold measurements of triceps and calf muscles.

Grade 3: Students will . . .

- Move with smoothly integrated body action.
- Achieve skill levels that boost self-esteem.
- Use balls and hoops in response to rhythm patterns.
- Perform a variety of multicultural dance patterns.
- Perform a sequence of movement patterns as the beat dictates.
- Identify social, emotional, mental, and physical components of a wellness program.
- Identify components of physical fitness such as muscular strength, endurance, flexibility, cardiovascular and body composition.
- Recognize the sense of well-being associated with fitness.
- Be introduced to team lead-up activities related to sports games.
- Reinforce rules, vocabulary, and sportsmanship of lead-up game activities.
- Perform and integrate a combination of developmental motor skills.
- Be introduced to basic rules and terminology of such selective individual activities as bowling and gymnastics.
- Integrate developmental motor skills into individual activities.
- Experience fun and enjoyment.
- Accept and respect achievement levels of others.
- Know and apply safety procedures.

Grade 4: Students will . . .

- Propel, track, and control manipulative objects with progressive skill.
- Take pride in quality of personal movement.
- Memorize and perform the sequence of movement patterns for a dance.
- Be aware of the ethnic or cultural origin of the dance.
- Recognize the importance of exercise, rest, nutrition, and relaxation for a healthy life style.
- Understand rules and vocabulary, and apply to group activities and team sports.
- Be introduced to such team games as soccer, volleyball, basketball, floor hockey, softball, and touch football.
- Reinforce concepts of selected individual activities such as jogging and roller-skating.

110. PHYSICAL EDUCATION — K-6 LEARNER OUTCOMES (SAMPLES), CONTINUED

- Be introduced to basic rules and vocabulary of selected individual activities—cross-country skiing, track and field, and so on.

Grade 5: Students will . . .

- Feel confident with their own motor skill levels.
- Perform a variety of square dance patterns.
- Be aware of the origin of square dance.
- Be aware of health screening (scoliosis).
- Show growth in understanding rules and vocabulary in team sports.
- Be introduced to strategy in team sports.
- Show growth in understanding rules and vocabulary of individual sports.
- Be introduced to strategy necessary for successful participation in competitive individual sports.
- Refine motor skills through observation and active participation.

Grade 6: Students will . . .

- Perform fundamental motor skills at a mature level while participating in activities.
- Feel confident with personal motor skill levels.
- Perform a variety of square dances with a more complex rhythmic pattern.
- Show growth in understanding, interpretation, and application of rules and vocabulary in team sports.
- Attain increasing competency that better enables participation in team sports.
- Appreciate the value and role of practice in assuring enjoyable participation.
- Show growth in understanding, interpretation, and application of rules and vocabulary in individual sports.
- Recognize and appreciate gender similarities and differences by demonstrating fairness, equality, and respect.

111. SCIENCE — K-6 LEARNER OUTCOMES
(SAMPLES)

Kindergarten: Students will . . .

- Show growing curiosity in living things.
- Observe the properties of trees in the schoolyard.
- Help plant and care for a tree.
- Compare leaf shapes to geometric shapes.
- Use pictorial experiences to heighten awareness of a variety of trees and leaves.
- Acquire vocabulary associated with the structures of trees.
- Observe and describe a variety of common animals.
- Compare structures and behaviors of different pairs of animals.
- Learn to handle animals carefully and help in the care and feeding of classroom animals.
- Show growing curiosity in the physical world.
- Observe the properties of different kinds of paper.
- Observe the properties of different fabrics.
- Acquire vocabulary associated with properties of paper and fabric.
- Observe the properties of a variety of wood.
- Change wood into a variety of properties.
- Understand the correlation between flowers and fruits' seeds.
- Observe and identify common birds living in the area in winter.
- Begin to develop an awareness and respect for nature.

Grade 1: Students will . . .

- Develop an interest in plants as living things.
- Experience the diversity of forms in the plant kingdom.
- Describe changes as plants grow.
- Become familiar with the structure of flowering plants.
- Recognize solids and liquids.
- Sort materials according to properties.
- Combine or separate solids of different particle size.
- Observe results of combining solids with water and liquids with water.
- Use information to investigate an unknown material.
- Sort earth materials based on properties.
- Observe properties in materials in a river rock mixture.
- Compare ingredients of different soils.
- Observe a variety of animal homes.

111. SCIENCE — K-6 LEARNER OUTCOMES
(SAMPLES), CONTINUED

- Distinguish between *hibernation* and *dormancy*.
- Understand animals' need for shelter.
- Observe and identify animal tracks in the snow.
- Describe plant parts and their function.
- Appreciate diversity in plants and animals.
- Develop a respect for natural resources.

Grade 2: Students will . . .

- Develop an interest in insects as living things.
- Experience the diversity of forms in the animal kingdom.
- Be familiar with the life sequences of different insects.
- Provide for the needs of insects (air, space, water, etc.).
- Solve problems through trial and error.
- Explore concepts of balance, counterweight, and stability.
- Develop an interest in air and weather.
- Describe weather changes over time.
- Be familiar with common weather monitoring instruments.
- Use a bar graph to compare weather conditions.
- Observe the force of air pressure.
- Compare the life history of honeybees and wasps.
- Understand the role of insects in pollination.
- Describe useful products of beekeeping.
- Appreciate the unique characteristics of insects.
- Describe the metamorphosis process in insects.

Grade 3: Students will . . .

- Gain experience with organisms (plants and animals).
- Investigate the effect of water on seeds.
- Observe properties of germinated seeds.
- Grow plants hydroponically.
- Observe crayfish structures and behavior.
- Develop responsibility for the care of living things.
- Compare sounds to develop discrimination.
- Communicate using a "drop code."
- Learn how sound originates (vibration) and is received.

111. SCIENCE — K-6 LEARNER OUTCOMES
(SAMPLES), CONTINUED

- Compare how sound travels through different substances.
- Compare methods to amplify sound.
- Explore liquid and solid states of water.
- Observe expansion and contraction of water.
- Investigate factors affecting evaporation and condensation.
- Be aware of the importance of water to life.
- Understand the necessity of standard units of measure.
- Understand the metric system.
- Measure objects in centimeters.
- Weigh objects in grams.
- Identify mechanisms of seed dispersal.
- Analyze a transect study area for seed variety.
- Understand what changes molecules of matter into crystals.
- Realize the insulating characteristics of snow.

Grade 4: Students will . . .

- Investigate the human skeletal and muscle systems.
- Build models to show how muscles cause movement.
- Investigate response times of hands and feet.
- Acquire vocabulary associated with skeletal and muscle systems.
- Compare effects of magnets on common materials.
- Discover the magnet's display functions of attraction and repulsion.
- Construct electrical circuits.
- Identify conductors and insulators.
- Learn how to make an electromagnet.
- Make a telegraph.
- Develop an interest in earth materials (rocks and minerals).
- Organize data about rocks.
- Seriate minerals on the basis of one property.
- Investigate the effect of vinegar on calcite.
- Use evaporation to investigate rock composition.
- Acquire the vocabulary of earth science.
- Explore the techniques of chromatography, rubbing, and carbon printing.
- Understand differences between deciduous and coniferous trees.
- Observe the process of converting sap into maple syrup.
- Compare the maple sugar-making process at the Ojibwa culture to modern methods.

111. SCIENCE — K-6 LEARNER OUTCOMES
(SAMPLES), CONTINUED

Grade 5: Students will . . .

- Investigate the properties of food.
- Be aware of carbohydrates, proteins, fats, and vitamins as food components.
- Test for the presence of acid, vitamin C, and sugar.
- Be aware of guides for healthy nutrition.
- Become informed consumers of food products.
- Gain experience with the concepts of mixture and solution, concentration and saturation, and chemical reaction.
- Experience models and maps.
- Gain experience with the concept of erosion.
- Observe the effect of water on land features.
- Conduct stream table investigations.
- Become familiar with topographic maps.
- Understand contour and elevation.
- Experience the concept of variables.
- Understand the behavior of pendulums.
- Gain experience with buoyancy.
- Use data to make predictions.
- Record and graph data to discover relationships between variables.
- Experience the outdoor skill of snowshoeing.
- Understand how snowshoes disperse weight.
- Demonstrate proficiency in compass usage.
- Complete an orienteering course.

Grade 6: Students will . . .

- Gain experience with major environmental factors in terrestrial and aquatic systems.
- Determine an organism's optimum conditions and environmental preferences.
- Relate laboratory studies to natural systems.
- Gain experience with levers and pulleys.
- Understand the concept of advantage as it applies to simple machines.
- Use diagrams to translate three-dimensional space relationships into two dimensions.
- Acquire vocabulary associated with simple machines.

111. SCIENCE — K-6 LEARNER OUTCOMES
(SAMPLES), CONTINUED

- Understand solar energy as an alternative energy source.
- Observe changes in shadows resulting from relative positions of sun and earth.
- Become proficient in using a thermometer.
- Design solar water heaters and passive solar space heaters.
- Recognize relationships between structure and functions of materials and systems.
- Acquire vocabulary associated with engineering and technology.
- Learn that there is often more than one solution to a problem.
- Learn about frostbite and hypothermia.
- Demonstrate proper firebuilding technique as an outdoor survival skill.
- Know and apply proper outdoor winter attire.
- Recognize the result of habitual loss of Neotropical bird migrants.
- Acquire bird identification techniques.
- Observe the bird-banding process and understand its use in research.

112. SOCIAL STUDIES — K-6 LEARNER OUTCOMES (SAMPLES)

Kindergarten: Students will . . .

- Explain changes in human development (baby to adult).
- Understand that responsibilities change with maturity.
- Understand that rules promote health and safety.
- Appreciate that imagination makes individuals unique.
- Identify four basic needs met by families.
- Explain how families differ.
- Realize that families have traditions.
- Recognize types of knowledge and skills.
- Understand that students go to school to gain knowledge and acquire skills.
- Appreciate the value of school rules.
- Choose self-directed activities that enhance social and academic learning.

Grade 1: Students will . . .

- Classify places and services in a community.
- Realize that communities change.
- Evaluate roles and identify careers in a community.
- Be aware of newspapers as information sources.
- Appreciate the differences of people and cultures.
- Develop compassion for all peoples.
- Compare information from various media.
- Appreciate that different people celebrate different holidays.
- Recognize how holidays strengthen family and community ties.
- Identify symbols of the United States.
- Appreciate similarities and differences among the 50 states.
- Understand that our community is part of the United States and that the United States is part of the world.

Grade 2: Students will . . .

- Compare the local community with a foreign community.
- Understand the interdependence of countries.
- Develop global vocabulary.
- Understand maps and globes as models of the earth.
- Identify directions (north, south, etc.).

112. SOCIAL STUDIES — K-6 LEARNER OUTCOMES (SAMPLES), CONTINUED

- Know the relationship of community to state to nation to North America to the seven continents.
- Describe local, state, and national governments.
- Explain democracy.
- List local, state, and national leaders.
- Identify state capital cities.
- Explain taxes as a source of revenue.
- Begin to understand world affairs.
- Learn various types of information featured in the news.

Grade 3: Students will . . .

- Understand map keys and symbols.
- Compare different kinds of maps.
- Understand time lines.
- Realize that a community is a place to live, work, and play.
- Identify ways that communities respond to needs.
- Compare different types of communities.
- Evaluate the roles of citizens in a community.
- Understand types and interdependence of occupations.
- Know the difference between goods and services.
- Understand the role money plays in economics.
- Recognize the role of manufacturing to the economy.
- Analyze the validity of news sources.
- Discriminate between facts and opinions.
- Analyze what an informed citizen is.
- Recognize the need to conserve and recycle.
- Describe renewable and nonrenewable resources.
- Identify ways to conserve natural resources.
- List various means of transportation and communication.
- Evaluate the impact of communication and transportation inventions.

Grade 4: Students will . . .

- Understand that places are alike and different in land forms.
- Name the four hemispheres.
- Define *longitude* and *latitude*.

112. SOCIAL STUDIES — K-6 LEARNER
OUTCOMES (SAMPLES), CONTINUED

- Identify the seven continents and four main oceans of the world.
- Explain the five major climates.
- Realize that the earth is constantly moving and changing.
- Know that natural and manmade forces affect the earth.
- Understand the relationship between food gathering and environment.
- Be aware of the interdependence of countries for food.
- Understand the development and spread of tools and technology.
- Investigate the Industrial Revolution.
- Evaluate how machines and inventions change the way people live.
- Recognize the importance of human choices and planning in the use of natural resources.
- Understand the dangers of pollution.
- Evaluate wise and unwise uses of our oceans.
- Discuss different kinds of energy and how to save it.
- Identify traditional beliefs, customs, and lifestyles of Native American heritage.
- Demonstrate respect for Native American culture.

Grade 5: Students will . . .

- Study early explorers of our nation.
- Recognize exploration as a driving force in the development of the United States.
- Appreciate how geographical features influenced expansion.
- Identify causes of the Civil War.
- Be aware of how government changes.
- Understand the shared history of the United States and Canada.
- Compare geographical features of the United States and Canada.
- Recognize how Canadian government is similar to ours.
- Show awareness of world events.
- Analyze global interdependency.
- Recognize the validity of different governments and cultures.

Grade 6: Students will . . .

- Understand the impact of the settlement of the Great Plains.
- Identify changes caused by the Industrial Revolution.
- Analyze the emergence of America as a world leader.
- Investigate technological advances in the twentieth century.

112. SOCIAL STUDIES — K-6 LEARNER OUTCOMES (SAMPLES), CONTINUED

- Identify causes and effects of the Great Depression.
- Analyze the role of the United States in war time.
- Appreciate our state's historical background, including the role of immigration.
- Describe our state's economic role today.
- Recognize the relationship between individuals and issues in today's world.
- Evaluate current events and understand major influences upon our behavior.

113. GRADE-LEVEL THEMES (SPECIAL STUDY TOPICS) FOR ELEMENTARY PUPILS
(EXAMPLES)

Many elementary schools use series of special themes as a vehicle for delivering the curriculum. These special topics spark student interest. Below is an illustrative list of grade-level themes common in many elementary programs.

KINDERGARTEN

Rain Forest

Dinosaurs

Butterflies

Bears

Apples

Pumpkins

Farm

Birds

Body Organs

FIRST GRADE

Letter Writing

I Can Do It

Fables

Charlotte's Web

Cats

Surprises

Scared Silly

Holidays

Hawaii

Polar Regions

Animals

Seven Continents

SECOND GRADE

Experts

Native Americans

113. GRADE-LEVEL THEMES (SPECIAL STUDY TOPICS) FOR ELEMENTARY PUPILS
(EXAMPLES), CONTINUED

Bird Watch
Mexico
Whales
Heroes
Solar System
Book Making
Bodies
Communities
Lots of Math

THIRD GRADE

Under the Sea
Japan
Maps and Globes
Fairy Tales
Friendship
Magic
Body
Research Papers
Earth (Rocks)
Tangrams

FOURTH GRADE

Endangered Animals
Suspense
Mysteries
Dear Diary
Humor
USA
Battle of Wits
Solutions

113. GRADE-LEVEL THEMES (SPECIAL STUDY TOPICS) FOR ELEMENTARY PUPILS
(EXAMPLES), CONTINUED

FIFTH GRADE

Going to Extremes
Words, Words, Words
Games People Play
Tales and Tails
Faces and Places
Author, Author
Trip to Africa

SIXTH GRADE

Egypt
Wolves
World War II
Folk Tales
Oceans
Bubbles
Survival Black History
Optics
Models and Designs

114. COMPREHENSIVE MIDDLE SCHOOL/JUNIOR HIGH COURSE OFFERINGS
(EXAMPLES)

Communities across the country continue to vacillate between middle schools and junior high schools, trying to find the right fit for pre- and early-adolescent learners. Whichever organizational pattern is adopted, exploration is the key to the curriculum for students in the middle years. Following is a representative course of study for grades 6-8:

Grade 6

Full Year:

    Math

    Science

    Reading

    Social Studies

    English

    Spelling

    Handwriting

Semester:

    Physical Education

    Music

    Life Skills (Home Ec. and Ind. Tech.)

Quarter:

    Art

    Health

    Keyboarding (20 hrs.)

Grade 7

Full Year:

    English

    Social Studies

    Math

    Science

    Reading (if necessary)

114. COMPREHENSIVE MIDDLE SCHOOL/JUNIOR HIGH COURSE OFFERINGS
(EXAMPLES), CONTINUED

Semester:

Art

Music

Physical Education

Life Skills

Introduction to World Language

Exploratory French, German, and Spanish

Reading and Study Skills

Grade 8

Full Year:

English

Social Studies

Math

Science

Reading (if necessary)

Semester:

Physical Education

Health

Electives:*

Art Workshop

Exploratory Business

Keyboarding

Oral Communication

Exploratory French

Exploratory German

Exploratory Spanish

Nutrition/Foods

Consumer Clothing

114. COMPREHENSIVE MIDDLE SCHOOL/JUNIOR HIGH COURSE OFFERINGS
(EXAMPLES), CONTINUED

Industrial Technology Communications

Energy, Power, and Transportation Production

Computer Applications

Band, Chorus, and Orchestra

Advanced Reading

Study Hall

*One-semester elective offerings

115. COMPREHENSIVE SENIOR HIGH COURSE OFFERINGS (EXAMPLES)

Although the size of the school's enrollment drives the curriculum to some extent, most communities attempt to provide a comprehensive program of course offerings at the senior high level. The goal is to meet the needs and abilities of all students by including courses for both college and vocational preparation. Below is a typical program of senior high school curriculum offerings:

Language Arts

English 9, 10, 11, and 12

Popular Literature

Reading and Study Skills

World Literature

Modern Literature

Imaginative Literature

Advanced Placement English

General Writing

School Literary Magazine

College Prep Composition

Creative Writing

School Newspaper

School Yearbook

Journalism

Speech/Debate

Argumentation and Formal Speech

Art of the Cinema

Reading Aloud and Performing

Media Production

Science

Science Nine

Biology

Advanced Biology

115. COMPREHENSIVE SENIOR HIGH COURSE OFFERINGS (EXAMPLES), CONTINUED

Anatomy and Physiology

Honors Chemistry

Advanced Chemistry

General Chemistry

Advanced Physics

Honors Physics

General Physics

Foreign Language

French I-V

German I-V

Spanish I-V

Japanese I-V

Mathematics

Computer Mathematics

Advanced Computer Math

Algebra

Math Exploration

Geometry I-II

Formal Geometry

Higher Algebra

Trigonometry and Analysis of Functions

Analysis of Functions II

Honors Geometry

Honors Algebra and Trigonometry

Honors Precalculus

Calculus

Discrete Math and Calculus

Introduction to Calculus

115. COMPREHENSIVE SENIOR HIGH COURSE OFFERINGS (EXAMPLES), CONTINUED

Social Studies

Advanced Placement European History

Advanced Placement American History

American Studies 9-10

Western Civilization

Former USSR and Eastern Europe

World Cultures

World Religions

Economic Issues and Public Policy

Political Behavior

Psychology

Sociology

Criminal Justice

Anthropology

Additional Elective Courses (by departments)

Art

Business

On-the-Job Career Programs

Life Management (Home Economics)

Industrial Technology

Music: Vocal, Band, Jazz, and String

Physical Education

Vocational Technical

Community Involvement

116. ALTERNATIVE METHODS OF OBTAINING HIGH SCHOOL CREDITS

In addition to regular courses offered by the school, many high schools will approve or grant credit(s) earned through a variety of alternative learning activities and experiences including the following:

1. *Credit by Performance:* Some schools establish guidelines by which credit may be given on a performance basis by means of approved assessments of varying kinds.

2. *Independent Study Programs*: Some schools provide planned programs of independent learning whereby students do not attend classes for a specific amount of time. Credit may be granted for performance on proficiency exams or completion of curriculum units identified as comprising the equivalency of a unit of work.

3. *Work-Study Programs*: Credit is commonly given for work experience (on-the-job) programs under the supervision of the school.

4. *Study Abroad*: Students who have attended foreign schools may have credits verified by evaluation of their transcripts or passing a proficiency exam. The same procedure usually applies to credits earned through the American Field Service International Program.

5. *Credit Through Military Service*: Schools may grant credits for the following types of educational experiences received while in military service:

   a. U.S. Armed Forces Institute Courses

   b. U.S. Armed Forces Institute Subject Exams

   c. High School Courses Offered Through USAF

   d. Marine Corps Institute Courses

   e. Basic (Recruit) Training in Lieu of Physical Education and Health Requirements

   f. Service School Training

   g. PREP (Predischarge Education Program)

6. *Credit Through Extension, Correspondence, and TV Courses*: Some schools accept credit from extension correspondence and television courses if they are sponsored by an accredited institution.

7. *Credit for Summer School Study*: Credit is often granted for summer courses offered by the local high school or other accredited high schools in the area.

8. *G.E.D. (General Education Development)*: Most schools honor equivalency certificates from accredited G.E.D. programs. Many issue regular diplomas for successful G.E.D. participants.

117. GRADUATION STANDARDS FOR THE FUTURE

Many states are in the process of upgrading standards for high school graduation in the twenty-first century. Many of these efforts focus on demonstrated competencies and outcomes. Following is a prototype of graduation standards for the future:

GRADUATION STANDARDS*

Basic Requirements:

Demonstrated competency in the skills of—

> Reading
>
> Mathematics
>
> Geography
>
> Science
>
> Government
>
> Physical Health and Safety

Required Profile of Learning:

Demonstrated record of academic work, with achievement measured against a high standard in the following areas—

1. Understand what they read, hear, and see

2. Write and speak effectively

3. Develop artistic pursuit

4. Know when and how to use math

5. Gather and use information

6. Understand the world through science

7. Understand interactions between people, their world, and their cultures

8. Make informed decisions

9. Know how to manage a household or business

10. Learn another language (optional)

*Draft of proposed graduation standards proposed by the Minnesota State Department of Education, 1995.

118. COMMON TYPES OF LEARNING STATIONS

Many elementary and middle schools employ learning stations to convey the curriculum. Such stations permit flexibility, use of multiple resources, personalized instruction, and individually paced learning. The most common types of learning stations include:

Interest Stations—Centers that capitalize on students' interests, avocations, and hobbies.

Exploratory Stations—Stations that introduce and open up doors to current events, hot topics, and new career opportunities.

Skill Stations—Opportunities for drill, practice, and hands-on activities.

Reinforcement Stations—Stations that offer students varied ways to use and apply new skills.

Enrichment Stations—Centers packed with teasers and activities designed to extend or enrich students' grasp of previously taught curriculum content.

119. IT'S NOT JUST SHOP CLASS ANYMORE

The traditional woodshop (fondly remembered by many adults from their own school days) is rapidly disappearing from today's public secondary schools. To prepare students for a twentieth-first century technology-dominated economy, more and more schools are replacing historic industrial arts programs with a state-of-the-art Industrial Technology curriculum. Below are Industrial Tech topics now commonly offered to students in grades 9-12 in schools in all parts of the country:

Planning and Design

Power and Energy

Graphic and Electronic Communications

Power and Transportation

Electricity and Electronics

Production Metals/Woods

Offset Lithography

Photography

Small Gas Engines

Consumer Mechanics

Automotive Technology

Digital and Solid-State Electronics

Machine Trades

Welding Trades

Metal Technology

Cabinetry and Furniture

Building Construction

Computer-Aided Graphics

Technical Illustrations

Machine Drawing

Architectural Drawing

120. LEARNER OUTCOMES FOR DRUG EDUCATION

The best drug-use prevention and education programs are built around essential learner outcomes. The student competencies below are typical outcomes and expectations of an effective prevention curriculum:

1. Recognizing and understanding the functions of various drugs, chemicals, and other mood modifiers.

2. Self-understanding of personal strengths and weaknesses.

3. Understanding the biological and social determinants of behavior.

4. Knowing where to go for help and information, and how to evaluate sources of information.

5. Understanding the legal issues involved in drug possession, sale, and consumption.

6. Developing understanding of a wide range of values about drugs.

7. Recognizing personal values concerning drug issues.

8. Developing techniques and coping skills for handling peer pressure and stressful situations.

9. Self-acceptance (a sense of personal autonomy).

121. SEX EDUCATION GUIDELINES

Most adults in America support responsible sex education as part of the school's regular curriculum. In some communities, however, the subject generates heated controversy. The best interests of students are seldom served when emotions tear a community apart. The following guidelines can help any school to initiate an acceptable and beneficial program of sound sex education for elementary, middle, and secondary school pupils.

1. Before any instruction takes place, the School District should have in place a clear-cut policy statement supporting and validating sex education as a legitimate part of the school's program.

2. A citizen-staff advisory committee should be formed to assist in planning the sex education curriculum. Parents, clergy, and members of the medical community should be included on the advisory board.

3. Content should be acceptable by community standards.

4. Administrative support (including that of the School Board) is crucial to the success of any sex education program.

5. Teachers must receive special training before being assigned to the course.

6. Instruction should be based on fact (not opinion) and geared to the maturity level of the students involved. It is never helpful to overwhelm students or to talk down to them.

7. Objectives of a sound sex education curriculum should include the following:

    a. To provide accurate information concerning the physiology of sex and the causes and effects of unsafe sex;

    b. To foster positive student self-images;

    c. To assist students in understanding sexual feelings;

    d. To prepare students for personal decision making;

    e. To promote sexually responsible behavior;

    f. To foster emotional maturity; and

    g. To engender respect for human sexuality.

8. Keep parents fully informed about the program. (Evening preview classes for parents have been popular in many schools.)

9. Parents and other citizens should be permitted to review all materials used in instruction.

10. Scare tactics and sermonizing should be avoided.

11. Individual differences and beliefs should be respected at all times.

12. Students should have opportunities to submit anonymous questions.

13. Students should be excused from participating in sex education instruction upon written parental request.

121. SEX EDUCATION GUIDELINES, CONTINUED

14. Materials should be reviewed annually to assure up-to-date authenticity and accuracy.

15. In addition to the school's program, school leaders should champion improved sex education in the home, the church, and youth agencies.

122. GAY-LESBIAN CURRICULUM ISSUES

Principals and other officials are in a quandary about how to deal with homosexuality (with information about gays and lesbians) in the school and in the curriculum. Whatever position the school takes, the overriding concern should be the welfare and best interests of all students. It is important that school leaders remain sensitive to the painful issues confronting many gay and lesbian students and adults in our society.

Public Attitudes and Prejudice (Homophobia)

"Coming Out"

Dating

Safe Sex

AIDS and Other STD's

Job Discrimination

Denial of Employee Benefits

Gay and Lesbian Marriages

Child Custody and Adoption by Gays

Gays in the Military

Violence Against Gays (Gay Bashing)

Physical and Sexual Abuse

Rape

Pornography

Name Calling

Stereotyping/Labels

Prostitution

Hate Crimes

Self-esteem Issues

Sexual Identity Issues

Gays in the Church

Gays in the Clergy

Housing

Credit

Gay Humor

Gays in Politics

Gay Subculture

Gays in the Media

Gays in Literature

Origins and Causes of Homosexuality

Gays and Morality

123. INFORMATION SOURCES ABOUT AIDS

Teaching about AIDS and other Sexually Transmitted Diseases (STD's) may or may not be part of the school's curriculum. In any event, students, parents, and educators alike need to know where to get accurate, unbiased, and nonjudgmental information about these diseases. The agencies below are credible resources for anyone interested in getting valid information about AIDS and other STDs:

- National AIDS Hotline   800-342-AIDS
- Spanish Language Services   800-344-7432
- TTY Services for the Deaf   800-243-7889
- National STD Hotline   800-227-8922
- National Herpes Hotline   919-361-8488
- American Social Health Association 919-361-8400

124. SPECIAL EDUCATION CURRICULUM SERVICES

Curriculum services for the following types of disabilities or handicaps are available in most places through the public schools, special intermediate school districts, private schools, or clinics or cooperatives:

Early Childhood Health and Developmental Problems

Physically Impaired

Vision Impairment

Hearing Impairment

Mental Disabilities

Learning Disabilities

Attention Deficit Disorders (ADD)

Emotional/Behavior Disorders (EBD)

Communicative Disorders

Speech/Language Disorders (e.g., articulation, sound production, fluency, stuttering, language delays)

Needs for Occupational and Physical Therapy

125. CURRICULUM GOALS FOR GIFTED/ TALENTED STUDENTS

Many curricular programs for high-potential students are designed to capitalize on the unique abilities, talents, interests, and needs of these pupils. The following goals commonly serve as the foundation of such programs:

- To identify pupils who are intellectually gifted
- To understand the abilities, needs, and interests of each student
- To enable gifted students to develop their abilities to the fullest potential
- To help students gain a realistic, healthy self-concept
- To develop students' ability to recognize, integrate, and use potential to become self-actualizing individuals
- To prepare students for responsible and productive roles in the future
- To develop students into creative, productive, and compassionate human beings
- To ensure that students understand, accept, and appreciate individual differences
- To help gifted students become issue-oriented
- To foster higher-order thinking skills, creativity, and motivation
- To help gifted students acquire skills of future thinking
- To nurture leadership skills coupled with personal and social responsibility

126. CURRICULAR AND EXTRACURRICULAR PROGRAMS FOR GIFTED STUDENTS

All Principals are committed to meeting the needs of all students—including the gifted and talented. In addition to special local grouping, tracking, or pull-out programs, many schools offer gifted and talented students supplemental enrichment programs, opportunities, and services, including the following:

- Advanced Placement
- Special Elective Courses
- College Prep
- Concurrent College Course Enrollment
- Mentorship Connections
- Independent Study
- College and Career Exploration
- Counseling and Advocacy
- Cocurricular and Extracurricular Activities
- Special Camps and Summer School Programs
- Acceleration
- Inventors' Fairs
- Junior Great Books
- Omnibus
- Math Olympiad
- Olympics of the Mind
- Minicourses
- Early Entrance

127. 10 CRITERIA FOR SELECTION OF MULTICULTURAL CURRICULUM MATERIALS

Increased emphasis is being placed on the selection of multicultural and gender-fair curriculum and instructional materials in today's schools. The criteria below can help guide Principals and other professionals in the selection process.

1. Contributions of all groups are represented fairly and proportionately.

2. Reporting is objective and honest.

3. All information is factual, well researched, and documented.

4. Sources include authentic, native authors representing the groups included.

5. Language is chosen carefully to avoid any racist name-calling, racial slurs, or racially sensitive terms.

6. Information regarding cultural and religious beliefs, customs, values, rites, and traditions is treated respectfully.

7. Stereotypes are avoided.

8. All forms of editorial discrimination and prejudice are absent.

9. All cultures and groups are represented and presented with pride.

10. Individual role models representing both sexes and a variety of ethnic and cultural backgrounds are included.

128. TEXTBOOK PUBLISHERS

Textbooks shouldn't drive the curriculum or be the curriculum. They are, however, critical tools in every school's instructional program. The following list of publishers specializing in textbooks and related curriculum resources can assist Principals and teacher committees in locating and ordering appropriate materials. (A more exhaustive list of all U.S. publishers appears in *Literary Market Place*, published annually and available in most libraries):

Addison-Wesley, P.O. Box 10888, Palo Alto, CA 94303

Allyn & Bacon, 160 Gould St., Needham Heights, MA ;02194

American School Publishers, 11 W. 19th St., New York, NY 10011

Apple Computer, Inc., 20525 Mariani, Cupertino, CA 95014

Avon Books, 1350 Ave. of the Americas, New York, NY 10019

Bantam Books, 1540 Broadway, New York, NY 10036

The Center for Applied Research in Education, 113 Sylvan Ave., Englewood Cliffs, NJ 07632

CTB/McGraw-Hill, 20 Rlyan Ranch Rd., Monterey, CA 93940

The Continental Press, Inc., 520 East Bainbridge St., Elizabethtown, PA 17022

Curriculum Associates, Inc., 5 Esquire Rd., No. Billerica, MA 01867

DLM Publishing, One DLM Park, Allen, TX 75002

Dutton/Signet, 375 Hudson St., New York, NY 10014

Educator's Publishing Service, 31 Smith Place, Cambridge, MA 02138

Encyclopaedia Britannica Educational Corp., 310 S. Michigan Ave., Chicago, IL 60604

Ginn Publishing Canada, Inc., 160 Gould St., Needham Heights, MA 02194

Globe Fearon Educational Publisher, One Lake St., Upper Saddle River, NJ 07458

Harcourt Brace Jovanovich School Dept., 6277 Sea Harbor Drive, Orlando, FL 32887

HarperCollins Children's Books, 10 E. 53rd St., New York, NY 10022

D. C. Heath & Co., 125 Spring St., Lexington, MA 02173

Henry Holt & Co., 115 West 18th St., N.Y., NY 10011

Houghton Mifflin Co., Elementary School Division, 222 Berkeley St., Boston, MA 02116

IBM Corp., 1133 Westchester Ave., White Plains, NY 10604

Kendall/Hunt Publishing Co., 4050 Westmark Dr., Dubuque, IA 52002

Alfred A. Knopf, Inc., 201 E. 50th St., New York, NY 10022

Little, Brown and Co., 34 Beacon St., Boston, MA 02108

Macmillan/Merrill Pub. Co., 866 Third Ave., New York, NY 10022

McDougal, Littell/ALM, P.O. Box 1667, Evanston, IL 60204

128. TEXTBOOK PUBLISHERS, CONTINUED

Milliken Publishing Co., 1100 Research Blvd., St. Louis, MO 63132

Modern Curriculum Press, Inc., 299 Jefferson Rd., Parsippany, NJ 07054

Monitor Book Co., Inc., P.O. Box 3668, Beverly Hills, CA 90212

William Morrow & Co., 1350 Ave. of the Americas, New York, NY 10019

National Textbook Company, 4255 W. Touhy Ave., Lincolnwood, IL 60646

Oxford University Press, Inc., 198 Madison Ave., New York, NY 10016

The Psychological Corporation, 555 Academic Court, San Antonio, TX 78204

G. P. Putnam's Sons, 200 Madison Ave., New York, NY 10016

Random House, Inc., 201 E. 50th St., New York, NY 10022

Scholastic, Inc., 555 Broadway, New York, NY 10012

Science Research Associates (SRA), 155 N. Wacker Drive, Chicago, IL 60606

Scott, Foresman & Co., 1900 East Lake Ave., Glenview, IL 60025

Silver Burdett Ginn, 299 Jefferson Rd., Parsippany, NJ 07054

Simon & Schuster, Rockefeller Ctr., 1230 Avenue of the Americas, New York, NY 10020

Prentice-Hall School, One Lake St., Upper Saddle River, NJ 07458

Steck-Vaughn Co., P.O. Box 26015, Austin, TX 78755

Teachers College Press, 1234 Amsterdam Ave., New York, NY 10027

H. W. Wilson Co., 950 University Ave., Bronx, NY 10452

Workman Publishing Co., 708 Broadway, New York, NY 10003

Zaner-Bloser, Inc., P.O. Box 16764, Columbus, OH 43216-6764

129. TECHNOLOGY RESOURCES FOR LEARNERS

Today's learners increasingly rely on technology to deliver the curriculum. The following technologies are becoming commonplace as part of the school's program of Resource-Based Instruction (RBI):

Computers/modems

Cassette tapes

Filmstrips

Camcorders

Videotapes

Telephones

Teleconferencing

Hypermedia

Cable TV

Interactive videodisc players

Microfilm/microfiche

TV/VCRs

Hard disk players

CD-ROM systems

Satellite Transmissions

Film slides

Fax machines

Virtual reality

Optical Character Recognition (OCR)

130. ROLE OF EVALUATION AND CURRICULUM

In winning schools, evaluation drives instruction. Comprehensive evaluation is critical to monitoring and measuring curriculum success, as well as to assessing student progress. The primary functions and limitations of curriculum evaluation include the following:

Functions

To communicate progress to students.

To help teachers diagnose student strengths and weaknesses.

To determine instructional direction.

To inform interested parties (parents, employers) about student competence.

To provide information for administrative planning.

To familiarize learners with targets and goals.

To promote educational equality.

To provide a basis for improvement.

Limitations

Some evidence is nonobservable.

Some objectives are intangible.

Performance criteria may vary due to circumstances.

Different evaluation mechanisms are needed for different outcomes (i.e., knowledge, skills, values, etc.).

The merits of varying outcomes are arguable.

Some evaluation measures may be biased against one sex or certain racial or ethnic groups.

131. THE LANGUAGE OF EVALUATION
(COMMON TESTING TERMS)

Principals and teachers have to use tests and test results to make decisions about students and programs. They are also called on to interpret examination results to students, parents, the media, and community members who may be unfamiliar with the language of test makers. It pays to be sure that common test terms are always used correctly.

Here's a quick refresher course in the "language of evaluation":

Achievement Test—A test measuring how much students have learned in a specific subject area.

Aptitude Test—A test that tries to measure potential learning capability.

Criterion-referenced Test—A test that compares student performance with a predetermined standard or criterion.

Diagnostic Test—A test designed to identify students' strengths and weaknesses in a given subject area.

Grade Equivalent Scores—The grade level for which a score is the "average."

Mean—Arithmetic average of scores.

Median—The middle score in a group.

Mode—The most frequent score.

Norm-referenced Test—A test comparing the performance of current test takers with the results of others who have previously taken the test.

Percentile Rank—A comparison that tells the test taker the percentage of other test takers whose scores fell below her or his score.

Reliability—A measure of a test's consistency.

Standard Deviation—A way of expressing the variability (range) of scores.

Standard Error of Measurement—An estimate of the degree of error in a test (i.e., how much a test taker's current score may vary from his or her hypothetical "true" score).

Standard Test—A test with norms determined by giving it to large numbers of students (norm group) under standardized conditions.

Validity—The extent to which a test actually measures what it purports to test.

132. COMMONLY USED STANDARDIZED TESTS

Standardized tests are essential to assess curriculum and measure pupil progress, achievement, intelligence, or interests. Although not exhaustive, the list below includes 46 of the standardized tests, measures, and profiles most commonly used in elementary and secondary schools across the country:

1. ACT Assessment (American College Testing): Used by colleges and universities to predict first-year college success.

2. ACT Proficiency Examination Program (American College Testing): Exams used by students to get college-level credits for advanced high school work in selected subjects.

3. AGS Early Screening Profiles (American Guidance Service): An early screening device for preschool readiness.

4. Basic Economics Test (Joint Council on Economic Education): Tests the basic understanding of economic issues for upper elementary students.

5. Basic Test in Arithmetic (Associated Examining Board): An assessment of work-related knowledge needed in mathematics for high school students.

6. Basic Test in Computer Awareness (Associated Examining Board): An assessment of awareness of the names and functions of the various parts of a computer.

7. Basic Test of Geography (Associated Examining Board): Assesses basic geography knowledge of high school students.

8. Basic Test in Fitness and Safety (Associated Examining Board): Assessment of understandings and skills related to safety, personal fitness, and hygiene.

9. Brigance Diagnostic Comprehensive Inventory of Basic Skills (Curriculum Associates, Inc.): An elementary school assessment of skill sequences. Designed for use in programs emphasizing individualized instruction.

10. California Achievement Tests (CTB/McGraw-Hill): Complete battery of standardized achievement tests for grades K-12.

11. Canfield Learning Styles Inventory (Western Psychological Services): An inventory given to middle/high school students to help identify varying learning styles.

12. CAP Assessment of Writing (American Testronics, Inc.): A holistically scored writing assessment with national norms for secondary school students.

13. CAT Writing Assessment (CTB/McGraw-Hill): A holistically scored writing assessment for elementary, middle, and high school pupils.

14. Chicago Effective Schools Project (Sylvia Brandon): A Likert-scale instrument to assess areas of school environment/climate.

15. Children's At-Risk Screener (CTB/McGraw-Hill): A screening test to determine needs for special education testing of preschool children.

16. Comprehensive Test of Basic Skills (CTB/McGraw-Hill): A complete standardized achievement test battery for K-12.

132. COMMONLY USED STANDARDIZED
TESTS, CONTINUED

17. Computer Aptitude-Literary-and Interest Profile (Psychological Corporation): A measure of computer literacy and interest for high school students.

18. Cornell Critical Thinking Test (Midwest Publications): A test of problem solving and critical thinking for secondary-age pupils.

19. Critical Reasoning Test (Midwest Publications): A test of general problem solving and creativity for secondary age-pupils.

20. Cultural Literacy Test (Riverside Pub. Co.): Assesses general knowledge about culture and cultural differences (for high school students).

21. Culture Fair Intelligence Tests (Institute for Personality and Ability Testing): A nonverbal measure of general ability.

22. Ennis-Weir Argumentation Test (Midwest Publications): Test of problem solving and critical thinking in the context of argumentation for high school students.

23. Fitness Knowledge Test (*Journal of Physical Fitness*): A short test for assessing elementary students' knowledge about physical fitness.

24. Gates MacGinitie Reading Test (Riverside Publishing Co.): A standardized survey of achievement in reading.

25. High School Subject Tests (American Testronics, Inc.): A series of tests designed to be used at the end of selected high school courses.

26. Integrated Literature and Language Arts Portfolio (Riverside Publishing Co.): Performance assessments in literature and reading for elementary and middle school students.

27. Iowa Test of Basic Skills (Riverside Pub. Co.): A standardized achievement test battery for grades K-9.

28. Kindergarten Readiness Test (Slosson Educational Publications): A test for preschoolers to assess reading readiness.

29. Language Assessment Scales (CTB/McGraw-Hill): A measure of oral proficiency.

30. Metropolitan Achievement Tests (Psychological Corp.): A standardized achievement test battery for grades K-12.

31. Minnesota Prekindergarten Inventory (Behavior Science Systems): A brief questionnaire related to child development status and early childhood readiness.

32. National Achievement Tests (American Testronics, Inc.): A standardized achievement test battery for grades K-12.

33. National Proficiency Survey Series (Riverside Pub. Co.): A series of course-based high school subject tests that can be given at the beginning or end of selected courses.

34. Non-Reading Intelligence Tests (Hodder & Stoughton): A nonreading ability measure for elementary-age pupils. Can be used for the early identification of special needs children.

132. COMMONLY USED STANDARDIZED
TESTS, CONTINUED

35. Otis-Lennon School Ability Test (Psychological Corp.): A general ability test.

36. Peabody Individual Achievement Test—Revised (American Guidance Service): A short (quick look) battery of tests in six basic subject areas.

37. Secondary Mathematics Item Bank (NFER-Nelson): A bank of items from which high school math teachers can select to meet their own needs.

38. Slosson Test of Reading Readiness (Slosson Educational Publications): An individually administered reading readiness test.

39. Stanford Achievement Test (Psychological Corp.): A standardized achievement test battery for grades K-12.

40. Stanford Writing Assessment Program (Psychological Corp.): A writing test based on student essays.

41. Strong-Campbell Interest Inventory (Consulting Psychologists Press): A career guidance instrument for high school students.

42. Test Anxiety Profile (Rocky Mt. Behavioral Science Institute): A brief scale that assesses anxieties about specific kinds of tests by high school students.

43. Test of Nonverbal Intelligence (PRO-ED): A nonverbal test of general ability.

44. Woodcock Language Proficiency Battery (DLM Teaching Resources): A test battery assessing general language skills of high school students.

45. Woodcock Reading Mastery Tests—Revised (American Guidance Service): A battery of reading tests for elementary through high school.

46. Written Language Assessment (Academic Therapy Publications): A direct assessment of writing (essay) for elementary, middle, and high school pupils.

133. COLLEGE AND PROFESSIONAL ENTRANCE OR LICENSING EXAMS

One measure of the effectiveness of the curriculum is how successful students are in gaining admission to the college or career of their choice. This often requires scoring well on a gateway examination. Student scores on these entrance or licensing exams offer another indicator of curriculum success. A partial list of common admission or licensing examinations appears below:

American College Testing Assessment Program (ACT)—commonly used by colleges and universities for admission and placement

Armed Services Vocational Aptitude Battery (ASVAB)

CIA (Central Intelligence Agency) Entrance Examination

General Educational Development (GED)—high school equivalency exam

General Test (for Federal Civil Service positions)

Graduate Management Admissions Test (GMAT)—commonly used for admission to business graduate schools

Graduate Record Exam (GRE)—commonly used for admission to graduate school

Law School Admission Test (LSAT)

Medical College Admission Test (MCAT)

National Teacher Examination

Nursing School Entrance Exam

Real Estate Licensing Exam

SAT (Scholastic Aptitude Test)—commonly used by colleges and universities for admission and placement

134. NONTEST TECHNIQUES FOR EVALUATING CURRICULUM AND SPECIFIC SCHOOL PROGRAMS

In addition to standardized, teacher-made, and criterion-referenced tests, many schools now use a number of nontest techniques for diagnosing and documenting program success or failure including:

- Consumer surveys (of student, parents, community, etc.)
- Classroom observations
- Performances, demonstrations, and exhibits
- Analysis of teaching materials and lesson plans
- Follow-up studies
- Monitoring subject area trends
- Curriculum mapping (tracking)
- Writing samples and portfolios
- Check lists
- Interviews
- Professional judgments
- Research investigations
- Accrediting association's evaluations
- Progress charts
- External evaluations by outside consultants
- Video portfolios
- Student logs

135. STANDARD TEACHER COMMENTS ON REPORT CARDS

The payoff of the curriculum is whether or not students learn what's taught and use what's learned. In addition to letter grades, many schools now use a preselected list of standard comments to convey how well pupils are mastering the curriculum, performing, progressing, and behaving in the classroom. A typical list of teacher comments for report cards includes:

Understands and applies content

Actively participates

Applies skills

Is conscientious

Displays self-control

Follows directions

Has mastered concepts

Is a good listener

Has good study habits

Shows improvement

Seeks help if needed

Assignments are late

Is disorganized

Makes insufficient effort

Needs more practice

Learns beyond the curriculum

Has a positive attitude

Respects self and others

Is responsible

Uses study time well

Shows initiative

Is well organized

Is well prepared

Helps others

Works independently

Takes pride in work

Uses time poorly

135. STANDARD TEACHER COMMENTS ON REPORT CARDS, CONTINUED

Fails to complete work

Lacks interest

Needs to make more effort

Creates disturbances

Is lost in the curriculum

136. STUDENT PORTFOLIO CONTENTS
(EXAMPLES)

Portfolios are being used increasingly by teachers to document, measure, and communicate how well individual students engage in and progress through the curriculum. Portfolios are simply systematic collections of student work products over time. These collections help assess student growth and development. Student portfolios typically include such samples of student accomplishments as the following:

Art work

Illustrations

Tests

Daily assignments

Written reports (first and second drafts)

Creative writing samples (i.e., poems, stories, etc.)

Letters

Outlines

Reading logs

Journal entries

Handwriting samples

Anecdotal observation notes

Audiotapes/Videotapes

Projects

137. CHARACTERISTICS OF EFFECTIVE STAFF DEVELOPMENT PROGRAMS

The following characteristics can guide the Principal in developing a solid professional growth program for teachers:

- Learning opportunities should deal with both the science and the art of teaching.
- Programs should improve teachers on both the <u>professional level</u> (theory, knowledge, skills) and the <u>personal level</u> (health, wellness, morale).
- Programs should stress philosophy and rationale as well as practical applications. (Teachers must believe in what they are teaching.)
- Teachers need to see some payoff for participation in an inservice program. The WIFM factor (What's In It For Me) is important to program success.
- Programs should include choices for teachers.
- Varied delivery systems should be used throughout the program. (Teachers have differing learning styles, too.)
- One-shot inservice infusions don't work. Programs must allow for feedback, follow-up, and follow-through.

138. GUIDELINES FOR EFFECTIVE STAFF DEVELOPMENT PROGRAMS

Staff development is the second half of the curriculum. Without effective teacher training, the best curriculum can flop. In designing a successful overall program of staff development, many school leaders have found the guidelines below helpful:

1. The total staff (teachers, administrators, counselors, aides, etc.) and parents should be included as appropriate.
2. All levels of staff should participate in identifying needs and developing programs.
3. The overall program should include a variety of growth experiences (varied times, locales, presentation styles, and formats, etc.).
4. The program should be personalized and targeted toward individual building staffs wherever possible.
5. Both individual and group needs should be addressed.
6. Feedback and evaluation are critical to the continuous improvement of the program.

139. CHECK LIST FOR EVALUATING STAFF DEVELOPMENT PROGRAMS

The check list below can serve as a useful tool for assessing the effectiveness of specific staff development programs:

_____ The program was relevant and important.

_____ The program achieved its purpose.

_____ Presenters were effective.

_____ Handout materials can be put to use in the classroom.

_____ The level of presentations was suited to the audience.

_____ Program activities were varied and appropriate.

_____ The program was useful to me personally.

_____ The program was useful to the staff as a whole.

_____ The session(s) was . . .

    _____ Too long

    _____ Too short

    _____ About right

_____ I would appreciate follow-up and/or further training on this topic.

140. QUOTES ON SCHOOLS AND CURRICULUM

"Moving a cemetery is easier than changing the curriculum."—*Anon.*

"Spoon feeding in the long run teaches us nothing but the shape of the spoon."
—*E.M. Forster*

"Soon learned, soon forgotten."—*Proverb*

"They know enough who know how to learn."—*Henry Brooks Adams*

"Perhaps the most valuable result of all education is the ability to make yourself do
the thing you have to do, when it ought to be done, whether you like it or not."
—*Thomas Huxley*

"The only real object of education is to have a man in the condition of continuously
asking questions."—*Bishop Mandell Creighton*

"We must open the doors of opportunity. But we must also equip our people to walk
through those doors."—*Lyndon B. Johnson*

"A school should not be preparation for life. A school should be life."—*Elbert Hubbard*

Section Four

ATHLETICS AND ACTIVITIES

141. GOALS OF THE STUDENT ATHLETIC AND ACTIVITY PROGRAM

The goals of the school's student athletic and activity programs include the following:

- Develop interests and provide alternative uses of discretionary time.
- Promote a positive attitude toward self and others.
- Develop new skills.
- Promote physical and mental fitness.
- Instill a sense of fair play and good sportsmanship.
- Develop leadership.
- Develop healthy interpersonal relationships.
- Develop commitment.
- Provide opportunities for socialization and making new friends.
- Have fun.
- Experience success.
- Stimulate student involvement in the school.

142. ROLE OF THE PRINCIPAL IN PROMOTING SPORTSMANSHIP

The role of the Principal in promoting good sportsmanship throughout the school and the community should be as follows:

1. Work with athletic personnel in the development, implementation, and coordination of an overall sportsmanship program.

2. Help educate the student body and adult spectators regarding proper conduct at school athletic contests.

3. Encourage the faculty to support the sportsmanship program.

4. Help coordinate the efforts of all groups involved, including coaches, team members, cheerleaders, pep club, band, and booster clubs.

5. Deal with and hold accountable any individuals or groups who may violate the principles of good sportsmanship.

143. EARMARKS OF AN EFFECTIVE ACTIVITY PROGRAM

The criteria below may assist school Principals in putting together a well-rounded package of extracurricular and cocurricular experiences and opportunities for all pupils:

—Is fluid in fitting the ebb and flow of student interests, needs, and priorities.

—Involves real learning.

—Is accessible and affordable.

—Is democratic and nondiscriminatory.

—Stresses cooperation as well as competition.

—Includes equal opportunities for both sexes.

—Eliminates elitism and strives to tap the uninvolved.

—Maximizes participation.

—Recognizes and fosters ethnic pride and awareness of cultural diversity.

—Provides adapted activities and opportunities for students with disabilities.

—Features qualified and interested advisors, coaches, and other adult leaders.

—Uses community resources.

—Opens up leadership opportunities to members of all student groups.

—Provides appropriate rewards and recognition.

144. BOYS' AND GIRLS' GENDER-FAIR SPORTS PROGRAM (SUGGESTED SPORTS OFFERINGS)

A typical program of boys' and girls' sports reflecting gender equity is represented below:

A. Fall Sports

Boys	Girls
Cross-Country Running	Cross-Country Running
Football	Soccer
Soccer	Swimming/Diving
	Tennis
	Volleyball

B. Winter Sports

Boys	Girls
Basketball	Basketball
Hockey	Gymnastics
Swimming/Diving	Cross-Country Skiing
Cross-Country Skiing	

C. Spring Sports

Boys	Girls
Baseball	Golf
Golf	Softball
Tennis	Synchronized Swimming
Track/Field	Track/Field

D. Most Popular Boys' and Girls' Sports*

Most Popular High School Girls' Sports	Most Popular High School Boys' Sports
1. Basketball	1. Football
2. Track/Field	2. Basketball
3. Volleyball	3. Baseball

---

*As reported by the Amateur Athletic Foundation, Los Angeles, CA.

144. BOYS' AND GIRLS' GENDER-FAIR SPORTS PROGRAM (SUGGESTED SPORTS OFFERINGS), CONTINUED

E. Notes

Specific sports for boys and girls vary somewhat in different regions of the country. Increased interest in gender equity has led to new developments across the nation such as the following:

- Interest in establishing girls' hockey or ringette programs
- Interest in bowling as a co-ed sport
- Consideration of sanctioning cheerleading and danceline as competitive sports for girls

145. REPRESENTATIVE LIST OF NONATHLETIC ACTIVITIES

Student activities can be as rich and varied as the interests of individual student bodies. Some activities are topical. Others are timeless. A typical list of non-athletic activities appears below:

Activities for Drug Awareness

Bands

Chess Club

Choruses

Community Service

Debate

Drama

International Club

Jazz Ensemble

Literary Arts Magazine

Math Team

Mock Trial

Natural Helpers (Peer Counselors)

Newspaper

Odyssey of the Mind

Orchestra

Radio Station

SOS (Save Our Surroundings)

Science Challenge

Ski Club

Speech Activities

SADD (Students Against Drunk Driving)

Student Council

Thespians

Video Yearbook

Yearbook

146. ACADEMIC COMPETITIONS

Increased demands for academic rigor have resulted in a growing number of such academic competitions for students as the following:

- Debate Tournaments
- Inventors' Fairs
- Math Teams
- Mock Trial
- Quiz Bowl
- Science Olympiad
- Speech Teams
- Odyssey of the Mind

147. ELEMENTARY AFTER-SCHOOL ACTIVITIES (EXAMPLE)

As the number of families in which both parents work has expanded, the need for after-school activities for elementary-age students is increasing. Following is a list of school-sponsored activities appropriate for younger pupils:

- Babysitting classes
- Karate instruction
- Foreign language classes or camps
- Sign language courses
- Dance classes
- Piano classes
- Art classes
- Drama classes
- Computer classes
- Aquatic activities
- Private music lessons
- Chess clubs

148. CRITERIA FOR ADDING OR DROPPING SPORTS

Adding a new sport or deleting an existing one is a far-reaching decision that can affect large numbers of people. The factors listed below can assist decision makers in weighing whether to take such action:

1. Level of student interest

2. Costs involved

3. Availability of qualified coaching personnel

4. Availability and accessibility of appropriate facilities

5. Impact on gender equity

6. Conflict or lack of conflict with other established sports

7. Opportunities for competition

8. Level of community support

9. Long-range prospects for continuation

10. Transferability of skills to lifetime sports activities

11. Experience elsewhere with the sport

149. GUIDELINES FOR GENDER EQUITY IN SPORTS

Gender equity in sports requires more than an equal number of offerings. It also requires equivalent efforts and considerations in the areas below:

- levels of competition
- length of seasons and number of contests
- access to practice facilities
- access to prime time and dates for contests
- locker room accommodations
- number and quality of coaches
- budget allocations
- supplies
- uniforms
- travel budget and accommodations
- quality of officiating

150. GUIDELINES FOR SPECTATOR SPORTSMANSHIP

Many schools or athletic conferences have adopted standards of appropriate crowd conduct similar to the following:

1. Maintain individual self-control at all times.

2. Show respect for opponents.

3. Show respect for officials.

4. Understand the rules of the game(s).

5. Recognize and appreciate skill in performance regardless of team affiliation.

6. Show a positive attitude in cheering. Booing officials or opponents is never appropriate.

7. Refrain from use of obscene or abusive language.

8. Refrain from using noise-makers (e.g., cowbells, whistles, air horns).

9. Refrain from throwing objects.

10. Refrain from bringing alcohol or other drugs to athletic contests.

151. ATHLETIC DIRECTOR—LIST OF DUTIES

1. Provide vision and leadership for a comprehensive athletic program.

2. Continually evaluate the overall athletic program.

3. Provide leadership in the selection and evaluation of qualified coaching and other athletic personnel.

4. Implement appropriate staff development programs for athletic personnel.

5. Maintain an effective program of student, parent, and community communication, including working with an Athletic Advisory Council.

6. Coordinate all athletic programs and services.

7. Secure necessary help to conduct games and events.

8. Arrange for proper supervision of all athletic contests.

9. Publicize the interscholastic athletic program.

10. Implement an appropriate awards program, including athletic banquets, as needed.

11. Prepare and manage the annual athletic department budget.

12. Maintain an efficient financial recordkeeping and reporting system.

13. Determine facility and equipment needs for athletics and make recommendations for improvement.

14. Assume responsibility for the proper care of all facilities and equipment.

15. Schedule facilities for all interscholastic athletic contests.

16. Keep the Principal informed of all matters related to the athletic program.

152. HEAD COACHES—LIST OF DUTIES

1. Instruct athletes in the fundamental skills, strategy, and physical training necessary to achieve a degree of individual and team success.

2. Generate an attitude of good sportsmanship and fair play.

3. Establish the fundamental philosophy, skills, and techniques to be taught student athletes.

4. Maintain discipline, adjust grievances, and work to increase morale and cooperation.

5. Provide proper safeguards for maintenance and protection of assigned equipment and facilities.

6. Supervise and evaluate all assigned assistant coaches.

7. Provide training rules and any other unique regulations of the sport to all participants.

8. Understand, support, and implement the school's chemical awareness policy.

9. Monitor student athletes' grades, behavior, and school attendance.

10. Initiate procedures for handling injuries and emergencies.

11. Provide direction for assistants, team captains, and student managers.

12. Determine discipline when necessary and adhere to required due processes.

13. Maintain open communication with students and athletes.

14. Assist in preparation of the athletic department budget.

15. Provide for inventory control of all equipment.

16. Conduct pre-season meetings for all athletes and parents.

17. Promote the sport within the school.

18. Maintain good public relations with news media, support groups, parents, officials, volunteers, and fans.

153. ASSISTANT COACHES—LIST OF DUTIES

1. Carry out objectives of the sport program as outlined by the Head Coach.

2. Instruct athletes in fundamentals, strategy, and training.

3. Assume supervision and control of student athletes as assigned.

4. Carry out all responsibilities as designated by the Head Coach.

5. By presence at all practices, games, and trips, provide assistance and guidance for individual participants.

6. Maintain the discipline philosophy as outlined by the Head Coach.

7. Be accountable to the Head Coach for all assigned equipment.

8. Help maintain locker room security and cleanliness.

9. Maintain a record of team statistics.

10. Carry out scouting assignments as directed.

11. Assist in implementation of appropriate conditioning and weight programs.

154. 5 EXPECTATIONS OF ALL COACHES

1. Leadership

2. Discipline

3. Self-improvement

4. Cooperation

5. Rapport

(*Note:* "Winning" did not make the list.)

155. RESPONSIBILITIES OF ALL COACHES

To players:

- Provide leadership and set an example.
- Be fair and unprejudiced with all players.
- Have a genuine, up-to-date knowledge of the sport.
- Put the safety and welfare of players first.

To school district:

- Reflect confidence and respect for the district.
- Maintain a high level of confidence in the overall athletic program and the school district.

To the school:

- Strive for excellence in all areas of the school.
- Treat the faculty, players, and general students with honor and respect.
- Be an integral part of the educational program of the school.
- Support all endorsed activities of the school.

To the community:

- Continue personal and professional growth.
- Maintain membership in appropriate coaching and professional associations.

To fellow coaches:

- Provide an open exchange of ideas.
- Praise assistants and award recognition when appropriate.
- Contribute a full measure of time, effort, thought, and energy at all times.

To coaches of other sports:

- Support, promote, and cooperate with all other coaches and activity sponsors.
- Support and serve fellow coaches.
- Reflect confidence in fellow coaches.

To faculty members:

- Cooperate with all faculty members.

To the physical plant:

- Keep practice areas and locker rooms in order.
- Use and store equipment properly.
- Maintain security of all storage areas.

156. COACH'S CODE OF ETHICS*

As a professional educator and coach, I will:

1. Strive to develop in each athlete qualities of leadership, initiative, and good judgment.

2. Respect the integrity and personality of the individual athlete.

3. Encourage the highest standard of conduct and scholastic achievement among all athletes.

4. Seek to inculcate good health habits and to establish sound training rules.

5. Fulfill responsibilities to provide health services and an environment free of safety hazards.

6. Exemplify the highest moral character, behavior, and leadership.

7. Promote ethical relationships among coaches.

8. Encourage a respect for all athletics and their values.

9. Abide by the rules of the game in letter and spirit.

10. Respect the integrity and judgment of sports officials.

11. Display modesty in victory and graciousness and courage in defeat.

12. Demonstrate a mastery of, and continuing interest in, coaching principles and techniques through professional improvement.

13. Be loyal to superiors and peers and support school policy.

14. Be a goodwill ambassador between the school and the community.

15. Neither knowingly nor unethically strive for another coach's job.

16. Offer congratulations in public—win or lose.

17. Never "run up" the score.

*Adapted for the Minnesota State High School Coaches' Association Code of Ethics.

157. SAFETY GUIDELINES FOR COACHES

1. *Fitting Equipment*: All equipment should be properly fitted according to manufacturer's instructions.

2. *Equipment Inspection*: All equipment should be checked regularly for safety. Particular care should be taken in inspecting protective gear.

3. *Facility Inspection*: All facilities should be checked regularly for safety. Inspection should include fields, gyms, pools, rinks, courts, tracks, and apparatus of all kinds.

4. *Team Supervision*: Proper supervision should be provided for all participants at all practices, games, and pre- and postgame activities.

5. *Training Kit*: A properly stocked training kit of first-aid supplies should be readily available during all practices, scrimmages, and games.

158. HEAD COACH EVALUATION CRITERIA

1. Follows athletic policies and job description criteria.

2. Continually strives to improve coaching performance.

3. Develops sound public relations.

4. Understands and follows regulations of all governing agencies.

5. Maintains suitable sideline conduct.

6. Cooperates and communicates with all parents and participates in parent nights, banquets, awards programs, pep assemblies, etc.

7. Develops respect by example in appearance, manners, behavior, language, and conduct.

8. Is knowledgeable in all aspects of the sport.

9. Maintains appropriate individual and team discipline.

10. Is fair, understanding, and patient with all team members.

11. Provides leadership and attitudes that produce positive efforts by participants.

12. Is competent in the medical aspects of coaching (i.e., first aid, treatment of injuries, etc.).

13. Follows proper purchasing procedures and operates sport within budget.

14. Follows proper procedures in the issuance, collection, inventory, and storage of equipment.

15. Team performance is consistent with quality of talent available.

16. Keeps Athletic Director informed of important developments.

159. ASSISTANT COACH EVALUATION CRITERIA

1. Loyalty to Head Coach and program.

2. Care of equipment.

3. Knowledge of sport.

4. Teaching ability.

5. Ability to motivate.

6. Rapport with coaches and players.

7. Supervision of student athletes.

8. Interest in coaching.

9. Acceptance of duties assigned by Head Coach.

160. EXPECTATIONS OF STUDENT ACTIVITY ADVISORS

To implement the goals of the student activity program, the following standards and expectations should be established for all advisors:

1. Enthusiasm for the activity is part of the professional pride expected of all advisors.

2. Appropriate discipline is the responsibility of all advisors. The advisor should model observation of school codes and rules, ideals of fair play, and appropriate behavior at all meetings, rehearsals, and events associated with the activity involved.

3. Students have a right to expect advisors to have a genuine interest in, and up-to-date knowledge of, the specific activity involved.

4. Advisors should continually seek self-improvement. Keeping abreast of new developments in the area of the assigned activity is expected.

5. The District expects full cooperation among all individuals associated with the activity program.

6. Sound principles of teaching and learning should be used in advising all activities.

7. Advisors should be fair and unprejudiced with all activity participants.

8. The safety and welfare of all participants should be uppermost in the advisor's mind.

9. The advisor should give support to all endorsed activities of the school.

10. The advisor has a responsibility to promote the specific activity throughout the school and community.

11. Each advisor is responsible for protecting and maintaining the physical plant for the school.

161. ACTIVITY ADVISORS—LIST OF DUTIES

1. Provide a safe and supervised environment at all times.

2. Be accountable for all assigned activity funds.

3. Develop and implement an appropriate recognition and award program.

4. Maintain accurate records of each student's activity participation.

5. Schedule and reserve appropriate space for activities and events.

6. Follow school policy regarding a chemical-free environment.

7. Maintain proper discipline and follow appropriate due process procedures.

8. Monitor each student's eligibility (e.g., satisfactory progress toward graduation) to participate in the activity program.

9. Follow established procedures for requisitioning materials and claiming reimbursement for expenses.

10. Follow school policy regarding prohibition of sexual harassment.

11. Arrange for appropriate and safe transportation for all activities and events under your responsibility.

12. Assume responsibility for supervision of participants at all times.

162. GUIDELINES FOR NONFACULTY COACHES AND ADVISORS

Nonfaculty coaches and advisors must place special emphasis on becoming familiar with the philosophies, goals, and objectives of the athletic and activity programs by:

1. Meeting the qualifications required of all coaches and advisors.

2. Meeting with the Principal, Athletic Director, or designee prior to the start of the season for orientation and goal setting.

3. Calling the Principal's or Athletic Director's office as determined on a pre-arranged basis.

4. Holding periodic conferences with the Principal or Athletic Director.

5. Following all procedures outlined in the job description.

6. Setting aside a regular time to meet individually with assistants and student participants.

7. Conferring with the Principal or Athletic Director during the last week of the season or activity to plan for awards presentations, year-end reviews, and the collection of equipment.

8. Being loyal to the school's traditions and supporting all of the school's programs by attending as many events and activities as possible.

163. OFFICIAL NATIONAL AMATEUR SPORTS GOVERNING BODIES

Sport	*Governing Agency*
Baseball	U.S. Baseball Federation (USBF)
Basketball	Amateur BB Assoc. of the USA (ABAUSA)
Diving	U.S. Diving, Inc. (USD)
Gymnastics	U.S. Gymnastics Federation (U.S.G.F.)
Ice Hockey	Amateur Hockey Assoc. of the U.S. (AHAUS)
Skiing	U.S. Ski Association (U.S.S.A.)
Soccer	U.S. Soccer Federation (USSF)
Softball	Amateur Softball Assoc. of America (ASA)
Swimming	U.S. Swimming, Inc. (USS)
Synchronized Swimming	U.S. Synchronized Swimming, Inc. (USSS)
Tennis	U.S. Tennis Association (USTA)
Track	The Athletic Congress (TAC)
Volleyball	U.S. Volleyball Assoc. (USVBA)
Wrestling	U.S.A. Wrestling (USAW)

164. PRE-SEASON CHECK LIST FOR COACHES

_____ 1. Meet with Athletic Director

     _____ Discuss objectives, responsibilities, and player handbook.

_____ 2. Check out keys for locker room and coach's office.

_____ 3. Check all equipment and facilities for safety.

_____ 4. Review League Official Handbook and Rules for your sport. Pay special attention to new rule changes.

_____ 5. Check time and date of rules interpretation meetings.

_____ 6. Review Conference policies and procedures.

_____ 7. Review eligibility procedures regarding physical exams, insurance, and participation fees. Do not allow participation of an athlete until all requirements are met.

_____ 8. Hold a pre-season meeting with parents/guardians, squad members, and coaching assistants.

_____ 9. Submit space use needs to Athletic Director.

_____ 10. Submit a practice, game, and scrimmage schedule to the Athletic Director.

_____ 11. Provide pre-season information to the media as requested.

_____ 12. Meet with equipment manager to review procedures.

_____ 13. Meet with weight training coach to set up team orientation.

_____ 14. Communicate with potential players via individual letters, posters, school public address announcements, and other personal contacts.

165. IN-SEASON CHECK LIST FOR COACHES

_____ 1. Check first-aid supplies, emergency procedures, and athletes' telephone numbers.

_____ 2. Check with Athletic Director to confirm player eligibility (i.e., payments, physicals, academic standing, etc.).

_____ 3. One week prior to first contest, submit team rosters for printing of programs.

_____ 4. Check bus times, field locations, and other transportation arrangements as appropriate.

_____ 5. Secure approval for any overnight trips.

_____ 6. Check with equipment manager for issuance of game uniforms.

_____ 7. Instruct team members about game etiquette.

_____ 8. Provide score books for the official scorer.

_____ 9. Provide for proper care of all equipment and uniforms.

_____ 10. Distribute scores to media.

_____ 11. Prior to the last contest, inform athletes of their responsibility to check with Athletic Office regarding eligibility for a letter or other awards.

166. POST-SEASON CHECK LIST FOR COACHES

_____ 1. Check in all equipment.

    _____ Collect all gear, including locks.

    _____ Inventory all equipment and supplies.

    _____ Make a final review with equipment manager.

_____ 2. Inform Athletic Director of equipment needing repair.

_____ 3. Follow up on all obligations incurred by your athletes.

_____ 4. Notify Athletic Office of players eligible for lettering.

_____ 5. Notify Athletic Office of any special honors earned by athletes in your sport.

_____ 6. Turn in a season evaluation form to Athletic Director and Principal.

_____ 7. Notify Principal and Athletic Director of any banquet plans.

_____ 8. Complete all final reports within one week.

_____ 9. Hold a post-season evaluation conference with the Athletic Director (and Principal as appropriate).

    _____ Discuss future equipment and capital outlay needs.

    _____ Review past season.

    _____ Make recommendations for the coming season.

    _____ Sign voucher for final payment.

167. RULES FOR CHEERLEADERS

Cheerleaders have a unique opportunity to influence spectators and create a positive atmosphere. The following rules can assist in promoting good sportsmanship.

1. Be courteous to opposing teams and cheerleaders.

- Allow visitors the first opportunity to cheer.
- Cheer for opponents when they have an outstanding effort.
- Use only positive cheers and actions.
- Allow visitors to cheer without interruption.

2. Be courteous to game officials.

- All comments to officials should be courteous and respectful.
- Show consideration for all players and fans.
- Stay off the field of play as much as possible.

3. Keep fans in a positive, supportive frame of mind.

- Select cheers that are positive and supportive.
- React positively to opposing players.
- Select appropriate times to encourage your team.
- Stay in control of cheerleading equipment (i.e., megaphones, pom-poms, etc.).
- Follow Conference guidelines for good sportsmanship.

168. CHEERLEADER ADVISOR—LIST OF DUTIES

1. Be responsible for supervision and instruction of cheerleaders.

2. Be responsible for conduct of cheerleaders at all practice sessions and contests.

3. Encourage good sportsmanship by example and leadership.

4. Initiate an energetic public relations program.

5. Be responsible for uniforms and supplies.

6. Conduct a four-week clinic for prospective cheerleaders.

7. Conduct a fair tryout and selection process.

8. Issue awards to deserving participants at the conclusion of the season or year.

9. Coordinate transportation to all athletic contests.

10. Manage the cheerleading budget.

169. EQUIPMENT MANAGER—LIST OF DUTIES

1. Regularly inspect all equipment for safety.

2. Maintain an effective system of inventory control.

3. Implement a systematic process for checking equipment and uniforms in and out.

4. Maintain tight security for proper storage of all equipment.

5. Arrange for equipment repairs as needed.

6. Arrange for timely laundering and cleaning of towels and uniforms.

7. Collect restitution for lost or abused equipment.

8. Advise the Athletic Director regarding the need for new and replacement equipment.

170. WEIGHT TRAINING COORDINATOR—LIST OF DUTIES

1. Check weight training equipment regularly for safety.

2. Provide thorough orientation and instruction on the use of weight equipment to all team members.

3. Supervise all weight training sessions.

4. Work with team members to develop individualized weight training and conditioning programs.

5. Stress safety at all times.

6. Maintain strict security for storage of equipment when not in use.

171. UNIFORM PURCHASING ROTATION SCHEDULE (SAMPLE)

Basic athletic supplies need to be purchased annually. Because of high costs, however, it is usually necessary to establish a rotation system for the purchase of new team uniforms. Below is a sample four-year rotation schedule that ensures fair treatment for all boys' and girls' sports and teams.

Year I

Baseball — Junior Varsity Jerseys

Basketball, Boys — Uniforms

Basketball, Girls — Uniforms

Football — Jerseys

Hockey — Jerseys (2 sets)

Volleyball — B Squad — Uniforms

Year II

Cross-Country Running, Boys and Girls

Football — Game Pants

Hockey — Breezers

Soccer, Girls — Game Uniforms

Swimming, Boys/Girls — Warmups

Synchronized Swim — Warmups

Track/Field — Sweatsuits

Year III

Baseball — Varsity Pants

Cheerleaders — Sweaters

Gymnastics — Warmups

Football — Game Uniforms

Soccer — Game Uniforms

Tennis, Girls — Jerseys/Sweaters

171. UNIFORM PURCHASING ROTATION SCHEDULE (SAMPLE), CONTINUED

Year IV

Baseball — Varsity Jerseys

Basketball, Boys — Warmups

Basketball, Girls — Warmups

Hockey — Game Uniforms

Tennis, Boys — Jerseys/Sweaters

Volleyball — Varsity Uniforms

172. ACTIVITY EVALUATION CRITERIA

To remain dynamic, relevant, and effective, student activities must be evaluated on a regular basis. The criteria below can serve as the basis for making judgments regarding a specific activity.

1. The activity is challenging enough to meet my needs.

2. The advisor was accessible for interaction.

3. There was enough time during sessions for interaction and socialization with peers.

4. The length of the activity was adequate.

5. The advisor had adequate knowledge of the activity.

6. The advisor was able to motivate participants.

7. The advisor listened to participants.

8. The advisor was enthusiastic.

9. The advisor handled difficult situations.

10. Practices/rehearsals were well organized.

11. All participants were treated fairly.

12. Proper discipline was maintained.

173. PROCEDURES FOR HANDLING PLAYER OR PARENT COMPLAINTS

The coaching staff is responsible for determining: team selection, length and content of practices, game strategy, and individual playing time. These decisions will be based on the best judgment of the coach. If concerns arise on any of the above, the procedure below should be followed:

1. The player should talk to the captain(s).

2. The player (and team captains, if appropriate) should talk to the coach.

3. The player and parent should talk to the coach.

Such other concerns as illegal activities, immoral conduct, disrespectful treatment of players, failure to follow school policies, or behavior that is unbecoming or degrading to the athletic program, the school, or the community should be handled as follows:

1. Discuss concern with Athletic Director. If no resolution . . .

2. Discuss concern with the Principal. If no resolution . . .

3. Discuss concern with Superintendent. If no resolution . . .

4. Discuss concern with School Board.

Parents, players, and others should feel free to express concerns, register complaints, or protest unfair actions without fear of retaliation or future prejudice.

174. STEPS FOR DEALING WITH DRUG USE BY STUDENT ATHLETES (EXAMPLE)

1. During the school year, student athletes shall not:

    a. use alcoholic beverages;

    b. use tobacco; or

    c. use, consume, possess, buy, sell, or give away any other controlled substance.

2. On the first confirmed violation, the student shall lose eligibility for the next two consecutive contests or two weeks of a season, whichever is greater.

    • It is recommended that the school offer an educational program for students to get information about the effects of abuse or misuse of drugs.

    • It is recommended that, when appropriate, the student be referred for an outside assessment of potential chemical health problems.

3. On the second confirmed violation, the student shall lose eligibility for the next six consecutive contests.

    • It is recommended that before being readmitted, the student show evidence of seeking chemical counseling as appropriate.

4. On the third confirmed violation, the student shall lose eligibility for the next twelve contests.

    • If the student voluntarily participates in a chemical treatment program, the student may be certified for reinstatement after a minimum period of six weeks.

5. Penalties shall be cumulative, beginning with and continuing throughout the student's participation in the school's athletic program.

175. WHAT WINNERS SAY ABOUT ATHLETICS
(QUOTES)

"As I understand it, sport is hard work for which you do not get paid."
   —*Irvin S. Cobb*

"The game isn't over till it's over."—*Yogi Berra*

"Show me a good and gracious loser and I'll show you a failure."—*Knute Rockne*

"In order to have a winner, the team must have a feeling of unity; every player must put the team first—ahead of personal glory."—*Paul "Bear" Bryant*

Justifying the role of athletics: "It's kind of hard to rally 'round a math class."
   —*Paul "Bear" Bryant*

"Winning is not everything—but making the effort to win is."—*Vince Lombardi*

"Success is peace of mind in knowing you did your best."—*John Wooden*

"For when the One Great Scorer comes
To write against your name,
He marks—not that you won or lost—
But how you played the game."—*Grantland Rice*

Section Five

DISCIPLINE

176. WHY STUDENTS MISBEHAVE

Although human behavior is complex, most experts agree that children and youth usually break rules, misbehave, or challenge authority for one of four basic reasons:

1. To signal for attention

2. To exercise or gain power

3. To retaliate

4. To cry for help

177. WHO'S ON THE SCHOOL'S DISCIPLINE TEAM?

Who's on the school's discipline team? Everyone! Discipline is too big a job for a single "vice principal" any more. Today, every adult in the building must assume responsibility for making and keeping the school safe, orderly, and businesslike.

The following staff members have specific discipline responsibilities in a modern elementary or secondary school:

Principal

Assistant Principal

Dean

Counselor

Social Worker

Chemical Health Specialist (Drug Counselor)

Police Liaison Officer

Teachers

Hall Monitors

Crossing Guards

Playground Aides

Cafeteria Aides

Parking Lot Supervisors

Security Aides

Discipline Aides

Management Aides

Diversity Specialists

Ombudsmen/Advocates

Note: Most schools don't have all of the specialized discipline personnel identified above, but every school should have as many of these positions as needed to get the job done.

178. DISCIPLINE QUESTIONS FOR NEW TEACHERS

The questions below can help beginning teachers find out all they need to know about discipline before the first day of school:

- What is the school's discipline plan?
- How do the students find out about these policies?
- What classroom rules do I need?
- What consequences will I impose?
- How do I send problem students to the office? For what offenses?
- Does the school have an in-house suspension program?
- Does the school have a detention program?
- Does the school have a Saturday School program?
- Does the school have a Teacher Assistant Team (TAT) program?
- What are the school's policies on attendance and tardiness?
- What records do I keep on attendance, tardiness, and discipline problems?
- What are my supervisory responsibilities outside of the classroom?
- How and when do I involve parents in discipline problems?
- What help is available to me in handling difficult discipline problems?
- How will I reward good behavior?
- How does the school recognize positive behavior?

179. STEPS IN PROGRESSIVE DISCIPLINE FOR STUDENTS

Every individual classroom or schoolwide discipline plan should provide progressive consequences for persistent or escalating infractions. A typical sequence of progressive disciplinary actions includes such steps as the following:

1. Verbal reminder
2. Verbal reprimand
3. Change of seating
4. Isolation
5. Loss of privileges
6. Parent conference
7. Removal from class (Principal referral)
8. Detention
9. In-school suspension
10. Out-of-school suspension
11. Saturday school
12. Loss of credit
13. Expulsion

Note: Corporal punishment is not an option.

180. DUE PROCESS GUIDELINES

Protecting democratic standards and individual rights is basic to effective discipline in schools. All Principals must be champions of due process for every student—even the worst kid in school. Due process means guaranteeing certain procedural safeguards for everyone. The essentials of due process for students include the following:

- Reasonable rules
- Proper notification and explanation of all rules, regulations, and policies
- Awareness of specific allegations or charges
- Right to counsel
- A full and complete objective investigation
- Documentation of all findings and actions
- Fair, equitable, and consistent disciplinary action
- Opportunity to file a grievance
- Right to a hearing
- Appeals provision

181. STEPS IN EXPULSION (EXAMPLE)

Expulsion from school is always serious business. The process is usually governed by carefully prescribed legal requirements. Principals should always check with the District Office or legal counsel before initiating the process of expulsion. The following model step-by-step expulsion procedure is typical of the process required in many states:

1. Principal initiates a certified letter to parents stipulating the cause/reason(s) for expulsion, and the expulsion and hearing procedure that will be followed. A return receipt should be requested.

2. A waiver of hearing form and copies of all applicable Board policies and State rules and statutes should be included with the parent letter.

3. Copies of all correspondence and enclosures should be filed with the Superintendent and with legal counsel.

4. If the student and parents sign the waiver of hearing form, the Superintendent's office should be notified immediately so that a School Board meeting can be scheduled as soon as possible.

5. If a hearing is waived, the expulsion can be acted on at a regular School Board meeting. Otherwise, action shall be at a Special Meeting of the Board.

6. If a hearing is held, it may be open or closed at the student's/parent's request. The student must have access to legal counsel.

7. Action to expel must be taken only by a roll call vote of the School Board.

8. Following Board action, the Clerk must provide written notice to the student and parents. (An alternative education plan for the pupil may also be required.)

Caution: Additional or alternative procedures may be required if the affected student is receiving special education services. Professional legal counsel should always be consulted before taking any expulsion action involving a special education student.

182. CHARACTERISTICS OF EFFECTIVE DISCIPLINE POLICIES, RULES, AND PROCEDURES

Good discipline begins with clear-cut, reasonable expectations. It helps if these expectations are written down. All written discipline codes should meet the following criteria:

- Plain language (no jargon or legalese)
- Honesty (no phony or cosmetic rules)
- Fairness (no favoritism or discrimination)
- Simplicity (a few, well-defined rules)
- Flexibility (capacity to adjust to unique circumstances)
- Consistency (same rules for all)
- Reasonableness (a good reason for every rule)

183. SHORTEST DISCIPLINE CODE (SCHOOL RULES)

1. Show Up
2. Obey Laws
3. Respect Others

184. STEPS TO ESTABLISHING GOOD DISCIPLINE

Although there are no magic formulas, the steps below can serve as a model process for achieving desired discipline goals (within the classroom or throughout an entire school):

1. Develop rapport.
2. Establish routines.
3. Look for causes of problems.
4. Involve all affected parties.
5. Provide options.
6. Spell out rules.
7. Enforce consistently.
8. Document infractions.
9. Follow due process.
10. Review and adjust policies and procedures.

185. REINFORCERS OF POSITIVE BEHAVIOR

Achieving positive student discipline involves reinforcing appropriate behavior as well as punishing inappropriate acts. Examples of common reinforcers include the following:

Individual Reinforcers

Opportunity to eat lunch with the Principal

Free computer time

"Happy Grams" to parents

Special privileges

Blue Ribbon Awards

Tokens or candy

Stickers or temporary tattoos

Opportunity to assist teachers

Selection as "Student of the Week"

Group Reinforcers

Popcorn party

Special field trips

Special games

Surprise party

Free passes

Recognition at all-school assembly

Talent show

Self-directed time

Visits from celebrities

186. 12 DISCIPLINE PRINCIPLES FOR PRINCIPALS

1. The basis for positive discipline is good teaching.

2. Every school is a mix of positive and negative factors.

3. Individualized discipline is as important as individualized instruction.

4. The only way to change behavior is to change feelings.

5. Discipline gets better only when everyone affected is involved.

6. Most students want to do the right thing.

7. How students behave (or misbehave) is largely the byproduct of how adults treat them.

8. Victimization is reduced in schools characterized by close teacher-principal cooperation.

9. Principals must understand the law and know the legal limits and requirements of disciplinary actions.

10. One out-of-control classroom can infect an entire school.

11. Discipline that has eroded gradually can only be restored gradually.

12. The determinant of all disciplinary action should be what's best for the student, now and in the future.

187. CAUSES OF TRUANCY

- Moving from elementary to secondary school
- Being bullied by peers
- Being an incest victim
- Parental illiteracy
- Perceived irrelevance of the school curriculum
- Poor teacher-student relationships
- Low self-esteem
- Being thrown out of the home
- Cry for attention or help
- "Broken homes"; neglectful, noncaring families; and socially disadvantaged backgrounds
- Peer influence
- Alienation from school
- Poverty (Almost 25% of all children live in poverty.)
- Lack of learning readiness from the first years of school
- Boredom with school
- Academic failure

Source: Review of literature by Susan Carstens, Crystal (MN) Police Department.

188. TRUANCY PREVENTION STRATEGIES

- Distribution of attendance policies to all students and parents
- Parent education regarding the importance of consistent attendance
- Computerized telephoning to homes of all absentees
- Annual attendance reviews prior to opening of school
- Interviews with poor attenders from the previous year
- Weekly/monthly assessments of poor attenders
- Loss of credit for excessive absences
- Attendance incentive programs
- Special activities on Mondays and Fridays
- Counseling for students with ongoing health problems
- Electives for students with limited ability
- Teacher training to identify at-risk students
- Community-based truancy prevention committee
- Publicity about truancy
- Tutorial help for students with academic problems
- Work permits for students with acceptable attendance
- Establishment of dropout prevention programs
- Competitive, spirited attendance campaigns
- Use of peer counseling
- Excluding children from businesses during school hours
- Employing students *only* after school
- Creation of neighborhood watch programs
- Recruiting students for clubs and recreation programs

Source: National School Safety Center.

189. WHY STUDENTS SKIP SCHOOL

Truancy is a symptom; there is always a reason why students skip school. It usually indicates a broader or deeper problem. The most common causes of unexcused absence from school include the following:

- Boredom
- Fear of school (school phobia)
- Conflicts with teachers or administrators
- Fear of bullies or gangs
- Falling behind in school work
- No one at home to get the student off to school
- Peer pressure
- Problems with drugs or alcohol
- Difficulty with the law
- Physical or sexual abuse
- Low self-esteem
- Depression

190. TIPS FOR HANDLING FIGHTS IN SCHOOL

1. Use a forceful, authoritative voice to get combatants' attention.
2. Quickly and emphatically remind the parties of school policy and the consequences of fighting.
3. Get the help of other adults to separate and subdue the students involved.
4. Check immediately for weapons and don't take any foolish risks. (There's a difference between bravery and bravado.)
5. Separate the students who are fighting so that others do not join in the fray.
6. If necessary, use mace or a fire hose to subdue the parties.
7. Try to "talk the parties down."
8. Get medical help if needed.
9. Disperse onlookers as soon as possible.
10. Get someone to record the names of witnesses.
11. Inform authorities as appropriate.
12. Preserve the fight scene until cleared by authorities.
13. Write up the incident as quickly as possible.

191. TIPS FOR MAINTAINING PLAYGROUND DISCIPLINE

- Limit the number of students on the playground at one time.
- Provide up-to-date playground equipment.
- Separate age groups on the playground.
- Strengthen supervision on the playground with the use of volunteers.
- Provide planned activities at all times on the playground.

192. CAFETERIA RULES (RESPONSIBILITIES)
(EXAMPLES)

1. Talk quietly.
2. Stay in place in the line.
3. Take only needed silverware.
4. Refrain from making loud noises (popping bags, banging on tables, etc.).
5. Remain seated while eating.
6. Don't throw anything.
7. Practice reasonable manners.
8. Walk at all times.
9. Follow established procedures for dismissal.

193. TIPS FOR MAINTAINING CAFETERIA DISCIPLINE

- Improve the physical appearance of the cafeteria (e.g., murals, round tables).
- Introduce better menu choices.
- Simplify and publicize cafeteria rules.
- Use student service groups to help keep the cafeteria clean.
- Limit length of cafeteria lines and the number of pupils eating at one time.
- Use a Stop Light (red and green lights) to signal appropriate and inappropriate noise levels.
- Initiate a "Cafeteria Pride" campaign.
- Establish a way of isolating chronic troublemakers.
- Encourage staff members to eat with students.
- Reward good behavior with special privileges.
- Invite parents and community members to eat with students. (Adult presence is a calming influence.)

194. SCHOOL BUS RULES (EXAMPLES)

1. Be at assigned bus stop three to five minutes before arrival time.

2. Respect home owners. Do not walk or stand on lawns. Avoid flower beds.

3. Ride only assigned bus and use only assigned bus stop.

4. Enter the bus in an orderly manner. Move directly to an open seat and remain seated until appropriate destination has been reached.

5. Younger pupils should board the bus first.

6. Seats in the rear should be filled first.

7. Keep hands, arms, and head inside the bus.

8. Keep aisles clear at all times.

9. Be courteous.

10. Don't throw snowballs at school buses or other vehicles.

11. Never hitch a ride on the back of the bus.

12. Don't throw items on the bus.

13. Don't distract the driver.

14. No eating or drinking on the bus.

15. No pets or large items (i.e., skis, large musical instruments, etc.) should be brought onto the bus.

16. The emergency door must be used exclusively for emergencies under adult supervision.

17. Any activity that is unsafe, dangerous, or disrespectful is not allowed.

18. All directions given by the bus driver should be followed at all times.

195. COMMON BUS INFRACTIONS

The most frequently reported school bus infractions include:

- Use of profanity, or obscene or abusive language or gestures
- Distracting noise
- Throwing objects
- Window breakage
- Fighting
- Harassment
- Smoking
- Mooning
- Drug use
- Weapon possession

196. PROGRESSIVE BUS DISCIPLINE

Consequences for student bus misconduct should follow a pattern of progressive disciplinary action such as the following:

1. Verbal warning or reprimand.

2. Report to parent and/or parent conference.

3. Temporary suspension of bus privileges. (Caution: Offenders should never be put off the bus without informing building officials and parents.)

4. Permanent withdrawal of transportation privileges.

Note: Certain serious violations (i.e., drug use, weapon possession, etc.) may necessitate bypassing the normal sequence of consequences, resulting in immediate withdrawal of bus service.

197. WHY KIDS TAKE DRUGS

- Peer pressure
- Boredom
- Experimentation
- Fun (getting "high")
- Escape from pain (school, home, or personal problems)
- Low self-esteem
- Thrill-seeking
- Media and/or street models
- Gang influence
- Abuse (physical, sexual, etc.)
- Coercion

198. INDICATORS OF POSSIBLE STUDENT DRUG USE

- Physical changes (weight loss, etc.)
- Fatigue or excessive drowsiness
- Radical mood or behavior changes
- Secretive behavior
- Loss of interest in favorite activities
- Dropping old friends—making new associations
- Unexplained sources of money
- Drop in school attendance and grades
- Appearance of drug paraphernalia
- Sudden reliance on eyedrops
- Slurred speech/incoherence
- Hyperactivity
- Paranoia
- Uncharacteristic apparel (long sleeves, sunglasses, etc.)
- Loss of interest in grooming and appearance
- Decline in personal hygiene
- Distorted sense of time

199. GLOSSARY OF DRUG TERMS

The language of the drug culture changes constantly. It is important that Principals and key staff members remain current on popular drug terms as they evolve over time. The words and phrases below illustrate common drug culture terms today:

Bag	Packet of drugs
Cap	Capsule containing drugs
Cut	Adulterating drugs
Fruit Salad	Mix of drugs
Mule	Drug carrier/courier
Roll Over	Giving evidence to authorities
Spike	Hypodermic needle
Toke	Drag on a marijuana cigarette
Yard	$100
Zigzag	Papers for rolling cigarettes

200. DRUG INTERVENTION GUIDELINES
(SAMPLE)

The sample guidelines below illustrate a typical process for staff members to follow in dealing with any students suspected of being intoxicated or high on drugs:

1. Any student suspected of being under the influence of alcohol or drugs should be referred as soon as possible. (It's permissible to have referred a student, even if the suspicion turns out to be false.)

2. Separate the student from curious onlookers.

3. Call the office for an escort (i.e., counselor, aide, police liaison officer, etc.) to remove the student.

4. Inform the escort of the specific behavior indicating drug use or influence.

5. The designated escort will accompany the student to the Principal or designee who will contact parents and the police as appropriate.

6. Place all suspicious substances in a sealed envelope labeled with the date and student's name. The envelope should be turned over to the Principal or designee.

201. 10 COMMON MISTAKES SCHOOLS MAKE IN COMBATING DRUGS

1. Denial—underestimating the scope of the problem

2. Using scare tactics

3. Starting too late

4. Emphasizing punishment

5. Ignoring tobacco and alcohol as gateway drugs

6. Keeping parents out of the loop

7. Assuming that all drugs work alike

8. Being overly judgmental

9. Presuming that all staff members are drug free

10. Engaging in pseudotherapy—acting like a treatment center

202. COMMON PROBLEMS OF FAS (FETAL ALCOHOL SYNDROME) CHILDREN

A growing number of pupils now entering school suffer from fetal alcohol syndrome, which can manifest itself in a variety of learning and behavior deficits. Some of the most common problems associated with FAS children are outlined below:

Social Deficits

- Limited initiative
- Lack of response to social cues
- Inability to form friendships
- Inability to consider consequences

Learning Deficits

- Short attention span
- Poor concentration
- Trouble with abstract concepts

Behavior Problems

- Stubbornness
- Bullying
- Impulsivity
- Anxious behavior

Effective instructional response techniques and strategies for dealing with these deficits include decreased stimuli, highly structured environment, and routine patterns.

203. 3-POINT TEST FOR SEXUAL HARASSMENT

To sort out harassing sexual behavior from innocuous flirtation or "horseplay" (flirting or hurting), many experts recommend applying this simple test:

1. Would you want your child treating others this way?

2. Would it be O.K. if your mother, sister, wife, or daughter were treated this way?

3. Would the behavior be viewed as offensive if videotaped and shown to girls or women you respect?

Any "No" answer indicates some level of sexual harassment.

204. WHY STUDENTS ARE RELUCTANT TO REPORT INCIDENTS OF HARASSMENT

Embarrassment

Fear of reprisal

Coercion

Guilt or self-doubt

Uncertainty about what is and what isn't harassment

Unfamiliarity with reporting procedures

Fear of being misunderstood, not believed, or not taken seriously

Reluctance to make waves

205. EXAMPLES OF SEXUALLY HARASSING BEHAVIOR IN SCHOOLS

- Name calling
- Leering/staring
- Unwelcome touching
- Suggestive comments
- Stalking
- Sexually-oriented graffiti
- Sexually-oriented jokes
- Dirty notes or letters
- Offensive clothing (T-shirts, etc.)
- Grabbing body parts
- Rumor spreading
- Date rape
- Simulated sex acts
- Teasing
- Whistling
- Pulling down shorts or pants
- Propositioning
- Unwelcome repeated requests for dates
- Sexual or sexist language
- Distributing nude pictures or pornography
- Rating the other sex's physical attributes
- Sexual threats

206. SEXUAL HARASSMENT CHECK LIST FOR PRINCIPALS (SAMPLE)

When a sexual harassment complaint is received, follow these procedures:

_____ If abuse or violence is suspected, report to authorities immediately.

_____ Determine seriousness of allegations. (Should a third party conduct the investigation?)

_____ Inform the District Office in writing within 24 hours.

_____ Initiate an investigation in a timely fashion (at least within two days).

_____ Inform involved parents of allegations and investigation in progress.

_____ Interview all parties separately and privately. (Have a third party sit in on all interviews.)

_____ Follow up all leads.

_____ Inform accused that reprisals will result in even stiffer penalties.

_____ If allegations cannot be substantiated, inform all parties.

_____ If infraction is first-time or minor, take appropriate progressive disciplinary action.

_____ If offense is major, consult with district administrators and legal counsel regarding appropriate disciplinary measures.

_____ Retain all documentation indefinitely.

_____ Report all general outcomes to all parties in writing within confidentiality and data privacy guidelines.

_____ Submit a final report to District Office.

_____ Place appropriate information in student or personnel files.

207. STEPS IN INVESTIGATING SEXUAL HARASSMENT COMPLAINTS

1. <u>Notification</u> (Notify all students and parents involved.)

2. <u>Interviewing</u> (Interview all parties and witnesses involved privately and separately.)

3. <u>Conclusion</u> (Reach judgments based on evidence and interviews.)

4. <u>Action</u> (Take action fitting the infraction. Sometimes, no action is warranted.)

5. <u>Documentation</u> (Maintain complete records of the allegations, investigation, findings, and actions.)

6. <u>Reporting</u> (Inform all parties of findings and outcomes.)

208. DO'S AND DON'TS OF HANDLING SEXUAL HARASSMENT COMPLAINTS

Do

Interview privately and separately.

Be sensitive.

Have females interview females and males interview males.

Have a third party witness interviews.

Probe for details.

Identify witnesses.

Remain neutral.

Keep detailed notes.

Get help if needed.

Continue to monitor after case is closed.

Caution against reprisals.

Don't

Ignore complaints.

Blame the victim.

Make snap judgments.

Protect accuser.

208. DO'S AND DON'TS OF HANDLING SEXUAL HARASSMENT COMPLAINTS, CONTINUED

Be confrontational.

Ask leading questions.

Threaten the accused.

Tape record interviews.

Be swayed by biases.

Make promises you can't keep.

Discuss with outsiders.

End investigation prematurely.

209. COMMON STUDENT PARKING LOT PROBLEMS

Repeated surveys of high school Principals identify the following problems most commonly associated with student parking lots:

Speeding

Reckless driving

Vandalism

Thefts from cars

Littering

Loitering

Noisy driving

Unauthorized traffic during the school day

Smoking

Alcohol or drug use

Sexual activity

210. STEPS TO STOP STUDENT STEALING

- Discourage locker/key sharing.
- Spot-check student lockers.
- Discourage having valuables at school.
- Bank cash daily.
- Mark all equipment for identification.
- Schedule evening cleaning hours.
- Rekey regularly.
- Rotate locker locks and combinations.
- Use "stakeouts" as needed.
- Install video cameras.
- Organize a "Crime Stoppers" campaign.
- Offer rewards.
- Provide opportunities to return goods with no questions asked.
- Prosecute offenders.
- Demand restitution.

211. WHY KIDS JOIN GANGS

Street gangs have powerful appeal for many at-risk students. The most common reasons for voluntary gang affiliation include:

Peer pressure

Identification

Recognition

Status (ego trip)

Security

Economics

Easy sex

"Herd instinct"

Rites of passage

Sibling imitation

Protection — safety

Charismatic leaders

Gang mystique

211. WHY KIDS JOIN GANGS, CONTINUED

Perceived glamorous lifestyles

Drugs

Excitement

Boredom

Purpose in life

Recreation

212. SIGNS OF GANG PRESENCE

Most gangs don't operate in secrecy. They like to announce their presence through a variety of articles, clothing, and other such signs as:

Graffiti

Hand signs

Hand shakes

Nicknames

Gloves

Buttons

Pacifiers

Jargon

Colors

Tattoos

Symbols (i.e., six-point stars, Playboy Bunny, top hats, pyramids, etc.)

Caps

Bandannas

Shoelaces

Scarves

Belts (buckles)

Jewelry

Haircuts

Slogans

Jackets

Body piercing

Note: Gangs are constantly evolving and may modify or change symbols from time to time.

213. ZERO TOLERANCE FOR GANGS

Tested ways to control gang activities in schools:

1. Eliminate gang-related graffiti promptly.

2. Block known gang members from enrolling in the school.

3. Keep in touch with local police for up-to-date information on gang presence, activity, and problems.

4. Separate rival gang members as much as possible.

5. Transfer troublesome gang members to another school or enroll hard-core gang leaders in alternative educational programs.

6. Involve gang leaders in positive leadership experiences within the school.

7. Provide support for gang members who are trying to get out of that way of life.

8. Provide "saturation supervision" for parking lots. (Parking lots are often where gang regalia first appear and where drug deals go down.)

9. Monitor outsiders and enforce trespassing ordinances.

10. Adopt strict anti-weapon and anti-violence policies.

11. Maintain a vigorous after-school activity program.

12. Meet face-to-face with gang leaders to lay down zero-tolerance guidelines.

214. SCHOOLYARD VIOLENCE SURVEY

The results of a 1993 survey of 16,000 students in grades 9-12 included the following findings regarding the incidence of school violence:

11.8%—reported carrying a weapon to school during the previous month

24%—had been offered, sold, or given an illegal drug at school during the previous year

16.2%—had a fight at school in the previous year

7.3%—had been threatened or injured with a weapon at school

4.7%—skipped school at least one day in the previous month because they feared for their safety

Source: 1993 survey conducted by the National Center for Disease Control and Prevention in Atlanta, GA.

215. CAUSES OF INCREASED VIOLENCE IN SCHOOLS

Child abuse
Negative role models
Gangs
Drug disputes
Vendettas
Jealousy
Media hype
Parent apathy
Sexual abuse
Racial clashes
Name-calling incidents
Fights over girls (or boys)
"Weaponization" of society

216. WEAPONS FOUND IN SCHOOLS

Weapons frequently seized in schools across the country include:

Firearms
Knives
Blackjacks
Billy clubs
Chains
Pipe bombs
Razors
Chuckka sticks
BB guns
Air guns
Acid
Brass knuckles
Choke wires
Ball bats

217. SCHOOL SECURITY AUDIT CHECK LIST

Security measures are more important than ever before in today's schools. The simple check list below can help audit security and surveillance provisions and practices in your school:

_____ School discipline policies are up-to-date, and are reviewed annually by school and legal personnel.

_____ All staff have received training on security procedures, ways to spot problems in the making, intervention techniques, and referral sources.

_____ A reception area has been established to receive, screen, and monitor all visitors.

_____ Notices have been posted directing all visitors to report to the appropriate reception area or to the Principal's office.

_____ Visitors, volunteers, and substitute teachers are identified by special name tags.

_____ The number of unlocked entrances has been limited in accordance with fire marshal requirements.

_____ Neighbors have been solicited to report all suspicious individuals and incidents.

_____ Zero-tolerance policies regarding alcohol, drugs, and weapons have been adopted and publicized.

_____ Closed-circuit video cameras have been installed in obscured or isolated areas of the building and on school buses.

_____ A modern sprinkler system has been installed in compliance with contemporary safety standards.

_____ Metal detectors have been installed or are ready for use as needed.

_____ A police liaison officer is on call and readily available at all times.

_____ A Blue Alert Crisis Intervention Team has been identified, trained, and equipped to act in emergencies.

_____ Custodial and supervisory personnel are equipped with walkie-talkies, beepers, or cellular phones.

_____ Magnetic locks have been installed where appropriate.

_____ Electronic intrusion alarms (audio and movement sensors) are in place, particularly in vulnerable areas (i.e., computer areas, music instrument storage areas, etc.).

217. SCHOOL SECURITY AUDIT CHECK LIST,
CONTINUED

_____ Mirrors provide surveillance for hard-to-see areas.

_____ Landscaping has been designed to reduce obscured areas and hiding places.

_____ Locks are rekeyed regularly.

_____ Locker sharing is discouraged.

_____ The number of master keys issued is limited and tightly monitored.

_____ Equipment items are routinely marked for identification.

_____ Students and staff have been advised to refrain from bringing valuables to school.

_____ Panic buttons have been placed in hazardous sections of the campus.

_____ Locker room and pool areas are monitored at all times when in use.

_____ Parking is restricted to registered vehicles only.

_____ The entire perimeter of the buildings and grounds (including parking lots) is well lighted.

_____ Emergency evacuation and bomb threat drills are practiced at regular intervals.

_____ Evening community classes and cleaning hours have been scheduled to reduce unsupervised time.

_____ Escorts are provided to bus stops and parking lots as needed.

_____ Student backpacks, book bags, and sports bags are restricted to lockers.

_____ An intelligence hotline has been established to receive tips about weapons, gang activity, or other potential problems.

_____ Police or private security guards patrol the buildings and grounds after hours as needed.

_____ Adequate liability insurance has been procured and is reviewed annually.

218. GUIDELINES FOR PEER COUNSELORS

Peer counseling programs are gaining acceptance in schools as a means for solving student problems without violence or other antisocial behavior. Simply defined, "peer counseling" is a student assistance program whereby kids help kids solve problems and act as resources for each other. Typical guidelines for peer counselors in working with other students include:

- Try to boost the self-esteem of both parties.
- Encourage open sharing of feelings.
- Value honesty.
- Respect privacy and confidentiality.
- Don't be judgmental.
- Accept differences of opinion.
- Demonstrate an interest in others.
- Avoid advice-giving.
- Encourage exploration of alternatives.
- Don't push; give all parties their time and space.
- Know when to refer students to an adult counselor.
- Support any measures that improve overall school climate.

219. PEER COUNSELORS BY ANY OTHER NAME

Peer counselors are known by many names in schools across the country including:

Natural Helpers

Peer Tutors

Peer Helpers

Peer Leaders

Peer(less) Leaders

Peer Assistance Leaders (PALS)

Peer Facilitators

Peer Partners

220. GUIDELINES FOR EFFECTIVE CONFLICT RESOLUTION PROGRAMS IN SCHOOLS

Many schools have now introduced conflict resolution programs as an alternative to violence for settling disputes. The guidelines below set up a framework for peaceful problem solving.

1. The process must be voluntary.

2. Parties must have the option to withdraw at any time.

3. Once a mediation session has begun, no interruptions are allowed.

4. All parties have full opportunity to present their cases.

5. Language must always be respectful.

6. The process remains as confidential as the parties want it to be.

7. The goal is to reach agreements that allow a continuing relationship between the parties.

8. Both parties must agree to, and sign off on, the settlement.

221. CONFLICT RESOLUTION CHECK LIST

Conflict resolution is a precise process that tends to follow a well-structured sequence of steps. The check list below can guide student mediators through the process.

_____ What is the real problem (conflict)?

_____ When/where did the incident(s) occur?

_____ Why did each party act as she or he did?

_____ What are all the possible solutions?

_____ What seems to be the best solution for all parties?

_____ Why is this solution best?

_____ What are the down sides to this solution?

_____ Who is going to do what?

_____ When?

_____ How will we know when it's done?

_____ Do both parties agree?

222. WHERE TO GO FOR HELP

Many discipline problems can't and shouldn't be tackled alone. It's not a sign of weakness to seek out advice, support, and assistance. It's called leadership.

Effective Principals actively seek out help and take it whenever and wherever they can get it. Many Principals are surprised by the amount of help available to every school. Here are some of the most common resources that can contribute to solving any school's discipline problems:

School Staff (Everyone on staff should be part of the school's discipline team. This includes assistant principals, deans, security personnel, regular and special education teachers, teacher assistance teams, peer coaching groups, etc.)

Parents

Students (Students know what's going on and often have practical ideas and suggestions for improvement.)

District Specialists (Psychologists, nurses, social workers, etc.)

Youth Ministers and Church Outreach Workers

Probation Officers

Child Protection Agencies

Family Counseling Centers

Battered Women Shelters

Juvenile Court Judges

United Way Agencies

Civic/Service Clubs (Lions, Rotary, Kiwanis, etc. Often these are the best source of funds for special projects.)

Youth-Serving Agencies (YWCA, Boys Club, Scouts, etc.)

Big Brother and Big Sister Organizations

Police

Sheriff's Department

Public Health Department

State Department of Education

Bureau of Alcohol, Tobacco, and Firearms

Minority Advocates and Organizations (NAACP, AIM, etc.)

Child Psychologists

Adult Activist Organizations (e.g., MADD)

Student Activist Organizations (e.g., SADD)

Police Reserve Units

222. WHERE TO GO FOR HELP, CONTINUED

Help "Hot Lines"

12-Step Recovery Programs

State Attorney General's Office

Highway Patrol

Psychiatrists

Pediatricians

Private Foundations (Often a good source of grants for new, innovative programs.)

State Teachers Association

College or University Faculty

Ad Hoc Task Forces (i.e., Governor's Task Force on Violence in Schools, etc.)

State Bureau of Investigation

Department of Public Safety

Safe Houses

Ex-Gang Members

Crime-Stoppers Organizations

Case Workers

Treatment Centers

Booster Clubs

Local Bar Association

FBI

Employee Unions

Chamber of Commerce

Alumni Groups

U.S. Department of Education

National Center for Disease Control

Center to Prevent Handgun Violence

American Federation of Teachers

American Association of School Administrators

National Education Association

Retired Teachers Groups

Faculty Spouses Groups

Fellowship of Christian Athletes

222. WHERE TO GO FOR HELP, CONTINUED

Homeless Shelters

Future Teachers of America

Phi Delta Kappa (and other fraternal organizations)

Insurance Investigators

National School Safety Center

Media

Professional Books on Discipline

Educational Research Service (ERS)

Security/Alarm Specialists

Block Clubs

Arson Investigators

Private Surveillance Firms

National Institute on Drug Use

Guardian Angels

Jacob Wetterling Foundation (and other missing children organizations)

Coaches Associations

National Institute on Alcohol Abuse and Alcoholism

School Legal Counsel

Children's Defense Fund

Network Contacts

223. THOUGHTS ON CHILDREN, SOCIETY, AND DISCIPLINE (QUOTES)

"It is true that many of the causes of discipline problems lie within the nature of our society as well as within the nature of our schools."—*Eugene R. Howard*

"It is a morally lost nation that is unable and unwilling to disarm our children and those who kill our children in their school buses, strollers, yards and schools, in movie theaters, and in McDonalds."—*Marian Wright Edelman*

"We are drowning our youngsters in violence, cynicism, and sadism piped into the living room and even the nursery."—*Jenkins Lloyd Jones*

"If poverty is the mother of crime, stupidity is its father."—*Jean de La Bruyene*

"The young always have the same problem—how to rebel and conform at the same time. They have now solved this by defying their parents and copying one another."
—*Quentin Crisp*

"Gangs are everywhere. Gangs are the catch-all of throwaway kids."—*Anon.*

"Violence is counterproductive. It is a very dangerous instrument and can destroy those who wield it."—*John Gardner*

"If the child is safe, everyone is safe."—*G. Campbell Morgan*

Section Six

EMERGENCY PROCEDURES

224. CRISIS MANAGEMENT GUIDELINES

A crisis can strike at any time. The only thing certain about crises is that they will occur from time to time. While you can't predict them, you can be prepared to deal with the unpredictable in your school. The suggestions below can help guide the preparation process:

1. Every school should have a written Crisis Plan. (The following pages in this section may serve as a model for such a document). All staff members should know where to find copies of the Crisis Plan—FAST!

2. A building floor plan should be attached to the Crisis Plan.

3. Each school should identify a Crisis Team with specific responsibilities in the event of an emergency.

4. All staff should have easy access to the names and phone numbers (extensions) of responsible designees when the Principal is away from the building.

5. One person should be identified as the school's official spokesperson in times of emergency.

6. When a crisis strikes, the Superintendent should be notified immediately and kept informed of continuing developments.

7. Not every contingency can be anticipated in a predesigned crisis manual. When all else fails, use COMMON SENSE.

8. Following each crisis, reevaluate the Crisis Plan and make necessary changes.

225. CRISIS PHONE DIRECTORY

Phone numbers for the following individuals and agencies should be readily available in times of crisis:

Superintendent

Police Department

Fire Department

Ambulance Service

Child Protection Agency

Poison Control Center

Utility Companies (water, gas, and electricity)

Weather Bureau

Civil Defense Office

Police Liaison Officer

Head Custodian

225. CRISIS PHONE DIRECTORY, CONTINUED

District Director of Buildings and Grounds

Designees (chain of command when Principal is unavailable)

Assistant Superintendent (Principal's immediate supervisor)

District Communications Coordinator

School Board Chair

District Legal Counsel

Media (contact for emergency school closing announcements)

226. "BLUE ALERT" TEAM

Many schools have established a "Blue Alert" team to provide initial medical care while waiting for paramedics or other professional medical help to arrive. These teams are usually made up of such specialized school personnel as:

- School nurse or health aide
- Health instructors
- Chemical health specialist
- Police liaison officer or security personnel
- Other staff with special skills or interest

EMERGENCY "BLUE ALERT" TEAM TRAINING

All members of the school's emergency "Blue Alert" team should receive specific training in such areas as:

- Cardiac-pulmonary resuscitation (CPR)
- First aid
- Safety measures
- Handling athletic injuries
- Nonviolent crisis intervention
- Crowd control
- Grief and trauma counseling
- Conflict resolution

Training in the above areas should be repeated and updated at regular intervals.

227. TIPS FOR CALLING 911

Most people know to call 911 for help in emergencies. Emergency response experts offer these suggestions for making such calls work most efficiently and effectively:

1. Stay calm.

2. State the problem accurately and completely.

3. State exact location of the emergency; include directions if necessary.

4. Answer all questions asked by the 911 telecommunicator.

5. Let the 911 telecommunicator guide and control the conversation.

6. Do not hang up! Stay on the phone until help arrives or the 911 operator terminates the call.

228. EMERGENCY FIRST-AID SUPPLY LIST

Every school should have the following first-aid supplies on hand and readily available at all times:

• Towels and wash cloths

• Cold packs

• Scissors (blunt end)

• Assorted bandages and Band-Aids

• Adhesive tape

• Antiseptic

• Sterile gauze pads

• Disposable plastic or rubber gloves

• Allergy kits

• Sweet candy or juice

• Updated list of current student medical conditions and medications

229. MEDICAL EMERGENCY PROCEDURES AND URGENT CARE DIRECTIONS

General

- Call health aide, school nurse, Blue Alert Team, or all as needed.
- Do not move a seriously injured person unless necessary for safety reasons.
- Staff or students experiencing any of the medical emergencies below should be evaluated further by medical professionals.
- Notify parents, guardians, or family member as soon as possible.

Bleeding

- Gently blot wound to remove foreign objects.
- Clean wound gently.
- Apply pressure to wound if bleeding is severe.
- Apply a dry cold pack to wounded area.
- Elevate wounded area above level of the heart if possible.
- Treat for shock if necessary.

Breathing Cessation

- Ensure that airway is open and clear.
- Give mouth-to-mouth respiration or CPR as necessary.

Choking

- Do not treat if victim can cough, speak, and breathe.
- If victim can't cough or speak, gestures for help or turns blue, apply the Heimlich maneuver.

Convulsions and Seizures

- Protect victim from self-injury.
- Support and protect victim's head.
- Protect yourself from being struck or kicked.
- Once seizure subsides or victim vomits, turn the body on the side.
- Do not force a blunt object between the victim's teeth.
- Do not give fluids to the victim.

229. MEDICAL EMERGENCY PROCEDURES AND URGENT CARE DIRECTIONS, CONTINUED

- If the victim stops breathing, give artificial respiration.

Eye Injuries

- For chemical burns, flush eye with a gentle stream of lukewarm water with eye open. Flushing should last at least 20 minutes. Watch that ears do not become contaminated by run-off.
- For penetrating injuries to the eye, do not attempt to remove the object or flush. Cover eye loosely. Keep victim quiet while lying on his or her back.

Neck Injury

- Ensure that victim has an open airway.
- Do not move or transport the victim unless absolutely necessary.

Shock

- Symptoms include cold, clammy skin; bluish face; sweating; and/or weak, rapid pulse.
- Have person lie down.
- Keep victim warm; cover victim only enough to prevent loss of body heat.
- Calm and reassure the victim.

230. BASIC EMERGENCY PREVENTION MEASURES FOR SCHOOLS

In a safety-conscious school, continuing efforts are made to prevent situations that can lead to an emergency. Preventive measures that can avert or minimize emergency occurrences include:

- Insist on a continuous program of quality maintenance.
- Assure that a custodian holding a current boiler operator's license is available or on call at all times.
- Maintain an up-to-date collection of safety manuals readily available in the school.
- Keep emergency exits and routes clear at all times.
- Comply with all fire, tornado, earthquake, and civil defense drill requirements.
- Install effective security systems in all key areas.
- Install a modern sprinkler system.
- Reduce or remove all "attractive nuisances," such as unlighted parking lots.
- Provide safety awareness training for all staff.
- Discipline safety violators.
- Provide an emergency radio at strategic locations throughout the building.
- Test all power sources regularly.
- Review accident reports and reports of inspections by OSHA or the fire marshal. Comply with all recommended corrective measures.
- Post procedures for calling 911 by all telephones.

231. CRISIS COMMUNICATION GUIDELINES

Communication is critical during crises. After an emergency has subsided, the Principal is often judged as much on how communications were handled as on how the actual crisis was resolved. These guidelines can expedite effective communication during a crisis situation:

1. Have up-to-date address labels for parents on hand at all times.

2. Have phone directories readily available throughout the school.

3. Inform parents of crisis communication procedures in advance.

4. Establish a telephone tree for disseminating information about a crisis.

5. During a crisis, refrain from taking a position on an issue until all facts are known. Don't jump to conclusions and don't feed the rumor mill.

6. Gather facts carefully and thoroughly. Verify accuracy.

7. Prepare written released statements carefully. Get help if needed. Misstatements can be embarrassing later on.

8. Stick with the facts. Don't babble, speculate, or editorialize.

9. Be positive and candid. Don't give the impression you're hiding something.

10. Mobilize communication immediately. Don't wait until the storm has passed.

11. After a crisis, always thank all appropriate parties for their cooperation during the emergency.

232. TIPS FOR DEALING WITH THE MEDIA DURING A CRISIS

Emergency situations in schools are "news." The presence of the media is inevitable (and sometimes can be helpful). The best Principals learn to deal with the media in ways that accurately inform the public, maintain perspective, and bolster confidence in the school's ability to manage adverse situations. Following the tips below can help convey an image of responsibility, credibility, and professionalism during periods of emergency:

• Remember, your goal is always to inform the public accurately, completely, and in a timely manner.

• Get help from the District Communications Coordinator if needed.

• Hold press conferences when appropriate.

• Be patient with questions from the media. Avoid using "No comment" as a response.

• Try to minimize media intrusion, distraction, and disruption if school is in session.

• Designate a spokesperson to handle media relations during an emergency. (It doesn't always have to be the Principal.)

• Don't try to second-guess the media as to what is newsworthy.

232. TIPS FOR DEALING WITH THE MEDIA DURING A CRISIS, CONTINUED

- Despite media pressure, always respect data privacy guidelines.
- Answer questions truthfully and accurately, without embellishment or editorializing.
- Never lie to the media!
- Tell the bad news first and quickly. Get it over with.
- Guard students from intrusion or harassment when grief is involved.
- Get parental permission before granting interviews with students.
- Don't stall. The media have deadlines.
- Avoid jargon.
- Always keep your promise to return calls to reporters.
- Avoid impromptu comments that may haunt or embarrass you later.
- Talk to reporters in a natural conversational manner. Avoid speaking too rapidly.
- Don't assume that anything is "off the record."
- Don't back away from microphones or cameras.
- Stay focused. Don't allow reporters to lead you away from the subject.
- Try to establish the school as the best source of information on the crisis.

233. SCHOOL EVACUATION PROCEDURES

Whenever emergency conditions necessitate evacuation of the school, the procedures below should be followed:

- Evacuation routes and procedures should be conspicuously posted in each room.
- Evacuation should be effected in accordance with procedures previously practiced during drills held regularly throughout the year.
- Special arrangements should be in place for the evacuation of disabled students.
- All occupants should be removed at least 500 feet (175 paces) from the building.
- All exits should be unlocked.
- Elevators should not be used in case of fire.
- Teachers are responsible for evacuating pupils in their classrooms, and are accountable for them throughout the duration of the evacuation period.
- Notify transportation service if necessary.
- Issue public announcements via the media if students are to be transported home at an unscheduled time.
- Seek shelter for evacuees if weather is inclement or severe. Consider the use of cars in the parking lot for temporary shelter.

234. FIRE EMERGENCY PROCEDURES

The procedures below represent a standard emergency plan in the event of the discovery of a fire in the school:

1. Activate the building alarm system. Notify the fire department.

2. Evacuate the school according to prearranged fire drill plans. All occupants should be removed 500 feet (approx. 175 paces) from the building. All roadways, driveways, and paths should be kept free for use by firefighting personnel.

3. Ensure that evacuation is complete and that all fire doors are closed.

4. Notify utility companies of any break that might cause a hazard. Direct maintenance staff to shut down all dangerous utilities if possible.

5. Notify the Superintendent and Supervisor of Buildings and Grounds.

6. Return to school only following an all-clear signal from fire department officials.

Caution: Emergency lighting should be available. Fire drills should be conducted regularly, including evacuation of students with disabilities.

235. UTILITY EMERGENCY PROCEDURES

In case of a utility emergency (i.e., electrical power failure, gas leakage, or water main break), follow the procedures outlined below:

Electrical Power Failure

- Notify the power and light company.
- Notify the Supervisor of Buildings and Grounds.
- Turn off all computers and other equipment that might be damaged by a power surge when electrical service is restored.

Gas Line Break

- Consider this a top-priority emergency situation.
- Clear the immediate area. Close school if necessary.
- Shut down all electrical equipment. Do not use electrical switches.
- Call the local gas company.
- Call fire department if necessary.
- Notify Superintendent and Supervisor of Buildings and Grounds.

235. UTILITY EMERGENCY PROCEDURES,
CONTINUED

Water Main Break

- Shut off water.
- Notify water department.
- Make plans to keep school closed until water service is restored.
- Call police department.
- Notify Superintendent and Supervisor of Buildings and Grounds.

236. EMERGENCY PROCEDURES FOR SEVERE THUNDERSTORMS

1. When weather is threatening, school personnel should stay tuned to radio or television for up-to-date advisory information.
2. If a severe thunderstorm strikes, initiate school warning system. Alert students to be prepared to take shelter.
3. Warn students regarding dangers from lightning or downed electrical wires, and possible flash-flooding in low-lying areas.
4. If storm occurs at dismissal time, hold all students until the danger has passed or students are picked up by responsible adults.

237. TORNADO EMERGENCY PROCEDURES

1. When tornadoes are a possibility, school officials should constantly monitor National Weather Service radio.
2. If a warning is issued, all occupants of the building should proceed immediately to predesignated tornado shelter areas. Appropriate shelter spaces include:

    a.) underground areas;

    b.) windowless, interior rooms (including bathrooms); and

    c.) interior hallways.

    Avoid windows, auditoriums, gymnasiums, or other structures with wide free-span overheads.

3. If the warning occurs at dismissal time, hold students until an all-clear has been announced or students are picked up by responsible adults.
4. Assign secretaries to close the school vault and lock files containing records.
5. Periodic tornado drills and classroom discussions of the above procedures should be conducted throughout the year, particularly during the tornado season.

238. EMERGENCY PROCEDURES IN THE EVENT OF A BLIZZARD OR SEVERE WINTER STORM

1. School personnel should be alert for possible public warnings by the National Weather Service over radio and TV whenever a bad storm is possible or anticipated.

2. Only the Superintendent of Schools has authority to close or dismiss school because of weather.

3. If school is closed or starting is delayed, an announcement will be made over designated radio and TV stations as early as possible. Principals should then use prearranged telephone trees to inform key personnel of the closing or late start.

4. If school must dismiss early because of inclement weather, public announcements should be made as early as possible. Regular transportation must be provided. Walkers should be directed to go directly home. Special provisions may need to be made for students with disabilities. Students should be reminded to dress properly. All extracurricular activities must be canceled.

5. In certain situations, it may be necessary to hold students until dangerous conditions have passed or students are picked up by responsible adults.

239. EMERGENCY PROCEDURES IN CASE OF A HAZARDOUS MATERIALS ACCIDENT

In a nuclear age, accidents involving radioactive or other hazardous substances are a possibility. Such accidents may include overturned tankers, train derailments, broken fuel lines, chemical fires, explosions, and so on. If they occur near any school grounds, winds may carry toxic fumes that can endanger students and staff members. If a hazardous materials accident happens close enough to the school to threaten the safety of occupants, use the procedures below:

1. Determine if evacuation is necessary. Sometimes, it is safer to leave students in school with all doors and windows closed and all ventilation systems closed down.

2. If it is necessary for building occupants to clear the area, move cross-wind to avoid toxic fumes.

3. Notify appropriate emergency response personnel.

4. Administer first aid as needed.

5. Notify the Superintendent

6. Do not allow students or staff to return to school until the area has been officially declared safe.

7. Inform parents about the accident, the emergency procedures taken, any symptoms to watch for, or further precautions that should be taken at home.

240. EMERGENCY PROCEDURES WHEN THERE IS SUDDEN DAMAGE TO THE FACILITY

Sudden damage to the school facility may be caused by a boiler explosion, a roof cave-in, a structural problem, and so on. When such an emergency occurs, the steps below should be followed:

1. If conditions pose a safety threat, evacuate occupants from the affected portion of the building.

2. Notify police or fire department immediately.

3. Designate someone to meet emergency crews and brief them on what has happened.

4. Notify the Superintendent and the Supervisor of Buildings and Grounds.

5. Arrange transportation for students if necessary and notify parents.

6. Do not return students to the damaged area until officials declare it safe.

241. BOMB THREAT EMERGENCY PROCEDURES

- Office personnel should be trained in procedures for tracing a telephone call.
- Any person receiving a bomb threat should secure a co-worker's attention (without tipping off the caller) so that tracing procedures can be initiated immediately.
- The individual taking a bomb threat call should keep the caller on the line as long as possible and write down as much information as possible (record caller's exact words).
- Try to obtain all possible information below from the caller:

    —Where is the bomb?

    —What does it look like?

    —When is it set to explode?

    —What kind of bomb is it?

    —What will detonate it?

    —Why did you set the bomb?

    —Who are you?

- Record the time and date the threat was received.
- Try to estimate the sex, age, and ethnicity of the caller and note any distinguishing background noises.
- Contact police immediately.
- Consult with police personnel in determining whether to evacuate the building.
- Inform the Superintendent of the nature of the threat and what response measures have occurred or are underway.
- If the decision is to evacuate the school, announce over the intercom that all individuals in the building should distance themselves at least 500 feet (175 paces) from the building.
- Teachers should make a visual check of classroom areas before evacuating. Anything suspicious should be reported, but <u>not touched</u>.
- Refrain from using radios, walkie-talkies, or cellular phones in the bomb threat area to avoid accidentally triggering the bomb.
- School personnel should not handle or move a suspected bomb. Leave this to professional police or bomb squad personnel.
- Do not return to the building until police or fire personnel give the all-clear signal.

242. LARGE GROUP EMERGENCY SITUATIONS—POISONING, DISEASE, ASPHYXIATION

In extreme situations, large groups of students may become involved in a mass crisis situation such as food poisoning, asphyxiation, or exposure to a communicable disease. When this happens, the simple guidelines below should be followed in order to limit and control the extent of the problem:

Food Poisoning

- Notify district nurse, the food services department, the Superintendent, and the local Health Department.
- Administer first aid to victims and transport affected parties to appropriate medical facilities as needed.
- Cooperate with local health officials to identify the source of the poisoning and to take corrective action.
- Follow all directives of medical authorities.
- Inform parents about the situation and alert them to further symptoms to watch for.

Asphyxiation

- Open all doors and windows.
- Evacuate the building if necessary according to prearranged procedures.
- Call fire department and medical emergency personnel for help.
- Apply first aid as needed to victims.
- Notify Superintendent and district nurse.
- Inform parents as soon as possible.
- Do not reenter building until the source of the problem has been identified and rectified.

Communicable Disease

- Notify school nurse and follow district policy on communicable diseases.
- Contact local health department for advice and assistance.
- Work with health department epidemiology officials to provide parents with necessary information, including symptoms to watch for and any needed precautions (e.g., vaccinations).

243. EMERGENCY PROCEDURES WHEN STUDENTS MUST BE KEPT AT SCHOOL

There may be situations (i.e., fires, gas leaks, downed electrical wires, etc.) that block traffic in the community or affect bus routes or stops. In these circumstances, students may have to be kept at school in accordance with the following procedures:

- Police or street department personnel should notify the school and appropriate transportation services.
- The bus company should inform the school of the bus numbers, routes, and stops affected.
- The school will identify and locate the children involved as soon as possible.
- Notify the Superintendent. Public announcements should be issued immediately.
- School staff should remain calm in dealing with upset students and parents.
- If time permits, the school should contact parents at home or work to explain the situation and why their children are being detained.
- Students should be assembled in a secure area where pickup by parents can be controlled and monitored.
- Parents should check in at the office so children can be called for pickup. Parents should sign out their children so that school personnel can keep accurate track of each student's whereabouts.
- Children should be released only to parents or guardians, unless they have contacted the school to grant permission for their child to go with another adult (day care provider, relative, neighbor, babysitter, etc.). All adults must sign out the children and designate relationship with them.

244. EMERGENCY PROCEDURES IF THERE HAS BEEN A BREAK-IN AT THE SCHOOL

When a break-in at the school is discovered, take these steps:

- Do not enter the building.
- Call the police from the nearest telephone.
- If you have already entered the building and then discover a break-in, do not touch anything. Leave the building and call the police.
- Notify the Superintendent and the Supervisor of Buildings and Grounds.
- Wait for police investigators to advise when clean-up and repairs can begin.

245. EMERGENCY PROCEDURES IN CASE OF STUDENT DEMONSTRATIONS OR DISTURBANCES

Since the activist era of the 1960s, schools have periodically been the sites of student protests, sit-ins, walk-outs, and other forms of demonstrations and disturbances. Open communication, student involvement, respectful treatment, due process, and user-friendly grievance procedures are the best preventive measures. When these fail, however, and a student demonstration or disturbance takes place, the action steps below can help neutralize and resolve the situation:

1. Consult with the Superintendent to determine if police assistance is needed.

2. The Superintendent may notify other area schools. Demonstrations can be contagious and often attract outside participants.

3. Students not involved in the disturbance should be kept fully informed to dispel rumors, and calm fears.

4. Try to meet with student protest leaders to discuss issues and seek solutions.

5. All staff members should be fully informed about the situation.

6. Normal classroom operations should be maintained as much as possible. Encourage all students to stay in the building.

7. The custodial staff should be responsible for building security, as long as the police are not involved.

8. Clerical staff should be responsible for the security of files and records.

9. All staff members should remain at their assigned duties unless otherwise directed by the Principal.

10. Parents and the public should be informed of the situation as soon as possible. The school should speak with a single voice (spokesperson) throughout the duration of the disturbance.

11. If media representatives appear at school, try to keep cameras out of the building or limited to a prearranged area.

12. If it is determined that the school should be closed, the following parties should be informed as soon as possible:

    a. Students
    b. Staff
    c. Parents
    d. Transportation Services
    e. Police
    f. Neighboring Schools

13. Staff members should supervise dismissal.

246. CONSIDERATIONS IN REPORTING CHILD ABUSE

Statutory requirements and protections for reporting suspected child abuse vary from state to state. School personnel must remain up-to-date on these matters. The considerations below can serve as a generic framework for dealing with abusive situations.

- School staff members should report immediately any suspected child neglect, physical abuse, or sexual abuse to the local Child Protection Agency or the police. (In many states, such reporting is mandatory.)

- Any report of suspected abuse should include the following information:
    - Child's name, birth date, address, phone number, and parent's (guardian's) name.
    - Name of anyone suspected of perpetrating the abuse or neglect.
    - Nature and extent of the abuse, including times, dates, locations, and witnesses if possible.
    - Name, address, and phone number of the reporting party.

- An oral report should be followed by a detailed written report as soon as possible.

- If it is suspected that the child is abandoned, in immediate danger, or in need of medical care, the police should be contacted immediately.

- Principals may permit police personnel to interview students at school upon receipt of written notice. In most situations, parents or guardians will not be notified until the interview (investigation) is concluded.

- In many states, school personnel reporting suspected neglect or abuse in good faith are provided with civil and criminal immunity. Anonymity is usually guaranteed except in very limited circumstances.

247. CHILDNAPPING—PREVENTIVE MEASURES AND EMERGENCY PROCEDURES

The abduction of children and youth has become a real threat that must be addressed by schools everywhere. The preventive steps and emergency response measures below have helped many schools respond to this growing concern:

Prevention Steps

- Maintain an up-to-date list of students who are not to be released to anyone except a particular parent or guardian. (The emergency cards for these students should be tagged or color-coded.)
- Before releasing any child to someone other than designated parents or guardians, check with the custodial parent. It's always good insurance to record the time and date of telephone approval.
- Always require anyone picking up a child from school to physically present himself or herself in the school office to pick up the child.
- In case of a parent's telephoning a request for a child to be released from school, confirm the identity of the caller by a separate, follow-up call.

Emergency Response (If an actual childnapping has occurred or is suspected)

- Phone police and/or police liaison officer immediately.
- Call the parent/guardian.
- Inform the Superintendent.
- Write down all pertinent information (description of the abductor, description of car involved, license tag numbers, etc.) as soon as possible.
- Any release of information to the media should come through the police, the parents, or the Principal or designee.

248. EMERGENCY PROCEDURES FOR DEALING WITH INCIDENTS OF ASSAULT OR RAPE

In the event of an occurrence of rape or serious assault of a student or adult, school personnel should follow these steps:

1. Provide first aid to the victim. Be sensitive to the emotional trauma being experienced by the victim.

2. Call police and/or police liaison officer.

3. Notify building Principal or designee.

4. Locate emergency card on file for the victim and inform parents, guardians, or family members as soon as possible.

5. Obtain as much information on the incident and the assailant as possible, as soon as possible.

6. Notify the Superintendent of the incident.

7. Stay with and comfort the victim until proper authorities or family members take charge.

8. Write down as much as can be remembered about the incident as soon as possible.

249. GUIDELINES FOR DEALING WITH SUICIDAL STUDENTS

Whenever a student threatens or hints at suicide, adults cannot afford to take the situation lightly. Any verbal, written, or behavioral suggestion of suicide may be a forewarning, an attention-getting device, or a cry for help. In any event, the matter must be treated with sensitivity and seriousness. The guidelines below can assist any staff member in dealing with a suicidal student.

1. In working with a suicidal student, the goals must always be (a) to evaluate the degree of imminent risk; (b) to allow the student to share feelings; (c) to diminish the student's sense of isolation; and (d) to build support and a follow-up plan for the student's future.

2. In interviewing any suicidal person, strive to remain calm, refuse to panic, be supportive, affirm that the person is right to share a suicidal concern, and listen more than you talk.

3. Focus on hope and try to expand available options. There are always choices other than suicide.

4. Watch for signs of serious intent (i.e., a well-defined plan for the suicide, hopelessness, depression, withdrawal, self-deprecation, etc.).

5. Avoid being critical or judgmental, or jumping to conclusions.

6. Be patient. Don't rush the student's story. Let it unfold.

7. Don't make promises you can't keep. Inform the person that the suicidal concern will have to be shared with others in order to get appropriate help and to make changes that will alleviate pressure.

8. Try to find out what is driving the student's suicidal intention, what would help change the situation for the better, and who is a positive role model or influence for the student.

9. Always arrange for a follow-up meeting with the student to discuss the situation further.

10. Seek proper help (Principal, social worker, counselor, psychologist, building crisis team, etc.). Inform the parents of the concern.

11. Responsible adults should then work together to develop an appropriate plan of action for the student, including continued monitoring, referral, and immediate intervention.

250. GUIDELINES FOR HANDLING TERRORISTIC ACTS IN THE SCHOOL

In today's violence-ridden society, the possibility of random violence, hostage-holding, terrorism—and even massacre—exists everywhere, including schools. It pays to be prepared for the nightmarish prospect of a terrorist on the school grounds. Experts offer the following suggestions for managing such unthinkable threats in a school:

1. Talk about such possibilities in advance. Have a general plan in mind.

2. Keep a list of emergency phone numbers readily available.

3. Always call 911 for help immediately.

4. Put your best person in charge of communicating with the terrorist.

5. Seal off the area of the school involved if possible.

6. Evacuate students not directly affected by the situation to a safe distance from the school.

7. Leave negotiating with the terrorist to experts (police, psychologists, etc.).

8. To the extent possible, follow the demands and requests of the terrorist until an experienced negotiator takes over. Try not, however, to agree to anything that worsens the situation or endangers more people.

9. Keep the terrorist talking until help arrives.

10. If known, try to contact someone close to the terrorist (i.e., family member, friend, co-worker, etc.) who may be able to help calm him or her down.

11. Designate one person to handle communications with the media, parents, and community members during the episode.

12. Be prepared to provide debriefings and counseling to all affected parties when the danger is over.

An emergency plan (even a rough one such as the suggestions above) works like an insurance policy. You hope you never have to use it—but if trouble strikes, it may be a lifesaver. Expect the best, but prepare for the worst-case scenario.

251. HOW TO BE A HOSTAGE—AND LIVE TO TELL THE STORY

The possibility of being held hostage may seem farfetched to many school personnel, but in today's violent and volatile society, it can happen. If it ever does, Frank Bolz, Captain of the NYPD Hostage Negotiating Team, offers these tips for getting through the experience safely:

- Follow instructions exactly during the first 15-45 minutes. This is the critical period when the terrorist is most emotional and most likely to be trigger-happy.

- Keep quiet and speak only when spoken to. Don't try to be friendly, phony, argumentative, or hostile.

- Don't make suggestions. *Reason:* Captors will suspect a trick.

- Be wary of attempting escape. If it fails, it's likely to bring violence.

- If you are released ahead of others, closely observe everything that goes on in order to help the police.

- Treat the hostage-takers like royalty, but try not to be condescending.

- Expect to be frisked or even treated roughly by police when released. Cooperate fully. *Reason:* Police aren't sure who is who and they don't take chances.

Author's Note: Don't try to be a hero. There's a difference between bravery and bravado. The latter can be life-threatening.

252. SOME THOUGHTS ON CRISES, EMERGENCIES, FEAR, AND PREPAREDNESS
(QUOTES)

"There cannot be a crisis next week. My schedule is already full."
  —*Henry Kissinger*

"I can see only one emergency following upon another as wave follows upon wave. . ."
  —*H.A.L. Fisher*

". . . Chance favours only the prepared mind."—*Louis Pasteur*

"Forewarned, Forearmed."—*Benjamin Franklin*

". . . The only thing we have to fear is fear itself."—*Franklin D. Roosevelt*

"It is by presence of mind in untested emergencies that the native metal of a man is tested."—*Abraham Lincoln*

"The crisis of yesterday is the joke of tomorrow."—*H.G. Wells*

HUMAN RESOURCES MANAGEMENT

253. IT'S THE PRINCIPAL'S JOB TO . . .

In the area of personnel,
It's the Principal's job to
HIRE;
INSPIRE; and
LIGHT A FIRE!

ESSENTIAL ELEMENTS OF AN EFFECTIVE TEAM

Principals get things done by working through other people. This takes teamwork. Effective teams don't just happen. They are developed, nurtured, and shaped by creative leadership and hard work on the part of all participants. Essential elements of an effective team include:

1. Team members share common goals and really care about achieving them.

2. Team members agree on priorities to achieve common goals.

3. Members understand their individual roles and respect one another's unique contributions.

4. Everyone understands who's in charge and how things get decided and get done.

5. Conflicts are recognized and resolved out in the open.

6. Personalities are valued, appreciated, and integrated toward a team effort.

7. People feel free to take risks and are supported in trying new things.

8. Team meetings are productive—and fun.

9. The team celebrates successes and shares credit.

10. Continuous improvement and lifelong learning are valued and practiced by all members.

254. 6 STEPS TO A WINNING TEAM

1. Define purpose (mission and goals).

2. Establish composition of the team and individual roles.

3. Clarify responsibilities.

4. Accommodate and integrate individual personalities.

5. Monitor and manage team performance.

6. Evaluate team outcomes and celebrate victories.

TEAM FUNCTIONS

To survive and succeed, every team needs to address these functions:

Getting Things Done:

- Initiating action
- Information and opinion sharing
- Data gathering
- Clarifying and elaborating
- Summarizing
- Consensus testing
- Decision making
- Action
- Evaluating
- Correcting and redirecting

Getting Along Together:

- Encouraging one another
- Expressing feelings
- Compromising
- Allowing mistakes
- Building on strengths
- Caring for each other
- Practicing loyalty
- Cheerleading
- Helping one another grow
- Celebrating together

255. BUILDING BLOCKS FOR BETTER MORALE (MORALE BOOSTERS)

Morale boosting is part of team-building. The Principal has more influence on school morale than any other single individual. To achieve an atmosphere of positive relationships and esprit de corps, Principals must address in specific ways each of the following four basic building blocks for better morale:

I. Personal Incentive Factors

- Achievement
- Recognition
- Advancement
- Responsibility
- Input
- Feedback
- Praise
- Reinforcement

II. Contractual Factors

- Salary
- Benefits
- Job security
- Working conditions
- Policies
- Grievance procedures
- Seniority
- Tenure

III. Professional Factors

- Adequate supplies and materials
- Flexible curriculum
- Planning time
- Growth opportunities
- Academic freedom
- Fair evaluation

255. BUILDING BLOCKS FOR BETTER MORALE (MORALE BOOSTERS), CONTINUED

- Discipline support
- Participatory decision making

IV. Social Factors

- Social affairs (luncheons, picnics, parties)
- Retreats
- Bowling leagues, softball teams, etc.
- Nights out (concerts, movies)
- Mixers
- Celebrations
- Fun

256. TEACHER (ELEMENTARY AND SECONDARY) — LIST OF DUTIES AND RESPONSIBILITIES (SAMPLE)

1. Plan, organize, and provide appropriate learning experiences within assigned area(s) of responsibility.

2. Establish and maintain a classroom atmosphere conducive to learning.

3. Evaluate and interpret student learning in a professional manner.

4. Identify special needs of students and seek help as needed.

5. Make reasonable efforts to promote and maintain appropriate student behavior.

6. Contribute to the continuous development of curriculum and the improvement of instruction.

7. Maintain and submit necessary records and reports.

8. Participate in faculty meetings, workshops, staff development programs, and other school-sponsored activities.

9. Assist in general building supervision and discipline control.

10. Adhere to the ethical standards adopted by professional teacher organizations.

257. SECRETARY TO ELEMENTARY PRINCIPAL—LIST OF DUTIES AND RESPONSIBILITIES (SAMPLE)

1. Organize and maintain student and teacher records and schedules as directed by the Principal.

2. Be knowledgeable of applicable legal requirements regarding student and staff records, including confidentiality standards.

3. Maintain inventory of office machines, equipment, and supplies.

4. Prepare correspondence, notices, bulletins, and reports as directed.

5. Be knowledgeable about employee contractual agreements.

6. Provide orientation for, and schedule substitutes for, certified and classified personnel.

7. Assist in establishing and monitoring student bus assignments.

8. Monitor all building budgets.

9. Foster an attitude of cooperation and positive public relations with school patrons.

10. Be knowledgeable about and interpret school policies and rules as applicable.

11. Handle immediate problems in the Principal's absence within delegated areas of responsibility.

258. SECRETARY TO JUNIOR HIGH PRINCIPAL—LIST OF DUTIES AND RESPONSIBILITIES (SAMPLE)

1. Maintain student records and schedules as directed.

2. Be knowledgeable about legal requirements regarding student and employee records.

3. Maintain inventory of office machines, equipment, and supplies.

4. Prepare correspondence, notices, bulletins, and other communications as directed.

5. Record staff absences and secure clerical substitutes as needed.

6. Be knowledgeable about employee contractual agreements.

7. Provide orientation for substitute teachers.

8. Account for and maintain budget records for the school and coordinate all purchases of textbooks and supplies.

258. SECRETARY TO JUNIOR HIGH PRINCIPAL—LIST OF DUTIES AND RESPONSIBILITIES (SAMPLE), CONTINUED

9. Foster an attitude of cooperation and positive public relations with all school patrons.

10. Be knowledgeable about and interpret school policies and rules as applicable.

11. Assist in administration and recordkeeping for the junior high athletic program.

12. Respond to student and parent inquiries and act in the absence of the Principal.

259. SECRETARY TO SENIOR HIGH PRINCIPAL—LIST OF DUTIES AND RESPONSIBILITIES (SAMPLE)

1. Compile and prepare all local, state, and federal reports as directed.

2. Act as liaison between the Principal and certified and classified staff members.

3. Maintain records of staff absences, calculate salaries for all substitutes (certified and classified), and procure classified substitutes when needed.

4. Assist in the selection and supervision of office staff and aides.

5. Maintain student credits and rank-in-class records and interpret transcripts for new students.

6. Prepare, compile, assemble, and distribute all materials for the opening and closing of the school year. Coordinate final check-out for all staff at the end of the school year.

7. Coordinate and prepare for graduation activities.

8. Receive, screen, and prioritize all calls and correspondence for the Principal and maintain her or his schedule and appointment calendar.

9. Maintain an adequate inventory of supplies and materials.

260. COUNSELOR (SECONDARY)—LIST OF DUTIES AND RESPONSIBILITIES (SAMPLE)

1. Provide individual and group counseling in the areas of educational, vocational, social, and emotional growth.

2. Assist students with registration, course selection, program changes, and post-high school planning.

3. Confer with parents regarding their students' progress and problems.

4. Assist students and parents in the transition from junior to senior high school.

5. Refer students and families to appropriate school and community resources.

6. Provide and interpret career information to students and parents.

7. Maintain and interpret student cumulative records.

8. Coordinate, administer, and interpret group and individual tests of scholastic, aptitude, achievement, vocational interests, and other tests as directed.

261. SCHOOL NURSE—LIST OF DUTIES AND RESPONSIBILITIES (SAMPLE)

1. Provide leadership in the development and administration of the total school health program.

2. Select, orient, direct, supervise, and evaluate individual building health aides.

3. Develop appropriate inservice programs in health education.

4. Provide direct classroom instruction and appropriate resource materials for health education as requested.

5. Prepare and submit all required records and reports.

6. Plan and implement appropriate vision, hearing, and scoliosis screening programs.

7. Manage the District's Blood Bank program.

8. Serve as resource person to school personnel in all matters of health concern.

9. Implement measures to prevent and control communicable diseases.

10. Develop a system of emergency care.

11. Assess and recommend school safety measures and provisions for a healthful school environment.

262. SOCIAL WORKER—LIST OF DUTIES AND RESPONSIBILITIES (SAMPLE)

1. Provide social work services to students and families with academic, social, emotional, or behavioral problems.

2. Confer with appropriate staff regarding individual student problems and classroom management strategies for particular students.

3. Consult with parents of students with problems.

4. Conduct home visits as necessary.

5. Be knowledgeable about community resources and make referrals as needed.

6. Prepare necessary reports for courts and other agencies and represent the school in court as needed.

7. Serve as a resource for developing effective classroom curriculum and activities.

263. SPEECH CLINICIAN—LIST OF DUTIES AND RESPONSIBILITIES (SAMPLE)

1. Identify children who have speech/language problems.

2. Provide speech/language assessment for students age 3-21.

3. Provide appropriate services for students who have speech/language problems including articulation, reception, expressiveness, stuttering, or voice disorders.

4. Assist with preschool screening.

5. Act as a resource person on speech and language development.

264. RECEPTIONIST/SWITCHBOARD OPERATOR—LIST OF DUTIES AND RESPONSIBILITIES (SAMPLE)

1. Act as receptionist and switchboard operator for the school.

2. Receive visitors and direct them to appropriate parties.

3. Respond to inquiries.

4. Prepare outgoing/bulk mail; sort and distribute incoming mail.

5. Open, sort, and date incoming invoices.

6. Maintain petty cash fund.

265. TEACHER AIDE—LIST OF DUTIES AND RESPONSIBILITIES (SAMPLE)

1. Type, duplicate, and collate materials for faculty.

2. Maintain files as directed.

3. Prepare correspondence, requisitions, and reports for the assigned department or grade level.

4. Assist in accounting for books and equipment assigned to the department or grade level.

5. Assist with supervision of lunchroom, playground, and classroom as directed.

6. Sell lunch tickets and assist with library book shelving as directed.

266. MANAGEMENT (BEHAVIOR) AIDE—LIST OF DUTIES AND RESPONSIBILITIES (SAMPLE)

1. Assist in developing behavior management programs.

2. Maintain baseline data on all referrals.

3. Provide one-on-one physical supervision for assigned students with emotional/behavioral problems.

4. Assist with crisis intervention.

5. Maintain parent contacts as appropriate.

267. SECURITY AIDE—LIST OF DUTIES AND RESPONSIBILITIES (SAMPLE)

1. Initiate preventive measures to reduce delinquent acts or violations of school rules.

2. Provide supervision and protective security for school buildings and grounds.

3. Assist in enforcement of all school rules while respecting the legal rights of all individuals.

4. Assist at school activities and functions as needed.

5. Assist in the investigation of criminal acts in the school.

6. Regulate traffic and parking on school property.

7. Be knowledgeable about

   - law enforcement procedures;
   - juvenile court procedures;
   - traffic control;
   - alcohol-drug control;
   - investigative protocol;
   - human relations; and
   - first-aid procedures.

8. Assist in maintaining student attendance.

Note: Security aides shall not be uniformed or equipped with side arms.

268. HEALTH AIDE—LIST OF DUTIES AND RESPONSIBILITIES (SAMPLE)

1. Provide first aid and emergency care as needed.

2. Arrange care for children who become ill at school.

3. Provide information on school accident prevention.

4. Be responsible for maintaining appropriate health records and reports.

5. Conduct routine vision and auditory screening.

6. Participate in preschool roundup and screening.

269. HALL MONITOR—LIST OF DUTIES AND RESPONSIBILITIES (SAMPLE)

1. Initiate preventive measures to reduce delinquent acts and school rule violations in school hallways and throughout the building.

2. Assist with emergency situations as directed.

3. Provide personal visibility and supervision in the hallways and throughout the building with special attention to the time periods before and after school and during passing time between classes.

4. Make periodic spot checks of restrooms, locker rooms, and practice rooms.

5. Provide surveillance of unauthorized persons on school premises and report their presence to the administration.

6. Assist in investigating all rule violations.

7. Assist with crowd control as needed.

270. PARAPROFESSIONAL—LIST OF DUTIES AND RESPONSIBILITIES (SAMPLE)

1. Tutor students individually and in small groups and provide homework support.

2. Administer makeup and retake tests.

3. Oversee standardized testing.

4. Supervise assigned study areas and periods.

5. Provide clerical assistance as needed.

271. CUSTODIAN—LIST OF DUTIES AND RESPONSIBILITIES (SAMPLE)

1. Perform basic mechanical and plumbing maintenance.

2. Carry out scheduled preventive maintenance on all building equipment.

3. Follow recommended and established cleaning procedures in assigned area of responsibility.

4. Assist in maintaining standards of building and site cleanliness to provide a healthy, safe, and attractive physical environment.

5. Assist visitors and building permit holders as needed.

6. Assist with building security by making routine facility checks, reporting any suspicious occurrences and activating security systems on schedule.

7. Follow established safety procedures at all times.

8. Be available for weekend building checks and emergency calls as needed.

272. COOK—LIST OF DUTIES AND RESPONSIBILITIES (SAMPLE)

1. Assist with cooking, baking, and food preparation as assigned.

2. Assist with food serving and kitchen clean-up.

3. Place food orders as directed.

4. Assist with ticket sales and ticket cash accounting as needed.

273. DEPARTMENT CHAIR—LIST OF DUTIES AND RESPONSIBILITIES (SAMPLE)

1. Act as liaison between the department and the building administration.

2. Work with the Principal to evaluate departmental procedures and individual teacher effectiveness.

3. Provide leadership in curriculum evaluation and development.

4. Encourage and facilitate the introduction of innovative instructional strategies and techniques.

5. Assist in the selection of new staff within the department.

6. Prepare and monitor departmental budgets.

7. Coordinate ordering and inventorying of texts, materials, and supplies.

8. Provide leadership in the implementation of appropriate staff development programs.

9. Assist in determining departmental schedules, teaching assignments, and room designations.

10. Encourage creativity and innovation that will result in enriched learning opportunities for all students.

274. LIST OF DUTIES FOR ADVISOR-ADVISEE PROGRAM ADVISORS (SAMPLE)

More and more schools are adopting or reinventing advisor-advisee programs in order to personalize the school experience. The roles below are representative of the expectations commonly assigned to student advisors:

1. Monitor each advisee's academic, extracurricular, and social development.

2. Build a relationship of mutual trust, confidentiality, support, and communication with all advisees.

3. Foster trust, cooperation, friendship, identity, and teamwork within the advisee group.

4. Serve as a liaison or ombudsman for each advisee with the remainder of the staff.

5. Foster and facilitate both formal and informal home-school communication, including conducting parent-teacher conferences.

6. Signal appropriate personnel about any problems in the making.

7. Assist students with solving school-related problems.

8. Follow the prescribed outline of advisor-advisee activities.

9. Celebrate every advisee's success (large or small).

10. Maintain a portfolio of each advisee's progress and accomplishments.

275. POLICE LIAISON OFFICER FUNCTIONS
(SAMPLE)

The roles and responsibilities of a Police Liaison Officer are many and varied as illustrated in the list of functions below:

1. Serve as a resource in the areas of prevention and resolution of juvenile delinquency behavior.

2. Consult with the Principal and staff on matters of school safety and security.

3. Work with juvenile court representatives concerning juvenile crime prevention and control.

4. Provide information and assistance to the PTA, service clubs, and other community groups.

5. Assist with crowd control in situations where it is needed.

6. Investigate incidents of crime in school.

7. Provide classroom lectures and other classroom presentations when appropriate.

8. Advise the school on discipline policy matters.

9. Assist with supervision of field trips and events.

10. Help organize safety and anticrime campaigns.

11. Maintain high visibility in the school as a deterrent to inappropriate behavior.

12. Participate in case conferences and parent conferences as appropriate.

13. Serve as a first call for help in incidents of abuse and harassment.

14. Improve communication between students, parents, the school, and the police department.

15. Be available to counsel students and parents on law-related matters.

16. Conduct background and follow-up investigations of students and staff members upon request of school administrators.

17. Keep school officials informed concerning police apprehension of students in and outside of the school.

18. Develop early identification of delinquent and predelinquent behavior and facilitate early intervention and referral as needed.

276. WHAT TO LOOK FOR IN THE STAFF OF THE FUTURE

Teaching is a dynamic profession in a rapidly changing society. What worked for teachers in the past isn't good enough anymore. Tomorrow's teachers will need new skills and attributes. Below is one community's list of desirable traits and characteristics that Principals should search for in hiring the staff of the future:

- Dedication to quality performance and service
- Enthusiasm, commitment, and exuberance in the classroom
- Ability to communicate effectively
- Willingness to work 101%
- Self-direction (ability to work with minimal directions)
- Capacity to be a self-starter
- Excitement about teaching and learning
- High expectations and high standards
- Optimism—hope for the future
- Unflinching faith in the next generation
- Genuine compassion for all children (and for their parents)
- Flexibility (capacity to change and learn new skills)
- Varied interests and experiences (hobbies, reading, travel)
- Ability to work with all kinds of people (experience with diversity)
- Understanding of and skill in modern classroom management
- Equal respect for both sexes
- Technological literacy
- "Street smarts"
- Consistent professional behavior
- Ability to provide work direction for other adults (i.e., aides, volunteers, interns, etc.)
- Some meaningful interest or experience in the arts
- Respect for childhood and adolescence
- Commitment to democratic values and practices
- Understanding of cooperative learning, resource-based instruction, and learning styles
- Pride in the profession and in the accomplishments of self and others
- Competency in a second language
- A healthy lifestyle
- Commitment to excellence
- Demonstrated commitment to lifelong learning

276. WHAT TO LOOK FOR IN THE STAFF OF THE FUTURE, CONTINUED

• Ability to convey a sense of joy and delight in learning
• Sense of humor!

Source: Staff of the Future Committee Report, St. Louis Park, MN, 1984.

277. 12 WAYS TO HIRE THE RIGHT PERSON— EVERY TIME

1. Insist that no one person hire or fire anyone.

2. Spell out exactly what's wanted and needed in every ad or job posting.

3. Use networks to identify and recruit qualified candidates.

4. Use a team to screen paper applications and reach consensus on finalists to be interviewed.

5. Use a structured interview, asking the same prepared questions of all candidates.

6. Get a writing sample and pay attention to it.

7. Be relentless in background checking.

8. Hire people better than yourself.

9. If you don't find the right fit, start over.

10. Conduct a criminal background check for all positions that involve contact with students.

11. Do everything you can to help new hires to succeed.

12. If it doesn't work, get rid of your mistakes early on. That's what the probationary period is for.

278. TEACHER RECRUITMENT SOURCES

Hiring is the most important long-term function Principals perform. Every school wants to hire the best teachers. Sometimes, shortages make it difficult to find even average teachers. The best Principals tap every available source to identify and recruit qualified candidates, including the following:

- Classified ads
- Teacher fairs
- College and university placement bureau postings
- Internal postings
- Networking
- Other districts (layoffs)
- Substitute teacher ranks
- Student teachers and interns
- Private and parochial school staffs
- Community and junior college staffs
- Day care center staffs

279. TIPS ON ATTRACTING AND HIRING MINORITY TEACHERS

Many school districts are competing for a limited pool of minority teaching candidates. The initiatives below can help to attract and hire minority teachers:

- Participation in minority teacher fairs
- Advertising in local media targeting minority populations
- Exchanging information with colleges noted for large minority enrollments
- Publicizing encouragement for persons of color to apply for all positions
- Running ads in national minority journals and other publications
- Networking (the most effective recruitment technique of all)

280. TIPS FOR SCREENING PAPER APPLICATIONS AND RESUMES

- Have more than one person screen papers.
- Spend no more than five minutes on any application or resume initially.
- Look for specific information (i.e., training, experience, technical skills, unique niches, etc.).
- Don't expect to find out about personality traits or motivation from written materials.
- Skim each application quickly to spot reasons for rejecting the application.
- Focus on "soft spots" (i.e., smoke screens, fuzzy answers, noncommittal responses, ambiguous recommendations, etc.).
- Notice what's not included or said.
- Don't get swept away by rhetoric. Look for a track record of accomplishment, not just a way with words.
- Reject sloppy or incomplete applications and applicants who do not follow instructions.
- Use the following criteria for initial evaluation of teacher applicants:
    - Above-average academic achievement
    - Direct teaching experience in a comparable, real-life situation
    - High score on National Teacher's Test
    - Positive evaluations and recommendations from credible sources
    - Specialized training, skill, or experience that sets the candidate apart
    - Commitment to or completion of postgraduate studies
    - Multiple licensure
    - Ability to coach or advise after-school activities
    - Leadership experience
    - Teaching style that fits your needs
    - Valuable summer employment experience
    - Evidence of successful adult relationships
    - Varied leisure and volunteer activities
    - Potential for growth
    - Good reasons for wanting to be a teacher (i.e., help others, benefit society, give back to community, etc.)
    - Possession of some quality you need and don't have

281. DO'S AND DON'TS FOR INTERVIEWING

Successful Interviewers Do:

- Put candidate at ease
- Treat candidates equitably
- Know what they want
- Prepare for each interview
- Use name tags to identify interviewers
- Avoid distractions
- Listen; give their full attention
- Observe body language
- Ask only job-related questions
- Avoid yes/no questions
- Value enthusiasm
- Probe beneath the surface
- Ask questions that reveal values
- Accommodate candidates with disabilities
- Use callback interviews if needed
- Let candidate ask questions
- Use common sense
- Explain what will happen next
- Defer judgment until all candidates are interviewed

Successful Interviewers Don't:

- Overglamorize the position
- Use tricks or play games with the candidate
- Waste time on irrelevant questions
- Make decisions based on first impressions
- Hurry
- Put up barriers between candidate and interviewers
- Weigh negative information more than positive information
- Ask for information they don't need
- Smoke
- Ask leading or loaded questions
- Talk too much
- Interview too many candidates

282. TABOO INTERVIEW QUESTIONS

To avoid the risk of possible discrimination claims or charges, Principals should never ask interview questions in the following areas:

Citizenship

National origin

Pregnancy or birth control

Disability

Economic status

Home ownership

Number of children

Race

Religion

Parents' place of birth

Military service

Arrest record

Marital status (maiden name)

Public assistance

283. MANDATORY INTERVIEW QUESTIONS

To satisfy legal requirements and avoid any possible future liability claims or litigation, personnel experts suggest that the three questions below be included in *all* interviews:

1. Have you ever been convicted of a felony?

2. Have you ever been disciplined by a professional organization?

3. Are you under court order to pay child support?

284. TIPS ON INTERVIEWING APPLICANTS WITH DISABILITIES

In interviewing candidates with disabilities, consider these tips from the Equal Employment Opportunity Commission (EEOC):

- Do not push or grab an applicant's wheelchair unless asked to do so by the applicant.
- Move any furniture that is in the way of an applicant in a wheel chair.
- Sit in a chair that allows your eyes to meet a wheelchair applicant's eyes at the same level.
- If an applicant is deaf, touch the person to get his or her attention.
- Use an interpreter (signer) if at all possible. Otherwise, the applicant will have to rely on lip reading, gestures, and note passing.
- Enunciate clearly if the applicant is lip reading and be sure you are facing the person.
- If an applicant is blind, be sure to identify yourself and others present.
- Cue a handshake with a blind applicant by saying, "May we shake hands?"
- Always be very clear and explicit in giving directions to a blind candidate (which direction to take, number of stairs, etc.).
- When interviewing retarded applicants, use simple terms, repeat questions or instructions, and give positive feedback when appropriate.

285. SUPPLEMENTAL SELECTION TOOLS
(BEYOND THE INTERVIEW)

A single interview isn't always enough on which to base a final hiring decision. Increasingly, Principals and other school leaders are employing multiple resources to aid in the hiring process. Among the most effective supplemental selection tools are the following:

- Work samples (paper marking, lesson design, etc.)
- Videotape auditions
- Portfolio of curriculum projects, lesson plans, and teaching units
- Guest teaching
- Writing samples
- Callback interviews
- Visitations to observe the candidate in action
- Evaluations by outside personnel consultants
- Use of simulated exercises (in-basket exercises, hypothetical problem situations, etc.)

286. 25 POWER INTERVIEW QUESTIONS

The questions you ask during the interview go a long way in determining whether you pick the right candidate. Following are 25 power questions appropriate for almost any interview:

1. Describe your teaching style.

2. How do you stay organized?

3. What excites you? Annoys you? Bores you?

4. What motivates you?

5. Whom do you admire?

6. Why do you want this job and what do you expect to get from it?

7. How do you keep from getting burned out?

8. What didn't you like about your last position?

9. What would you do if your Principal made a decision you didn't like?

10. What do you dislike about teaching?

11. What do you expect of your Principal?

12. Describe how you are a self-starter.

13. Give an example of how you handle conflicts.

14. If you had an idea for improving the school, how would you sell it to colleagues and the Principal?

15. Why did you want to be a teacher in the first place?

16. If you weren't a teacher, what would you be and why?

17. What gives you job satisfaction?

18. How do you get ready to teach a lesson?

19. Describe the best lesson you ever taught and explain why it worked.

20. How do you find out what students need to know?

21. If a lesson flops, what do you do?

22. How do you handle angry parents?

23. Give examples of how you handle pressure and stress.

24. Describe an ideal teaching-learning situation.

25. Why should we hire you over all the other candidates?

287. TIPS FOR CONDUCTING BACKGROUND REFERENCE CHECKS

Before making any final hiring decisions, it pays to verify and supplement the information and impressions gained through interviewing. This requires careful background checking. The suggestions below can help get the most valid results from reference checking:

- Talk directly to the candidate's previous supervisor.

- Give truthful references if you expect to get truthful recommendations and comments.

- Remember that the most reliable references are obtained from people you or someone else on your school staff knows personally.

- Always obtain a waiver or release from the candidate to obtain information in order to protect your sources.

- Ask candidates for self-references (recommendations) and compare these with the report from selected references.

- Go beyond the original reference. Ask about others who are familiar with the candidate's work.

- Protect your sources to assure truthful references in the future.

288. CHECK LIST OF INFORMATION FOR NEW EMPLOYEES

New employees frequently express frustration with the bureaucracy, mechanics, red tape, and paperwork of "getting started" with the system. They don't know what forms to fill out, what choices they have, when the deadlines are, or where to go for information and help. All of this detracts from the important work of getting geared up to be a dynamite teacher from day one. Good Principals help by guiding newcomers through the bureaucratic maze of start-up. Following is a comprehensive check list that should be carefully reviewed orally or in writing with each new employee:

_____ Absence and Substitute Teacher procedures

_____ Accident reporting procedures

_____ Benefit provisions

_____ Child abuse reporting procedures

_____ Child care programs and services

_____ Community background and information

_____ Contract provisions

_____ Credit Union information

_____ District discipline policies

_____ District personnel directory

_____ Drug policies and procedures

_____ Emergency closing information

_____ Flex benefit plans

_____ General leave

_____ Grievance procedures and process

_____ Insurance programs and options (health, dental, life, and income protection)

_____ Job descriptions and job posting procedures

_____ License renewal requirements and procedures

_____ Local travel reimbursement policy

_____ Mail services

288. CHECK LIST OF INFORMATION FOR NEW EMPLOYEES, CONTINUED

_____ Mentor teacher program

_____ Notary public services

_____ Part-time employees' work schedule

_____ Payroll schedule

_____ Policies (location and availability)

_____ Probationary teacher status and requirements

_____ Personnel records (what and where)

_____ Retirement systems and deductions

_____ Sabbatical leave provisions

_____ Salary schedule placement and lane changes

_____ School Board meeting dates

_____ School Calendar

_____ Seniority lists

_____ Sexual harassment and violence procedures

_____ Sick leave provisions

_____ Social Security

_____ Staff development programs

_____ Tobacco use policies

_____ Vacancy and transfer provisions

_____ Vacation schedules

289. GUIDELINES FOR TRAVELING TEACHERS

In many school systems, some teachers are assigned to more than one school. This is particularly true for specialists (e.g., music, physical education). Such assignments can cause confusion, resulting in the affected teachers' missing out on important communications, being doubled up with extra duty assignments, and so on. Guidelines like those outlined below have helped districts avoid these problems and assure equitable treatment of traveling teachers:

1. Traveling teachers shall receive paychecks and district communications at the school where they are assigned for the majority of the day. If assigned equally, these items shall be received at the school where the teachers report first in the day.

2. Traveling teachers shall attend faculty meetings and other functions at the school where they are assigned for the majority of the day. If assigned equally, they shall attend such activities at the school where they report first in the day.

3. Traveling teachers may be assigned proportionate supervisory assignments (hall duty, detention supervision, etc.) at the school where they are assigned for the majority of the day. If assigned equally, the Principals involved shall agree on an equitable supervisory duty load for the teachers.

4. Travel time should be considered in making extra duty assignments to traveling teachers. Prep time shall be provided to the teacher in addition to necessary travel time. (Travel time is not a substitute for prep time.)

5. Traveling teachers shall conduct parent-teacher conferences in all schools to which assigned according to a prorated schedule to be posted in each building.

6. Traveling teachers shall be evaluated by the Principal of the building to which they are assigned for the majority of the day (with input from the other Principal involved). If assigned equally, the Principal of the building to which the teacher reports first in the day shall conduct all evaluations (with input from the other Principal involved).

290. PHASES OF PROFESSIONAL LIFE

In education, as in other professions, most individuals follow a common pattern of personal and professional development. In making personnel and staff development decisions, it pays for Principals to consider the common stages of professional evolution as follows:

Phase 1. Protege (Young Turk)

Phase 2. Mature Pro (Being Your Own Person)

Phase 3. "Middle essence" (Midcareer Transition or Crisis)

Phase 4. Mentoring (Contentment or Disillusionment)*

*Sometimes, morale and productivity are greatest among mature professionals who have made peace with themselves—with their strengths and limits as professionals.

291. 10 OBSTACLES TO POSITIVE STAFF PERFORMANCE IN SCHOOLS

1. Overload of nonteaching chores (paperwork).

2. Rigid hierarchy and inflexible scheduling (limited personal autonomy and discretion in decision making).

3. Administrative dominance and interference ("Big Brother is watching you").

4. Low professional self-esteem. (Society does not demonstrate great respect for teachers.)

5. Substandard working conditions (large class size, inadequate materials, violence, run-down buildings, etc.).

6. Inconsistent policies and waffling leaders.

7. Lack of direction, leadership, and support from Principal.

8. Public criticism and lack of parental and community support.

9. Lack of specific personal and professional goals.

10. Boredom and burnout.

292. IMAGE OF AN EFFECTIVE TEACHER

Principals bear the brunt of evaluating all teachers, weeding out incompetents, and nurturing and empowering superstars. This process starts with an image of what an effective teacher looks like. The traits below are commonly agreed-upon characteristics of outstanding teachers at all levels:

- Positive self-image
- Confidence
- Optimism
- Love of students
- Youthful attitude
- Organizational skills
- Listening ability
- Openness
- Caring
- Resiliency
- Empathy
- Energy
- Exuberance

293. 10-POINT SUCCESS PLAN FOR PERFORMANCE APPRAISAL

The 10-point success plan for performance appraisal below highlights the necessary ingredients for an effective teacher evaluation program.

1. Teacher input and involvement in designing the process.

2. A focus on improvement of instruction and professional growth, rather than on fault-finding, personal criticism, or penalties.

3. Shared responsibility (evaluator and evaluatee) for identifying areas of improvement and appropriate growth plans.

4. A commitment to build on strengths.

5. Agreed-upon limitations that make improvement a manageable task.

6. Simplicity in process, procedures, paperwork, and recordkeeping.

7. Built-in provisions for monitoring progress and making midcourse corrections.

8. Periodic mutual (administrators and teachers) reviews and dialogue on the overall process.

9. Requirement of specific indicators for measuring progress (or lack of it).

10. Recognition of the right to fail. (Not all goals are met and not all plans work as planned.)

294. TIME LINE FOR TEACHER PERFORMANCE APPRAISAL (EXAMPLE)

The suggested timetable below illustrates how an effective teacher professional performance appraisal program can be implemented:

May 15–Sept. 15 — Teachers submit proposed goals or job targets.

Sept. 15–Oct. 15 — Principal schedules individual conference to review responsibilities, plans, and job targets.

Oct. 15–March 31 — Meetings are held as necessary to review progress toward agreed-upon goals.

April 1–April 30 — Teacher completes self-appraisal and submits forms to Principal.

May 1–June 5 — Principal conducts year-end appraisal conference. Review by a third party may be requested. Written appraisals are completed and filed in the personnel office.

295. QUALITY INDICATORS FOR PROBATIONARY AND TENURED TEACHERS

Standards are the first step toward the effective management, supervision, and evaluation of teaching personnel. Where such standards do not exist, the Principal should be proactive in initiating their development. A sample set of standards and quality indicators for probationary and tenured teachers appears below:

A. Instructional Skills

1. Uses a variety of effective teaching techniques and models.

2. Uses a variety of evaluative techniques to drive instruction, diagnose student needs, and measure learning.

3. Sets high expectations.

4. Plans instruction to meet specific objectives.

B. Focus on Students

1. Establishes a healthy, supportive classroom climate.

2. Generates interest and excitement in learning.

3. Knows each student and exhibits genuine interest in individuals.

4. Shows sensitivity to student needs and feelings.

5. Understands the basic principles of teaching and learning.

C. Knowledge of Content and Use of Materials

1. Demonstrates current knowledge of subject matter.

2. Demonstrates knowledge and use of district curriculum scope, sequence, and learner outcomes.

3. Designs and uses a variety of materials to supplement the textbook.

4. Uses multisensory approaches to accommodate differing learning styles.

5. Integrates real-life experiences and community resources into the classroom.

D. Classroom Environment

1. Organizes physical setting for effective and efficient learning.

2. Exercises classroom control in a positive manner, using a variety of effective behavior management techniques.

295. QUALITY INDICATORS FOR PROBATIONARY AND TENURED TEACHERS,
CONTINUED

3. Provides a positive environment conducive to learning.

4. Follows district and building discipline plans consistently.

5. Assists students to assume responsibility for appropriate behavior.

6. Establishes a climate where students feel free to question and think creatively.

E. Communication Skills

1. Communicates clearly in oral and written form.

2. Communicates students' strengths and weaknesses with honesty, tact, and understanding.

3. Encourages and initiates two-way communication.

4. Demonstrates responsibility in communicating student progress.

F. Interpersonal Skills

1. Recognizes responsibility to foster positive buildingwide morale.

2. Promotes teamwork within the staff.

3. Displays consistency and fairness.

4. Displays compassion and sensitivity.

5. Recognizes the importance of parent and community involvement.

6. Shows responsiveness to parent needs and community concerns.

G. Professionalism

1. Sets high expectations for personal performance.

2. Practices ethical behavior, respects confidentiality, and follows proper channels of communication.

3. Demonstrates continuing professional growth and development.

4. Actively participates in professional organizations and activities.

5. Holds the profession in high esteem.

6. Meets basic work expectations (promptness, etc.).

295. QUALITY INDICATORS FOR PROBATIONARY AND TENURED TEACHERS,
CONTINUED

H. Attitude

1. Exhibits enthusiasm, energy, and optimism.

2. Demonstrates a problem-solving attitude in the workplace.

3. Takes risks and is open to change.

4. Reflects self-confidence.

5. Exhibits a good sense of humor.

I. Adaptability

1. Monitors and adjusts teaching approaches as needed.

2. Recognizes personal needs and is willing to ask for help.

3. Handles change, interruptions, last-minute requests, and emergencies effectively and calmly.

4. Responds to frustrations and adversity with patience and renewed effort.

5. Anticipates problems and devises ways to overcome them.

Note: In most instances, these standards should be applied differentially, depending on the experience of the teacher involved. Probationary teachers will not be expected to meet or exceed these standards to the same degree as veteran staff members.

296. TIPS FOR CONFERENCING WITH TEACHERS

1. Use the teacher's name during the conference.

2. Read examples from Principal's script tape or observation notes.

3. Listen carefully during the diagnosis phase.

4. Actively involve the teacher in the conference.

5. Use notes to assist in the instructional phase.

6. Slow down. A conference is not a race.

7. Use transitional statements to move through the various phases of the conference.

8. Respect confidentiality.

9. Avoid "I like you . . ." statements.

10. Dignify all of the teacher's responses.

11. Use positive examples where possible.

12. Teach; don't preach. Use principles of learning.

13. Avoid long lists for the teacher "to work on."

14. Don't interrupt the teacher.

15. Be sincere. Establish a pleasant tone whenever possible.

16. Use questions to narrow the focus.

17. Have written objectives for every conference.

18. Use closure techniques.

19. Remain professional.

20. Have fun!

297. CRITERIA FOR CONSTRUCTIVE CRITICISM OF EMPLOYEES

Sooner or later, all Principals have to criticize some staff member and make suggestions for improvement. Constructive criticism is usually better than negative or destructive criticism. The criteria below pinpoint ways to maximize the positive potential of a constructive criticism approach:

- Avoid personalizing the criticism.
- Focus on behaviors—not personalities.
- Criticize in private.
- Avoid criticizing in anger.
- Stick to facts. Ignore rumors.
- Stress positive behaviors where appropriate. Build on strengths.
- Praise improvement.
- Convey support and a willingness to help.
- Limit written criticism.
- Return or destroy old letters of criticism if permanent improvement occurs.

298. PROGRESSIVE DISCIPLINE FOR EMPLOYEES

Employees, like students, occasionally need discipline. Below are the most common steps in progressive discipline for teachers and other staff members:

- Oral reprimand
- Written reprimand
- Written notice of deficiency
- Suspension with pay
- Suspension without pay
- Dismissal (discharge for cause)

299. 10-POINT ACTION PLAN FOR DEALING WITH STAFF CHEMICAL ABUSE AND DEPENDENCY ISSUES

1. Adopt a firm, forthright policy for handling drug use and abuse by employees.

2. Orient staff and the community to the disease concept of alcoholism and other drug addictions.

3. Employ a Chemical Health Specialist or Counselor or establish an Employee Assistance Program (EAP).

4. Provide easily accessible counseling and referral services, including evaluation, referral to appropriate in-patient or out-patient treatment, and follow-up support programs.

5. Initiate interventions where needed.

6. Implement appropriate staff development and public information programs.

7. Make available health insurance programs that cover the cost of treatment for chemical dependency.

8. Develop appropriate support groups for employees and family members.

9. Provide awareness training to assist in receiving and relating to recovering employees.

10. Maintain strict confidentiality regarding chemical health problems.

300. GUIDELINES FOR POLITICAL ACTIVITY BY TEACHERS

- Circulation of literature for or against any candidate through school facilities is prohibited.

- Teachers should not participate in political activities during the school duty day.

- Teachers shall not solicit, enlist, or organize students for any political activity during the regular school day.

- School equipment or supplies shall not be used in the preparation or distribution of political materials at any time.

- If candidates are invited to speak in school, all candidates for the same office should be invited to appear also. Teachers are responsible for arranging equal time for all candidates.

301. GUIDELINES FOR RELIGIOUS ACTIVITY IN SCHOOL

- The school's position on religions should always be instructional (educational), not devotional.

- Teachers may teach <u>about</u> a variety of religious beliefs and practices, but must refrain from imposing any particular view, attempting to indoctrinate students, or converting students to any specific religion.

- The school may sponsor the study of religion, but not the practice of any specific religious doctrine.

302. STANDARD TEACHER CONTRACT TOPICS

The master agreement has a powerful influence on conditions and relationships within the school. A good contract can ease or avoid many sticky situations and provide a framework for productive working relationships. A bad contract causes confusion, frustration, ill will, and disharmony between administration and teachers. The outline below represents the most common elements found in many effective teacher contracts:

1. Purpose of the agreement
2. Definitions
3. Recognition of the exclusive bargaining unit
4. Management rights
5. Association (union) rights
6. Length of school year
7. Length of school (duty) day
8. Basic compensation (salary schedule)
9. Extra compensation (extracurricular stipends, curriculum writing, etc.)
10. Group insurance benefits (health, dental, life, income protection)
11. Leave provisions (general, sick, emergency, bereavement, sabbatical, etc.)
12. Vacancies and transfers
13. Unrequested leave (layoff) and seniority policy
14. Severance pay and early retirement provisions
15. Performance appraisal (evaluation) criteria and procedures
16. Grievance procedure
17. Labor-Management committees
18. Miscellaneous provisions
19. Duration
20. Appendices and attachments

303. CONTRACTUAL RIGHTS OF TEACHERS

Under most master contracts, teachers are entitled to these rights:

- Right to express views and opinions on school matters and conditions of employment.
- Right to file a complaint or grievance in the case of perceived mistreatment or misapplication of the contract.
- Right to request payroll deductions for association or union dues.
- Right to payroll deductions for Credit Union savings or investments.
- Right to see their own performance appraisals and personnel files.
- Right to reproduce any contents of their personnel files (at the teachers' expense).
- Right to submit for inclusion in the file written information in response to any material contained therein.
- Right to a private and personal life that is not the appropriate concern of the district unless personal activities affect teaching performance.

304. DEFINITIONS OF TEACHER SALARY SCHEDULE TRAINING LEVELS

For purposes of placement on the teacher salary schedule, many school districts define training levels as follows:

Bachelor's Degree . . . at least a bachelor's degree in the field of licensure.

Bachelor's + 15 . . . at least 15 quarter hours beyond the bachelor's degree, either graduate or undergraduate, that are in a field related to the teaching assignment.

Bachelor's + 30 . . . at least 30 quarter hours beyond the bachelor's degree, either graduate or undergraduate, that are in a field related to the teaching assignment.

Bachelor's + 45 . . . at least 45 quarter hours beyond the bachelor's degree, including no fewer than 15 graduate credits, that are in a field related to the teaching assignment.

Bachelor's + 60 . . . at least 60 quarter hours beyond the bachelor's degree, including no fewer than 30 graduate credits, that are in a field related to the teaching assignment.

Master's Degree . . . a master's degree in a field related to the teaching assignment.

Master's + 15 . . . at least 15 quarter hours of graduate credit beyond the master's degree in a field related to the teaching assignment.

Master's + 30 . . . at least 30 quarter hours of graduate credit beyond the master's degree in a field related to the teaching assignment.

Master's + 45 . . . at least 45 quarter hours of graduate credit beyond the master's degree in a field related to the teaching assignment.

Master's + 60 . . . at least 60 quarter hours of graduate credit beyond the master's degree in a field related to the teaching assignment.

Doctorate . . . a doctor's degree in a field related to the teaching assignment.

305. EXTRACURRICULAR ASSIGNMENTS
(EXAMPLES)

Comprehensive secondary schools commonly have a wide variety of extra-curricular or cocurricular assignments for which teachers receive additional compensation. The list below is typical of the types of extra-duty assignments found in many schools:

Athletic Director

Baseball Head Coach (boys)

Baseball Assistant Coach (boys)

Basketball Head Coach (boys and girls)

Basketball Assistant Coach (boys and girls)

Cheerleading Coach (boys and girls)

Cross-Country/Track Head Coach (boys and girls)

Cross-Country/Track Assistant Coach (boys and girls)

Equipment Manager

Football Head Coach (boys)

Football Assistant Coach (boys)

Golf Coach (boys and girls)

Gymnastics Head Coach (boys and girls)

Gymnastics Assistant Coach (boys and girls)

Hockey Head Coach (boys)*

Hockey Assistant Coach (boys)*

Intramural Director (boys and girls)

Cross-Country Ski Head Coach (boys and girls)

Cross-Country Ski Assistant Coach (boys and girls)

Softball Head Coach (girls)

Softball Assistant Coach (girls)

Soccer Head Coach (boys and girls)

Soccer Assistant Coach (boys and girls)

Strength Coach (boys and girls)

Swimming Head Coach (boys and girls)

Swimming Assistant Coach (boys and girls)

Diving Coach (boys and girls)

Synchronized Swim Head Coach (girls)

305. EXTRACURRICULAR ASSIGNMENTS
(EXAMPLES), CONTINUED

Synchronized Swim Assistant Coach (girls)

Tennis Head Coach (boys and girls)

Tennis Assistant Coach (boys and girls)

Track Head Coach (boys and girls)

Track Assistant Coach (boys and girls)

Volleyball Head Coach (girls)

Volleyball Assistant Coach (girls)

Dramatic Advisor (Play Director)

Dramatic Musical Director

Choreographer

Concert Band Director

Pep Band Director

Orchestra Director

Vocal Music Director

Jazz Ensemble Director

Debate Director

Speech Director

Math Team Director

SADD Advisor

Mock Trial Advisor

Literary Magazine Advisor

Student Council Advisor

Radio Station Advisor

Cable TV Station Advisor

Newspaper Advisor

Yearbook Advisor

Video Yearbook Advisor

Club Advisor

Curriculum Writing

Extended Employment

Department Heads

Elementary Grade Level Chairs

*In some parts of the country, a few schools have introduced hockey for girls.

306. PAY EQUITY RESPONSIBILITY LEVELS
(CRITERIA FOR JOB EVALUATIONS BASED ON DECISION-MAKING STRUCTURE)

More and more school districts are implementing pay equity (comparable worth) programs whereby men and women are paid equal pay for equal work. Such programs require a job evaluation system for establishing the comparable worth of different jobs. One common method of job evaluation weighs positions on the basis of the level of decision-making responsibility as described below:

Level I—POLICY: Determines overall goals and direction of the organization.

Level II—PROGRAMMING: Determines the means of achieving overall goals of the organization.

Level III—INTERPRETIVE: Makes decisions on means of achieving specific goals handed down from above.

Level IV—PROCESS: Makes decisions on the processes of achieving the means identified above.

Level V—OPERATIONAL: Makes decisions on carrying out processes determined above (not what operations to perform, but *how* to carry them out).

Level VI—DEFINED: Decides only means and speed of performing operations defined from above.

307. TEACHER GRIEVANCE PROCEDURES
(SAMPLE LEVELS)

Most formal grievance procedures for teachers include a step-by-step process similar to the levels described below:

Level 1. The grievance is submitted to the responsible administrator, who tries to resolve the matter informally or meets formally with the grievant and issues a written response in timely fashion.

Level 2. If the grievance is unresolved, it can be appealed to Level 2 by submitting it to the Superintendent in writing. The Superintendent meets with the grievant to discuss the problem and issues a written response according to a prescribed time line.

Level 3. If the grievance remains unresolved, it may be appealed to the School Board for consideration. The Board has the right to review or not review the grievance. If the Board chooses, the entire Board or a committee thereof will meet to hear the grievance and answer in writing. If the matter is still not resolved, the grievant may request that the matter be submitted to arbitration. If the School Board rejects the request for arbitration, the Board's findings are final and binding.

Note: In most situations, the School Board reserves the right to review any decision under Level 1 or Level 2 and can affirm, reverse, or modify any decision made at these levels.

308. TIPS FOR HANDLING EMPLOYEE GRIEVANCES

Effective schools have a well-defined formal grievance procedure (a process for resolving disputes over contract interpretation or application). When a grievance arises, it's often up to the Principal to process the matter in a timely and professional manner. The tips below can help:

- Know the contract provisions thoroughly.
- Ensure that the parties fully understand what constitutes a grievable issue or offense.
- Follow the formal grievance procedure (i.e., hearings, time lines, etc.) to the letter.
- Try to resolve the grievance informally where possible.
- Don't treat any grievance lightly.
- Listen to all parties carefully.
- Assemble all pertinent facts. Interview witnesses when necessary.
- Don't ridicule any grievance or grievant.
- Avoid stalling or passing the buck.
- Rely on facts. Avoid guesswork.
- Don't lose your temper. Remain poised.
- Avoid any implication of a threat.
- Don't take complaints personally.
- Keep your sense of humor.
- Be direct in questioning.
- Have the courage to make unpopular decisions.
- Stick with your decisions.

309. SCHOOL DISTRICT GOALS DURING A TEACHER STRIKE

The six primary goals of the school district during any work stoppage are:

1. Work toward a realistic and reasonable settlement as soon as possible.

2. Maintain emphasis on the needs and interests of students.

3. Retain the dignity of the district.

4. Provide for the safety of all parties and the protection of all school facilities and property.

5. Preserve as much community good will and support as possible.

6. Pave the way for rapid healing and a return to business as usual following the eventual settlement.

310. WHAT TO EXPECT IN A TEACHER STRIKE

If teacher strikes are allowable in your state, it makes sense for school leaders to have a strike contingency plan. Advance knowledge of common strike strategies and tactics can help Principals and others develop appropriate preventive and response measures. The tactics below have been observed in many teacher strikes across the country in recent years:

- Adoption of a slow down ("work to rule") posture prior to a full-fledged walk out.
- Demands for around-the-clock bargaining.
- Establishment of "informational" picket lines.
- Stepped-up media messages with regard to teacher concerns or demands.
- Increase in letters to the editor and other communications from teachers.
- Creation of crisis centers, truth squads, and so forth.
- Increased calls for public forums.
- Pressure for School Board members to get personally involved in bargaining.
- Charges of unfair labor practices and bad-faith bargaining.
- Attempts to polarize the community (we-them, good guys-bad guys, etc.).
- Proliferation of rumors, innuendoes, and half-truths.
- Exploitation of students.
- Mass rallies and use of mob psychology.
- Formal, organized picket lines.
- Telephone campaigning and calls to parents.
- Intimidation of substitute or replacement teachers who cross picket lines.
- Announcement of a "war chest" of funds to support striking teachers.
- Expressions of support from other unions.
- Boycotting of businesses where Board members work.
- Harassment of negotiators, Board members, and other school officials.
- Picketing of Board members' homes.
- Distribution of leaflets from the teachers' union to homes, shopping centers, church parking lots.
- Pep rallies for striking teachers.
- Encouraging sympathy strikes in other school districts.
- Phone jamming.
- Vandalism to school property.
- Threats to Board members and others involved in negotiations.
- Violence on the picket lines.
- Disruption of the school transportation system.

311. CHECK LIST FOR PRINCIPALS DURING A TEACHERS' STRIKE

_____ Make every effort to collect all keys in advance.

_____ Collect grade books, lesson plans, seating charts, etc., before teachers walk out (if at all possible).

_____ Advise teachers to take home personal belongings for the duration of the strike.

_____ Lock up confidential files and records during the strike.

_____ Hold daily briefings for nonstriking personnel.

_____ If the school continues to operate, determine curriculum and program on a day-to-day basis.

_____ Take steps to protect the safety of all substitute or replacement teachers.

_____ Communicate with parents on a regular basis throughout the strike.

_____ Maintain a log of all communication.

_____ Advise work-study students to continue to report for work during the strike.

_____ Do not allow strikers in the building.

_____ Provide for around-the-clock security and surveillance.

_____ Lock all doors from the inside. Limit access to a single entrance if possible.

_____ Arrange for protected parking for nonstriking personnel.

_____ Avoid making unauthorized statements to the media.

_____ Advise nonstriking personnel to withdraw and call the police if they are physically prevented from crossing picket lines.

_____ Maintain optimism. Settlement will come.

_____ Keep your sense of humor.

_____ Don't hold grudges after settlement.

312. CHECK LIST FOR STAFF LAYOFFS

Implementing necessary staff layoffs should be more than a numbers game. It can and should be as humane a process as possible. The check list below can help guide Principals in humanizing the painful effects of staff retrenchment:

_____ Project staffing needs and anticipate reductions as early as possible.

_____ Be upfront and honest about cutback plans.

_____ Make pertinent data (enrollment projections, budget shortfalls, seniority lists, etc.) available to all affected parties.

_____ Communicate the mechanics of the layoff process to all staff members.

_____ Involve staff in formulating budget reduction plans.

_____ Humanize and personalize the layoff notification process. Avoid form letters with rubber stamp signatures.

_____ Deliver layoff notices in person and at a time that creates minimal disruption.

_____ Urge retiring teachers to give early notice to reduce the number of layoffs needed.

_____ Promote early retirements, general leaves, job sharing, and use of part-time personnel in order to minimize the number of terminated personnel.

_____ Provide outplacement services as soon as possible.

_____ Keep up-to-date in furnishing references and letters of recommendation.

_____ Pass on the names of laid-off personnel to other districts that are hiring additional teachers.

_____ Allow terminated teachers to participate in job interviews during regular school hours.

_____ Adhere strictly to all legal and contractual due process requirements and procedures.

_____ Sponsor job-change workshops for affected employees.

_____ Continue to show that you care about affected employees even after their release.

_____ Focus on healing within the organization.

313. 10 MOST COMMON SUBSTITUTE TEACHER COMPLAINTS

1. Low pay rates

2. Short notice

3. Delay in receiving payment

4. Lack of respect

5. Absence of daily lesson plans

6. Partial day assignments that don't cover expenses

7. Unrealistic expectations by regular teachers

8. Disrespectful, unruly students and lack of support in discipline matters

9. Inadequate communication and information

10. Lack of feedback

314. 10 STEPS FOR SUBSTITUTE TEACHER SUCCESS

Substitutes (reserve teachers) are valuable members of every school's professional team. The following ten-step program can help assure substitute teacher success in your school:

1. Select reserve teachers as carefully as you do regular staff members. Hold out for seasoned pros with a track record of success; don't settle for mediocre or unproven substitutes.

2. Hold a thorough building-orientation program for all reserve teachers you plan to use on a regular basis.

3. Limit the number of reserve teachers you use. Too many subs in the building at one time can disrupt discipline unduly. Substitute teachers can be lifesavers, but they shouldn't be a way of life.

4. Develop a comprehensive, user-friendly Substitute Teacher Handbook for your school.

5. Insist that teachers leave daily lesson plans for use by substitutes.

6. Treat reserve teachers as guests. Pamper them a little.

7. Assign a faculty host to each substitute.

8. Include reserve teachers in building and district staff development programs.

9. Evaluate every reserve teacher every time he or she works in your building.

10. Recognize successful substitutes (e.g., appreciation plaques, special luncheons).

315. 10 WAYS TO RECOGNIZE AND REWARD SUBSTITUTE TEACHERS

It always pays to recognize and honor effective reserve teachers. It's one way to keep them coming back. Here are ways some schools show respect for valued reserves:

1. Reward loyalty and good work with frequent assignments.

2. Use "Guest Teacher" tags.

3. Designate a student to introduce the Guest Teacher to the rest of the class.

4. Assign a Faculty Host to each substitute.

5. Reserve special parking spots for substitutes.

6. Send favorite reserve teachers appreciation cards from students.

7. Include pictures of regular substitutes in the school yearbook.

8. Let subs eat free in the school cafeteria.

9. Hold a year-end special luncheon or tea to honor substitutes.

10. Initiate an annual "Reserve Teacher of the Year" award program.

316. 10 WAYS TO RECOGNIZE VOLUNTEERS

Most schools couldn't operate without volunteers. Below are ten school-tested suggestions for showing volunteers that they are truly appreciated.

1. Provide special training programs for volunteers.

2. Issue personalized coffee mugs to volunteers.

3. Let volunteers go to the front of the cafeteria line.

4. Issue "We ❤ Volunteers" T-shirts or sweatshirts.

5. Celebrate volunteers' birthdays.

6. Give each volunteer an appreciation card signed by the students.

7. Give volunteers free passes to school events (games, plays, concerts, etc.).

8. Dedicate an assembly program or instrumental concert to a special volunteer.

9. Hold a special year-end party to celebrate volunteers.

10. Give successful volunteers first consideration for job openings.

317. CHECK LIST FOR CLERICAL PERFORMANCE APPRAISAL

Principals often devote considerable effort to evaluating the teaching staff, but neglect regular evaluation of clerical personnel. It pays to nurture, instruct, and empower clerical employees through positive performance appraisal. The simple check list below can be a useful tool in conducting such appraisals:

_____ The quality of work meets expectations.

_____ The quantity of work satisfies job requirements.

_____ Job knowledge is adequate and increasing.

_____ Performance is consistently dependable.

_____ Working relationships are positive and affirming.

_____ The attitude toward the job is positive and enthusiastic.

_____ Adapts readily to changing circumstances and demands.

_____ Exercises initiative in fulfilling job responsibilities.

_____ Communication skills are effective.

_____ Accepts responsibility willingly.

318. SUPERVISORY HINTS FOR WORKING WITH CUSTODIAL-MAINTENANCE STAFF MEMBERS

- Conduct weekly walk-through inspections and briefings with the Head Custodian.
- Have clearly defined job descriptions and standards of performance for custodial personnel, including specific work areas and responsibilities for each custodian.
- Use the probationary period to weed out incompetents.
- Secure substitutes to cover absences. Use commercial temporary help if necessary.
- Regulate vacation schedules to assure adequate help at all times.
- Provide paid training opportunities for custodial-maintenance personnel.
- Involve custodial personnel in decisions affecting their working conditions.
- Include custodial representatives on building committees and task forces.
- Furnish special name tags for custodial personnel.
- Host special appreciation events (i.e., barbecues, picnics, etc.) just for the custodial staff.

319. TOP 15 MOST STRESSFUL JOBS IN TODAY'S SCHOOLS

Although individual circumstances may vary, the following are the most stressful positions in the typical American urban or suburban school district today (ranked in order of priority):

1. Senior High School Principal

2. Superintendent

3. Junior High/Middle School Principal

4. Elementary Principal/Assistant Principal (secondary) (*tied for fourth place*)

5. Special Education Teacher

6. Drug Counselor

7. School Bus Driver

8. Regular Classroom Teacher

9. Police Liaison Officer

10. Athletic Director

11. High-Profile Coach

12. Personnel Director (if in charge of contract negotiations)

13. Business Manager

14. Hall Monitor (secondary)

15. Playground Supervisor (elementary)

320. THOUGHTS ON HUMAN RESOURCES MANAGEMENT (QUOTES)

"There are an enormous number of managers who have retired on the job."
—*Peter Drucker*

"I think that maybe in every company today there is always at least one person who is going crazy slowly."—*Joseph Heller*

"Guidelines for Bureaucrats: (1) When in charge ponder. (2) When in trouble delegate. (3) When in doubt mumble."—*James H. Bowen*

"I've been nitpicked to pieces by the goddamn bureaucracy."—*Travis Reed*

"So much of what we call management consists in making it difficult for people to work."—*Peter Drucker*

"Work is achieved by those employees who have not yet reached their level of incompetence."—*Laurence J. Peter*

"Only a mediocre person is always at his best."—*Somerset Maugham*

"The fellow who never makes a mistake takes his orders from one who does."
—*Hubert V. Prochnow*

"Treat people as if they were what they ought to be and you help them become what they are capable of being."—*Johann W. von Goethe*

"We work to become, not to acquire."—*Elbert Hubbard*

"Why in the world are salaries higher for administrators when the basic mission is teaching?"—*Governor Jerry Brown*

"Working with people is difficult, but not impossible."—*Peter Drucker*

Section Eight

LEGAL MATTERS

321. KEY FEDERAL LAWS AFFECTING SCHOOLS

- Elementary and Secondary Education Act (Titles I, II, and III)

  Part of the "Great Society" legislation passed under the Lyndon Johnson administration providing federal funding for remedial/compensatory education programs, libraries and library materials, and innovative practices.

- Civil Rights Act of 1964

  Antidiscrimination legislation.

- Federal Education Act of 1972 (Title IX)

  Bars discrimination based on sex (gender).

- Rehabilitation Act of 1974 (Sec. 508)

  Mandates handicapped accessibility.

- Family Education Rights and Privacy Act (Buckley Amendment) and the Privacy Act of 1974.

  Data privacy protection.

- PL 94-142

  Mandates special education services.

- Americans with Disabilities Act

  Requires reasonable accommodations for all persons with disabilities.

322. LANDMARK COURT DECISIONS AFFECTING SCHOOLS

Plessy vs. *Ferguson*—Allowed "separate but equal" segregation policies.

Brown vs. *Topeka Board of Education*—"Separate but equal" educational facilities declared unconstitutional.

Engel vs. *Vitale*—School prayer may not be required.

Alexander vs. *Holmes Co. Board of Education*—Demanded immediate desegregation of public schools.

San Antonio Ind. Dist. vs. *Rodreguez*—Education is a property interest protected under the 14th amendment and cannot be denied without due process.

Gross vs. *Lopez*—Even short-term suspensions require due process.

322. LANDMARK COURT DECISIONS AFFECTING SCHOOLS, CONTINUED

Wood vs. *Strickland*—School officials may be held personally liable for violations of students' rights.

Tinker vs. *Des Moines School Board*—(Famous "black arm band case") Pupils do not shed constitutional rights at the school door.

Johnson vs. *Paulsboro N.S.*—Established right of married students to participate in extracurricular activities.

State vs. *Stein*—Established that school officials may inspect student lockers to prevent illegal use without giving a "Miranda warning" in advance.

323. COMMON SOURCES OF LAWSUITS AGAINST SCHOOL PERSONNEL

The most common grounds for lawsuits against school personnel (particularly administrators) include the following:

- discriminatory practices
- violation of constitutional rights (assembly, free speech, etc.)
- violation of data privacy guarantees
- denial of due process
- misuse of corporal punishment
- punishment involving academic penalties (i.e., lowered grades, withholding diplomas, etc.)
- slanderous or libelous statements about students
- disregard for or neglect of safety concerns
- alleged sexual harassment or criminal sexual misconduct

324. TIPS ON RISK MANAGEMENT (HOW TO AVOID A LAWSUIT)

The following preventive measures can help Principals avoid lawsuits or minimize the risk or liability involved:

1. Be fully aware of current legislation and case law affecting school operations. Inform staff of all applicable legal requirements. Provide special training if necessary.

2. Maintain and publicize up-to-date policies in compliance with all legal requirements. Follow your own policies.

3. Know what's going on in your building.

4. Provide consistent supervision (of students and employees).

5. Provide proper notification of any rule changes.

6. Avoid distinctions based on race, religion, creed, sex, income status, marital status, age.

7. Maintain complete records and documentation of all disciplinary incidents and actions.

8. Avoid any searches unless there is substantive cause to believe that illegal items are present.

9. Avoid any restriction on freedom of expression unless it interferes with school work or orderly class conduct.

10. Respond in timely fashion to all allegations, charges, or complaints.

11. Allow students to present petitions, testimony, and witnesses in their own behalf.

12. Have a third-party observer sit in on all interviews and interrogations.

13. Whenever in doubt about the correct course of conduct, consult and follow legal counsel.

14. Maintain adequate liability insurance through a personal policy or a blanket policy provided by the District.

325. WHAT TO LOOK FOR IN A SCHOOL ATTORNEY

A legalistic world requires sophisticated legal counsel. In times of trouble, a lawyer can be a Principal's best friend. The characteristics of an effective legal advisor for Principals include the following:

- Experience in school law and labor relations
- Knowledge of legal precedents affecting schools
- Understanding of how schools work (familiarity with the language of the profession)
- Ability to draft clear policies, opinions, and other documents
- Effective communication and listening skills
- Impeccable integrity and credibility
- Rapport with school personnel
- Sense of humor

326. WHEN TO CALL YOUR SCHOOL ATTORNEY

Principals should never be afraid to use legal counsel when needed. Following are some of the most common ways in which school attorneys can help elementary and secondary Principals:

- To clarify what can and cannot be done under the law.
- To explain and interpret specific laws.
- To review building policies and procedures.
- To research legal precedents and court decisions regarding issues facing the school.
- To draft policies, letters of reprimand, and other quasi-legal documents.
- To conduct interviews and investigations.
- To draft responses to grievances, charges, allegations, etc.
- To negotiate settlements in disputes.
- To brainstorm solutions to sensitive legal issues.
- To arrange for hearing officers, mediators, arbitrators, court reporters, etc.
- To test whether proposed actions are legal and defensible.
- To help in preparation for testimony.
- To take depositions.
- To serve as public spokespersons when appropriate.
- To provide staff development on new laws, legal requirements and limitations, risk management, etc.

327. STEPS FOR INVESTIGATING COMPLAINTS WITHIN LEGAL BOUNDARIES

How an investigation is conducted is often as important as the outcome of the investigation. Procedural errors can jeopardize the legality of the results. To protect all parties involved (including yourself) and to preserve the integrity of the findings, all investigations of complaints and allegations should include the following steps:

1. *Notification*	Inform involved parents and students of the nature of allegations, and that an investigation must be undertaken.
2. *Interviewing*	Interview all involved parties separately with a witness present. The order of interviewing usually proceeds from the accuser and the accuser's witnesses to the accused and the witnesses for the accused.
3. *Conclusion*	Reach fair conclusions based on the credibility of the parties, the circumstances, corroborating evidence, motivation, history, attitudes, demeanor, and extenuating conditions.
4. *Action*	Action must fit the infraction and be consistent with that taken in similar situations.
5. *Documentation*	Accurate recordkeeping is essential.
6. *Reporting*	All parties should be informed of the investigation's findings and any resulting action(s).

328. GUIDELINES FOR DOCUMENTING INVESTIGATIONS AND ACTIONS WITHIN LEGAL LIMITS

The primary purpose of documenting disciplinary and other investigations and actions is to establish a paper trail showing a sequence of events. Sometimes, a Principal's notes and records take on legal significance. In today's court-conscious society, it's better to err on the side of overdocumentation than to underdocument. Experienced school attorneys offer the following guidelines for maintaining proper documentation:

- Record notes and summarize conferences as soon as possible while memories are fresh.
- Proofread notes and records carefully.
- Record only facts. Avoid editorializing, speculating, reaching conclusions, or making premature judgments.
- The essential specifics to document are who, what, when, where, how, and why.
- Try to include dates, times, locations, names, phone numbers, and addresses.
- Include exact quotes whenever possible.

328. GUIDELINES FOR DOCUMENTING INVESTIGATIONS AND ACTIONS WITHIN LEGAL LIMITS, CONTINUED

- Never assume that all personal notes are private. The power of the subpoena is far-reaching.

- Have parties sign off that pertinent documents have been received or reviewed.

- Retain notes and records indefinitely.

329. TIPS ON TESTIFYING

Principals are sometimes called on to testify in court or in other quasi-legal proceedings. It's not always as easy as it looks. All professionals are well advised to follow the tips below when testifying in any legal setting:

1. Prepare thoroughly. Review all facts, records, and your own recollections.

2. Rehearse testimony with your attorney.

3. Dress and act like a professional. It will enhance your credibility.

4. Listen carefully to all questions and to all instructions from the judge.

5. Don't be afraid to ask for clarification of a question or instruction.

6. Take your time. Think before you speak.

7. Answer only what is asked. Don't embellish, editorialize, or offer extraneous information.

8. Keep your answers as brief as possible.

9. Remain confident. Nobody knows what you know better than you do.

10. Don't guess, grandstand, bluff, or lie.

11. Glance at your own legal counsel for possible cues.

12. Remain calm. Stay controlled. Angry or emotional outbursts will not help your testimony.

330. SUMMARY OF LEGAL REQUIREMENTS FOR THE USE OF STUDENT RECORDS

The legal requirements below should be kept in mind when managing pupil records:

- Affected parents and students have a right to review and copy school records.

- The affected parties may challenge the accuracy of student records.

- If a request for a record change is denied, a hearing may be requested on the matter.

- If no change is made in a challenged record, the affected party has a right to file a statement of rebuttal.

- Most educational data, including health information, cannot be disclosed without proper consent.

- Appropriate staff members with a reasonable "need to know" may have legal access to student records.

- Officials in another district to which the student is moving may have access to the student's records. (Records that are hand-carried by the student should not be considered official.)

- State and federal education agencies may access pupil records in the course of authorized operations, but must maintain confidentiality.

- Records subject to a court order may be made available without consent.

- Release of pupil directory information (e.g., census data) is permissible after proper public notice of intent.

- Release of record information to other outside parties can be made only with proper consent.

- Postsecondary students may not review confidential recommendations if they have signed a waiver.

- Basic school records should be maintained for an indefinite period of time.

331. PROBLEMS WITH THE JUVENILE COURT SYSTEM

Schools count on the courts and court personnel (judges, referees, probation officers, etc.) to help punish and rehabilitate youthful offenders. In some areas, conditions within the juvenile court system have become part of the problem, rather than part of the solution. The most frequent complaints by school personnel against the court system include the following:

- Gridlock and long delays in bringing cases to trial
- Lack of communication between the courts and school personnel
- A tendency, in some courts, to sidestep issues and to refer discipline problems back to the school
- Lenient penalties that reinforce bad behavior and student perceptions that they are above the law
- Priorities within the court that give little emphasis to the most common violations (i.e., truancy, smoking, etc.).
- An attitude of blaming the school for problems of delinquency
- A willingness by the court to let parents off the hook
- Using school attendance as part of the penalty for student offenders
- Lack of follow-up on students placed on probation

332. CIVIL RIGHTS ORGANIZATIONS

During the 1900s, the nation has witnessed a proliferation of civil rights organizations. Part of the purpose of these groups is to keep society and the government honest in enforcing civil rights legislation and initiatives. The most prominent civil rights organizations today include:

- American Arab Antidiscrimination Committee
- American Civil Liberties Union
- Americans for Democratic Action
- Antidefamation League of B'nai B'rith
- American Indian Movement (AIM)
- Congress of Racial Equality
- National Association for the Advancement of Colored People (NAACP)
- National Urban League
- Operation PUSH (People United to Save Humanity)
- Southern Christian Leadership Conference
- Student Nonvolent Coordinating Committee

333. LAW-RELATED RESOURCES

In addition to regular law enforcement agencies and standard legal counsel, every state and community boasts a variety of governmental, public, and private organizations that can assist the school (i.e., administration, staff, parents, and students) with specific law-related problems. These agencies typically include:

Adult Protection Services

AFDC

Attorney General's Office

Bankruptcy Court

Battered Women Shelters

Better Business Bureau

Building Code Inspectors

Child Protection Agencies

City Attorney

Civil Rights Commission

Conciliation Court

Consumer Protection Agencies

County Attorney

Crisis Intervention Centers

Department of Commerce

EEOC

Family Violence Department (Police)

Gay and Lesbian Community Services

Internal Revenue Service

Jewish Family Services

Landlord and Tenant Services

Legal Aid Clinics

Legal Aid Society

Legal Services for Low-Income
    Families

Migrant Legal Services

NAACP

Native American Family Services

Poison Control Center

Public Defenders

Public Health Department

Rape and Sexual Assault Centers

Services to People with Disabilities

State Bar Association

State Department of Human Rights

Suicide Prevention Centers

Tenant Unions

334. SOME THOUGHTS ON LAWS, LAWYERS, AND COURTS (QUOTES)

"Lawyers spend a great deal of time shoveling smoke."—*Oliver Wendell Holmes Jr.*

"He that is his own lawyer has a fool for a client."—*Proverb*

"I don't want a lawyer to tell me what I cannot do; I hire him to tell me how to do what I want to do."—*J. Pierpont Morgan*

"To some lawyers all facts are equal."—*Justice Felix Frankfurter*

"A man may as well open an oyster without a knife as a lawyer's mouth without a fee."—*Barten Holyday*

"The Supreme Court has handed down the Eleventh Commandment: 'Thou shalt not, in thy classrooms, read the first ten.' "—*Thomas Reed Powell*

"Our court dockets are so crowded today it would be better to refer to it as the overdue process of law."—*Bill Vaughn*

"Fidelity to the law requires that the laws be as plain and explicit as possible." —*Samuel Cooke*

PARENT/COMMUNITY RELATIONS AND COMMUNICATIONS

335. LEVELS OF SCHOOL-HOME PARTNERSHIP

Schools must work with parents on many levels today. The role of the school in working with families encompasses seven distinct levels of interaction and support:

Level I	Supporting the family structure
Level II	Treating parents as valued customers
Level III	Keeping parents informed
Level IV	Bringing parents into the school as visitors and volunteers
Level V	Encouraging parent participation in learning projects
Level VI	Collaborating in developing behavior standards and enforcing positive discipline
Level VII	Involving parents in on-site decision making

336. A NEW BELIEF SYSTEM ABOUT FAMILIES

To form a successful partnership with all parents, schools need to adopt a new set of beliefs about what today's families are like and how they work, including these six tenets:

1. All families have strengths and weaknesses.

2. There are all kinds of families and all can be successful.

3. All parents want their children to succeed.

4. Parents know a lot about what works and what doesn't with their children.

5. Parents can learn new skills and techniques for raising their children.

6. A child's development depends on the strength of the family, as well as school.

337. TODAY'S PARENT AUDIENCES

In the 1990s, families come in many forms. Today's Principals deal with a variety of parent audiences including:

- Traditional parents
- Adoptive parents
- Single moms
- Single dads
- Foster parents
- Parents of twins
- Expectant parents
- Parents of infants
- Teen parents
- Parents with disabilities
- Non-English-speaking parents
- Parents of chronically ill children
- Later-life parents
- Unmarried parents
- Gay/Lesbian parents
- Open-enrollment parents living outside your district

338. THE PRINCIPAL'S ACCESS TO STAKEHOLDERS

It's important for Principals to tap the best ideas in the community for school improvement. Fortunately, every Principal has built-in access to parents and community members through a number of ready-made groups, organizations, and outlets such as those listed below:

Access to Parents	*Access to Community-at-Large*
PTA/PTO	Civic Clubs
Advisory Councils	Church Groups
Site Councils	Chamber of Commerce
Principal's Coffees	Neighborhood Meetings
Open Houses	Letters to the Editor
Conferences	Radio/TV Interviews
Newsletters	Town Meetings
Home Visits	Open Office Hours

339. PARENT ORGANIZATIONS

Every school has one or more formal parent organizations to promote, support, advise, and assist in a variety of ways. The most common ones include:

PTA/PTO

Parent Communications Network (PCN)

Site Council/Site Management Council

Curriculum Advisory Committee (CAC)

Principals Advisory Council (PAC)

Athletic Advisory Committee

Booster Clubs

Neighborhood Watch Groups (Block Mothers)

Ad Hoc Committees and Task Forces (i.e., fund-raising, diversity, playground equipment, etc.)

340. 10 COMMON COMMUNICATION BARRIERS

Good Principals must be good communicators. Following are ten common barriers that frequently impair communications with staff, students, and community members:

- Vagueness
- Too much information
- Too little information
- Biased (nonobjective) information
- Too much jargon
- Patronizing communications
- Pollyanna attitudes

341. 4 GOALS FOR DEALING WITH DIVERSITY

Every Principal needs to provide leadership for meeting the needs of and empowering all students in a diverse population. All efforts to deal with diversity inside and outside of the school should be guided by the following four common goals:

1. To develop and maintain an atmosphere of respect for all individuals, regardless of race, social class, sex, age, religion, or physical-psychological condition.

2. To understand and respect human differences in the school and community.

3. To promote individual participation in all facets of school and community life.

4. To confront prejudice in the school wherever it exists.

342. PARENT RESPONSIBILITIES

Parental support for the school sends an important message to students about the importance of education. Professionals suggest the following basic responsibilities of parents in supporting the school and helping their children to become successful learners:

- Be sure your child attends school regularly and arrives on time.

- Follow school procedures in reporting legitimate absences and readmitting pupils after an absence.

- Let the school know of any serious family or financial problems. They may be able to help or ease the way for your child.

- Attend Open House, parent-teacher conferences, PTA/PTO meetings, special programs, concerts, and other school events throughout the year.

- Support your school's discipline policies and bus safety rules.

- Let the teacher know about your child's special interests and needs.

- Volunteer as a room mother, library helper, playground aide, tutor, reader, resource person, field trip chaperone, picture lady, book nook leader, or PTA committee member—if you can.

- Stay tuned in to what's happening at school and help your child with homework.

- If a problem arises, try to resolve it by following the chain of responsibility below:
    —Classroom teacher
    —Principal
    —Assistant Superintendent
    —Superintendent of Schools

343. DANGER SIGNS OF DYSFUNCTIONAL FAMILIES

The following behaviors characterize many dysfunctional families:

- Violence is a way of life.
- Physical and sexual abuse are tolerated.
- Alcohol and drug use are common in all generations.
- Fear is a daily emotion.
- Mutual respect and appreciation are lacking among family members.
- Rules and standards are absent.
- Fault-finding and finger-pointing are commonplace.
- Put-downs and criticism are the norm in family communication.
- Blaming and shaming are routine.
- Inattentiveness abounds.
- There are no family rituals and traditions.
- Few, if any, special family events take place.
- Compliments and visible signs of support are lacking.
- There is little or no positive physical contact (absence of hugs).
- Children are viewed as burdens, not gifts ("albatross syndrome").
- Denial is commonplace.
- Home is a place to go, not a place to be.
- Dreams and goals are not apparent.
- Defeatism is a prevailing attitude.

344. WHAT PARENTS REALLY WANT TO KNOW

Most parents today really want to ask the following questions (but may be afraid to):

1. Who will be my child's teacher?

2. How large are your class sizes?

3. What are you doing about security and keeping my child safe?

4. Are there gangs in this school? What are you doing about them?

5. What are you doing about drugs and weapons in school?

6. What is your discipline plan?

7. Will my child be safe riding the bus?

8. What if my child is sexually harassed?

9. Where does my child catch the bus? When?

344. WHAT PARENTS REALLY WANT TO KNOW,
CONTINUED

10. How early can kids come to school?

11. What special help is available?

12. What do I do if my child is ill and can't attend school?

13. What if my child becomes ill at school?

14. How will I know if the school is closed or dismissed early due to severe weather or other emergency?

15. When will students learn to read?

16. Do you teach phonics?

17. How much homework will my child have?

18. Is my child at a disadvantage if we don't have a computer at home?

19. Should my child use a calculator for math assignments?

20. How will you grade my child?

21. Is the school lunch healthy? How much is it? How do we pay?

22. Whom can I contact if I have questions?

23. What if I have a complaint?

24. Are you going to ask me for extra money for field trips and other special things?

25. Will someone really get to know and care about my child??

345. 5 KEY QUESTIONS TO ASK ABOUT ALL SCHOOL COMMUNICATIONS

In every form of school communication, the key questions to be asked and answered are always the following:

1. What do you want to communicate?

2. Why do you want to communicate the information?

3. Who needs to get the information?

4. How should the information be communicated?

5. When is the best time to communicate it?

346. 25 COMMUNICATION TECHNIQUES YOU CAN USE TODAY

Following is a sampling of information strategies and techniques that have worked for schools in all parts of the country:

1. Start a parenting library, resource room, or toy check-out center in the school.
2. Include an "open mike" segment in each PTA/PTO meeting agenda.
3. Institute parent hotlines providing up-to-date information on school activities and events.
4. Hold coffee parties and brown bag minisessions for parents.
5. Place school messages on billboards and marquees throughout the community.
6. Conduct "whistle stop" tours by riding the school bus and stopping at regular stops to visit with residents and answer questions.
7. Hold neighborhood and town meetings.
8. Include noncustodial parents in all school communications.
9. Expand the number of advisory councils.
10. Provide incentives for teachers to make home visits.
11. Encourage local churches to include school information in weekly bulletins and newsletters.
12. Have students call citizens with invitations to special events.
13. Hold open evening and Saturday office hours.
14. Arrange for school displays in local stores and public buildings.
15. Conduct classes in a mall so shoppers can see students and teachers in action.
16. Plan a computer fair for parents. Students can demonstrate hardware and software.
17. Conduct regular opinion polls and focus group interviews.
18. Use spot announcements in conjunction with telecasts of athletic events.
19. Convert an old school bus into a "schoolmobile" to carry school displays throughout the community.
20. Conduct concerts and other performances in the neighborhoods (i.e., parks, parking lots, etc.).
21. Lobby for employers to let workers off to participate in school events.
22. Develop special "Parent Kits" with information on homework hints, summer activities, etc.
23. Issue press releases and hold press conferences when appropriate.
24. Place student newspapers and yearbooks in local physicians' and dentists' waiting rooms.
25. Develop an adult-in-the-classroom program so that parents and other grown-ups can audit high school classes at no cost.

347. 8 NEW WAYS TO GET AND KEEP PARENT SUPPORT

The home-school partnership is strained in today's fast-paced society. Single-parent families and families where both parents work are now the norm. Because parents are busier, more worn out, and more stressed out than ever before, it's not so easy to get them involved in the school. The following measures, however, have helped many schools to regenerate the partnership:

1. Provide babysitting services in conjunction with all parent meetings.

2. Provide food for the family at parent meetings whenever possible.

3. Arrange for transportation to and from meetings.

4. Never lecture parents about how and what they should do. (Most are doing their best already.)

5. Try to hold meetings in the neighborhoods (churches, parks, fast-food restaurants, etc.).

6. Conduct workshops on parenting. Stress parents helping parents (support groups, parent networks, etc.).

7. Make it easy for parents to help (i.e., let them make phone calls from home, send home materials so moms and dads can make learning aids, such as games or flash cards, on their own turf and on their own time).

8. Use today's technology (voice mail, E-mail) to boost home-school communication.

348. HIGH-TECH COMMUNICATION TOOLS

Schools and Principals everywhere are jumping on the information highway with such high-tech communication tools as the following:

- Beepers for the Principal and other key personnel
- Telephones in every classroom
- Modern school telephone systems (call-waiting, speed dial features, etc.)
- Voice mail boxes for all staff members
- Car phone for the Principal
- School fax machine for receiving parent messages, attendance information, home-work assignments, and so on
- School operated FM radio station and cable TV channel
- Videotapes and compact disks available for home checkout
- Teleconferencing
- E-mail and Internet messages where appropriate

349. VOLUNTEER OPPORTUNITIES IN SCHOOLS

Good schools are saturated with volunteers. The needs and opportunities for parent volunteers in schools are rich and varied. Examples of common volunteer slots in elementary and secondary schools include:

Room Parent

Teacher Aide

Tutor

Crossing Guard

Playground Supervisor

Library Helper

Minicourse Teacher

Resource Person

Bus Monitor

PTA/PTO Officer or Committee Chair

Fund-Raising Volunteer

Field Trip Chaperone

Caller

Driver

Site Management Council Member

Principal's Advisory Council Member

Parent Communications Network Chair

Mentor

Big Brother/Big Sister

Book Nook Chair

Jr. Great Books Leader

Block Home Parent

Interpreter (Signer) for Hearing Impaired

Club Advisor

Volunteer Coach

Task Force Member

Curriculum Advisory Council Member

School Store Manager

349. VOLUNTEER OPPORTUNITIES IN SCHOOLS, CONTINUED

Accompanist

Test Timer

Computer Aide

Office Aide

Scout for Athletic Deptartment

Usher

Ticket Taker

Prompter for School Plays

Costume Designer

Property Manager

Storyteller

Debate Judge

Gymnastics Spotter

Swim Meet Timer

Athletic Advisory Committee Member

Party Planner (Organizer)

Crowd Control Assistant

Get-Out-the-Vote Committee Member

Preschool Screening Helper

Artist in Residence

Consultant on Graphics and Publicity

Recycling Coordinator

350. PARENT ADVISORY COMMITTEE FUNCTIONS

The most common functions of Principal's advisory committees are:

- questioning/inquiring
- examining/studying
- research/fact finding/data gathering
- synthesizing
- identifying problem areas
- informing others
- suggesting/recommending
- evaluating
- reporting results

351. COMMON OBSTACLES TO EFFECTIVE ADVISORY COMMITTEES

Parent advisory committees have become an integral part of the school's decision-making process for many Principals. To assure positive results, it pays to avoid the common stumbling blocks identified below:

1. Ill-defined purpose
2. Too large or too small membership
3. Nonrepresentative membership
4. Bad timing (established prematurely or too close to the end of the year)
5. Lack of resources (funding, clerical support) for the committee
6. Information overkill (providing too much too soon)
7. The intrusion of politics
8. No provision for evaluation
9. Committee recommendations that leave no alternatives for the school staff
10. Lack of follow-up on committee work or recommendations

352. GUIDELINES FOR PARENT ADVISORY COUNCILS

I. Membership:

    A. Size should be limited to be workable. (Anything over 15 is probably too large.)

    B. Councils should be a mix of parents and staff members (should be a minority of the Council).

    C. Only one member from a family.

    D. Membership should represent all of the different grade levels in the school.

    E. Include a balanced number of males, females, and minorities.

    F. Limit terms to two years.

II. Officers:

    A. Officers should include (at least) chair, vice chair, secretary, and treasurer (if funds are involved).

    B. Officers should be elected by the members (not hand picked by the Principal).

III. Meetings:

    A. Regular meetings should be held at least quarterly.

    B. Meeting times should be set for the convenience of the members.

IV. Agendas:

    A. Agendas should be developed mutually by the Principal and the chairperson.

    B. Any member should be allowed to suggest agenda topics.

    C. Agendas should always be distributed in advance of each meeting.

353. 14 STEPS TO EFFECTIVE USE OF PARENT COMMITTEES, TASK FORCES, AND ADVISORY COUNCILS

1. Define general areas of responsibility for the group. Be sure everyone understands what such terms as "advisory" mean.

2. Limit the focus. Define the specific charge to the committee or task force.

3. Determine whether the group is ad hoc or continuing.

4. Determine membership requirements and parameters (i.e., representation, term limits, selection procedures, etc.).

5. Identify leadership.

6. Establish operating rules (formal bylaws if necessary).

7. Insist on setting starting and ending times for all meetings and enforce them.

8. Provide appropriate resources, materials, and background information.

9. Arrange for necessary recordkeeping and reporting.

10. Set time lines and target dates.

11. Provide help as needed.

12. Develop a process for keeping track of committee progress.

13. Evaluate each committee separately.

14. Get out of the way.

354. TIPS FOR BETTER OPEN HOUSES

The school's annual Open House is the first direct contact with the school for many parents. (For some parents, it is the only first-hand contact.) It is important to make the best possible impression. Here are school-tested ways to assure a successful Open House:

- Stress informal dress.
- Use school buses to provide transportation from low-income housing areas.
- Invite grandparents.
- Serve a free or low-cost meal (soup and sandwiches) if possible.
- Provide babysitting services.
- Saturate the building with displays of student work.
- At secondary level, use students to provide valet parking.
- Feature student performing groups (a sure-fire crowd gatherer).
- Provide signing interpreters for the hearing impaired and language interpreters for non-English-speaking families.
- Run videos depicting school events and activities at strategic locations throughout the building.
- Provide building maps and student guides to assist parents in finding their way around.
- Brighten up the school with banners and balloon bouquets.
- Give away donated door prizes.
- Have an inexpensive take-home gift for everyone. (School pencils make good gifts. The PTA can buy them.)
- Don't ask for money right away.
- Let students show their families around.
- Be sure that individual classroom teachers cover these crucial items:
    —attendance procedures
    —discipline policies and plans
    —grading standards
    —homework expectations
    —curriculum highlights
- Give handouts for parents to take home.
- Insist that parents make follow-up appointments to discuss individual issues. The Open House is for everyone and is not the appropriate setting for a private conference.
- Conduct a sign-up campaign for school volunteers.
- Start and end on time.
- Provide parking lot security and escorts if needed.
- Try to make it fun for everyone!

355. ADVICE TO PARENTS ON GETTING THE MOST OUT OF PARENT-TEACHER CONFERENCES

Principals and teachers offer the suggestions below to help parents get the most out of parent-teacher conferences:

- Decide what you want to discuss in advance. Ask your child about discussion topics. Write down questions to ask the teacher. For example, parents often want to find out about:

    special school programs and services

    discipline policies

    grading policies

    after-school activities

    daily schedule

    attendance/absence procedures

    homework policy

    your child's progress

    your child's relationships

- Also list such items you want to share about your child as:

    special health needs or problems

    outside interests and hobbies

    feelings/fears about school

    likes and dislikes

    sibling relationships

- Take notes during the conference.
- Ask the teacher how you can help your child, the teacher, the school.
- Follow up by discussing the conference with your child.
- Start immediately on any action steps you agreed to take.

356. PITFALLS AND IMPROVEMENT TIPS FOR PRINCIPAL'S NEWSLETTERS

The school newsletter is the Principal's most personal and powerful means of communicating with parents and other readers. Communication specialists offer the following advice for upgrading parent newsletters:

Avoid these pitfalls:

- Overuse of technical terms, jargon, and acronyms
- Running too long
- Coming across as too boastful, too preachy, or too defensive
- Sending mixed emotions
- Being too vague
- Talking down to readers

Try these improvements:

- Adopt a catchy name and logo that set your school apart (a readily identifiable masthead design is best).
- Use bold, attention-grabbing headlines.
- Limit use of statistics.
- Concentrate on a right-to-the-point writing style.
- Share your personal priorities as school leader.
- Insert clip-and-save calendars.
- Include lots of student quotes, student writing, and other examples of student work.
- Include clear photos and reproductions of student art work.
- Leave lots of white space. Crowded copy doesn't get read.
- Use tear-sheets to generate feedback and two-way communication.
- Proofread; proofread; proofread! (Dont't be embarrassed by unfortunate misprints.)
- Don't pussyfoot around controversial or sensitive issues or walk on eggs; face touchy subjects squarely with all the facts you can gather.

The school newsletter that goes into the home of every parent is the single most important public relations and communication tool available to the Principal. Give it your best effort and get professional help if you need it.

357. GUIDELINES FOR HOME VISITS

More and more schools are implementing programs of home visitations by teachers to enhance mutual understanding, to expand communication, and to promote home-school cooperation. Many Principals urge teachers to heed the guidelines and precautions below in making such visitations.

1. Don't go alone the first time. Be accompanied by a counselor, aide, or another teacher who has one of the family's children in class.

2. Call first to schedule the visitation. Don't show up unannounced.

3. If you can't visit every family represented in your classroom, try to visit every new family.

4. Begin by sharing nonthreatening school or community information as an ice breaker.

5. Concentrate on getting to know each other better; don't appear to be snooping.

6. Stress common goals shared by both home and school.

7. Avoid using any judgmental or belittling language.

8. Don't act shocked or surprised by anything you see or hear during the visitation.

9. Don't talk down to parents, but use everyday language instead of professional jargon.

10. Keep the tone of the visit friendly.

358. EARMARKS OF EFFECTIVE LETTERS TO PARENTS

When you send progress, disciplinary, or other kinds of letters to parents about their children, you may find the following advice of experienced Principals helpful:

- Write in an informal style (unless the letter is to be used as a legal document). Avoid stuffy educationese or jargon.

- Introduce yourself in the first sentence.

- Stick to hard data (i.e., grades, test scores, etc.) and firsthand observations. Avoid speculation or judgmental remarks.

- Keep the tone of the letter professional, friendly, and helpful.

- End on a positive and encouraging note if at all possible.

- Encourage the parent to respond in writing or by a telephone call.

- Follow up with a phone call of your own if necessary.

359. 5 TIPS FOR BETTER LETTERS

1. Omit irrelevant and extraneous material.

2. Get to the point—fast.

3. Avoid jargon, acronyms, and gobbledygook.

4. Keep the format logical.

5. Write as you speak.

360. PROTOCOL FOR CONDUCTING A TOWN MEETING

- A series of small town meetings is better than one large congregation.
- Invite the entire community via the media and individual notices.
- Videotape town meetings for replay over local cable TV channels.
- Have a well-defined purpose for every town meeting.
- Arrange chairs in semicircles (small groups of three to five participants).
- Present everyone in attendance with an agenda, a fact sheet, note paper, and "I want to know more" postcards.
- Suggested format:
    a. Introduction and overview
    b. Small-group conversations, with reports back to the total group
    c. Questions and answers
    d. Open microphone
    e. Summation and next steps

Collect notes, comment cards, written questions, and postcards. END ON TIME.

361. TIPS ON HANDLING COMPLAINTS

Every school receives some negative feedback and criticism. How these attacks are handled spells the difference between excellent schools and also-rans. Here's how the best schools deal with complaints:

- Take all complaints seriously. Listen to the caller's feelings and ideas.
- Never intimidate callers.
- No complaint should go more than 24 hours without some specific response.
- Refer the complaining party to someone who can do something about the issue or problem as soon as possible.
- Get all the facts. Don't make any premature promises.
- Don't attempt to bluff or lie to blunt criticism.
- Avoid use of any abusive or sexist language with any complainant (even if the caller uses such language).
- Rephrase what you've heard to verify understanding.
- Ask for clarification if needed.
- Record the time and date of the call, and make notes of what the caller tells you.
- Try to build understanding and provide straight answers or find someone who can.
- Promise to look into the matter.
- If you can't resolve the issue, tell the caller what options remain open.
- If nothing else, agree to disagree and remain calm and polite.

362. 8 WAYS TO BEAT THE GRAPEVINE OR RUMOR MILL

1. Always tell the truth.

2. If you don't know, admit it.

3. If you don't know, find out.

4. Pay attention to rumors to find out what are the current concerns.

5. Never try to use the grapevine for your own purposes.

6. If a rumor is a lie, pounce on it immediately and refute it with facts.

7. Communicate face-to-face and equally with everyone.

8. Be sure to avoid making racist, sexist, or other inappropriate comments in public.

363. GUIDELINES FOR COMMUNITY USE OF SCHOOL FACILITIES

Schools belong to the community and should be used, as much as possible, for public purposes and to promote community goals. Opening up the school to community members of all ages is one of the best ways to foster positive public relations. The guidelines below can help manage and maximize community use of school facilities:

1. Consider all events that must take place in the school before scheduling any event.

2. Schedule school-related and parent activities first, district activities second, and then consider other use requests based on established priorities (see item 3) or a first-come, first-served basis.

3. Priority categories for scheduling facilities for use by nonschool groups:

Priority 1 Groups	*Priority 2 Groups*
Local public agencies	Group 1 organizations that restrict participation
Civic/charitable groups	Religious groups for worship or fund-raising purposes
Neighborhood associations	Business or commercial groups
Youth-serving agencies	
City agencies	
Federal and state agencies	
Political organizations	
Local religious groups for recreational activities	

4. Schedule for optimum flexibility and minimum conflict.

5. Provide special rooms for special purposes.

6. Assign building use fees according to district policy.

7. Don't schedule meetings that may be prejudicial to the best interests of the school.

8. Don't hesitate to provide access for religious groups as required by federal regulations.

9. When conflicts arise, negotiate space use by trading off better facilities for less desirable hours.

10. Make it clear that authorization for use of school facilities should not be considered an endorsement or approval of the activity or group or the purposes they may represent.

364. ADVICE FROM THE PRINCIPAL: HOW TO HELP YOUR CHILD STAY OUT OF TROUBLE AND STAY IN SCHOOL

- Establish and enforce regular bedtimes.
- Subscribe to newspapers and magazines.
- Limit TV time.
- Talk about school and lifelong learning.
- Have books and maps around the house.
- Celebrate big and little successes at school.
- Make a big deal out of reading.
- Model patience and "stick-to-itiveness."
- Talk about values and what you believe in.
- Spend time in the classroom.
- Don't stop learning yourself.
- Show your children how mature grown-ups solve problems without violence.
- Model goal setting.
- Show interest in school work (even at the high school level).
- Support positive peer groups such as SADD.

365. PARENT TIPS ON BUILDING A CHILD'S SELF-ESTEEM

Schools should help parents understand the power of a child's self-esteem and how to nurture it. The following practical tips can go a long way in boosting any child's self-concept:

- Communicate one-on-one with your child every day.
- Act as if your children are important in your life.
- Treat kids as people, not property.
- Don't put your work before your children.
- Show your human side and your vulnerability.
- Be honest; keep promises; don't lie.
- Celebrate each child's unique personality.
- Hold high expectations, but remain flexible.
- Don't try to be perfect, and don't expect your kids to be either.
- Help your children overcome weaknesses without feeling inferior.
- Never belittle a child's dreams.

365. PARENT TIPS ON BUILDING A CHILD'S SELF-ESTEEM, CONTINUED

- Downplay competition and emphasize self-growth.
- Insist that no one is worthless.
- Show pride in your children, yourself, and your family.
- Reinforce positive behavior.
- Do lots of little things that show you care.

366. TIPS FOR PARENTS ON HELPING CHILDREN WITH HOMEWORK

Parents can play a crucial role in encouraging their children to study and learn. Here are tips on ways you can help your youngster:

- Teach (help) your child to organize, prioritize, and set goals.
- Provide an environment conducive to study. Eliminate as many distractions as possible.
- Remove barriers and don't accept excuses.
- Make homework time part of the regular family routine (like bathing, chores, bedtime, etc.).
- Encourage your children to do their own work. Don't let them copy (cheat) and don't do homework for them.
- Show your child how you remember and meet deadlines.
- Teach your children memory tricks (mnemonic devices).
- Let your children see how you do the homework required by your job.
- Provide your children with their own "In" and "Out" baskets.
- Pay attention to whether or not your child is keeping up. Check with teachers if necessary.
- Teach your child to break big assignments down into manageable tasks and to take one step at a time.
- Help your child understand her or his learning style.
- To the extent possible, provide your child with the tools for study (paper, pencils, dictionary, rulers, computer, etc.).
- Discuss current events as a family.
- Practice listening skills as a family.
- Praise effort, as well as results.
- Encourage your child to take risks and try new things.
- Celebrate successes; don't nit-pick or expect perfection.
- Don't threaten or offer bribes.

367. SUGGESTED RESPONSIBILITIES FOR MENTORS

Meet with the student's teacher(s) to learn about academic and personal needs.

Meet with parent and student to plan the year.

Attend school conferences with the parents and student when appropriate.

Be available by phone to confer with the student, parents, and teachers as needed.

Give fax number to student and family members.

Make personal contact with the student at least once a month for social activities.

Lead by example. (Be a role model.)

368. 6 LITTLE THINGS THAT BUG PEOPLE AND STIFLE COMMUNICATIONS

1. Being argumentative, intentionally starting controversies, and refusing to give ground.

2. Acting superior. Putting down other people.

3. Being rude, interrupting others, and cutting people off before they complete a thought or statement.

4. Being loud and bullying others.

5. Killing others' ideas and ridiculing suggestions from other people.

6. Consistently showing a lack of enthusiasm in contacts with others.

369. HOW TO DISAGREE WITHOUT BEING DISAGREEABLE

- Even if you don't agree with another party, remain pleasant and make an honest effort to understand the other's point of view.
- Listen carefully to *everything* the other party has to say.
- Avoid emotional or loaded language that only heightens the disagreement.
- Look for areas where you can agree.
- Repeat the other's position to verify understanding.
- Back up your own position with facts—calmly!

370. COMMON FAULTS OF PRINCIPALS THAT CAN HAMPER COMMUNICATIONS

- Failure to see the other's point of view
- Failure to show appreciation
- Lack of frankness and sincerity
- Arbitrariness
- Arrogance
- Lack of courtesy
- Sarcasm
- Nervousness
- Loss of temper

371. CHARACTERISTICS OF A FULL-SERVICE SCHOOL

In conjunction with Community Education departments, some Principals are now implementing a full-service concept. The best possible public relations program is simply for the school to become an integral part of community life for all ages. Features of a full-service school include:

- Regular classroom instruction for school-age children.
- Preschool/Day-care services.
- Evening enrichment classes for all ages.
- Recreation activities for all ages.
- Open gym and pool nights for families.
- Summer learning and play activities for all ages.
- Post Office drop-off and pickup box.
- Regular stop for public transportation.
- ATM machine.
- Drop-off box for library book returns.
- Registration desk for all school district, city, and recreation programs.
- Children and adult theater productions.
- Food shelves or co-op programs.
- Meals on Wheels headquarters.
- Seasonal tax advice.
- Meeting rooms for community and neighborhood groups.
- Satellite cop shop (community policing center).
- Counseling/ombudsman services for all ages.
- Congregate dining for senior citizens.
- Petting zoo.

372. I WISH I'D SAID THAT—QUOTES ON COMMUNICATION

"You will never really know what I mean and I'll never know exactly what you mean."—*Mike Nichols*

"To say the right thing at the right time, keep still most of the time."—*John W. Roper*

"Good communication is as stimulating as black coffee and just as hard to sleep after."—*Anne Morrow Lindbergh*

"The best argument is that which seems merely an explanation."—*Dale Carnegie*

"Communication is something so simple and difficult that we can never put it in simple words."—*T. S. Matthew*

"It is a luxury to be understood."—*Ralph Waldo Emerson*

"Be obscure clearly."—*E. B. White*

"'The Medium is the Message' because it is the medium that shapes and controls the search and form of human associations and actions."—*Marshall McLuhan*

Section Ten

PERSONAL AND PROFESSIONAL WELLNESS

373. ELEMENTS OF HOLISTIC HEALTH

Health is holistic, and its many components contribute to the total person. All components of the total person need nurturing, support and—sometimes—healing. The basic elements contributing to holistic health include:

Physical Elements

Exercise/Fitness

Diet/Nutrition

Stress Management

Substance Use

Lifestyle Management

Sexuality

Mental-Emotional Elements

Self-esteem

Affirmations

Acceptance

Relationship Elements

Family

Loved Ones

Colleagues

Friends

Associates

Acquaintances

Spiritual Elements

Life's Meaning

Philosophy of Life

Values

Ethics

373. ELEMENTS OF HOLISTIC HEALTH,
CONTINUED

Morals

Eternity

Work Life Elements

Goals

Success

Opportunity for Growth

Opportunity for Advancement

Work Ethic

Expertise

Pride

Economic Pressures

Ecological Elements

Pollution

Unsafe Conditions

Environmental Hazards

374. ABC'S FOR HEALTHY LIVING

A — Attitude

B — Beauty

C — Coping Skills

D — Diet

E — Exercise

F — Fun

G — Goals

H — Humor

I — Interests

J — Joy

K — Kindness

L — Laughter

M — Mental Growth

N — Nature

O — Open Communication

P — Peace

Q — Quietude

R — Relaxation

S — Spirituality

T — Time Management

U — Unconditional Love

V — Values

W — Work

X — X-rated Fun with Someone You Love

Y — Youthful Point of View

Z — Zero Tolerance for Nicotine, Alcohol, and Drugs

375. MEDICAL SPECIALTIES

As with most professions, the medical community has become increasingly specialized over time. The most common specialties today include:

Allergy - allergy disorders

Cardiology - heart disease

Chemical dependency - substance abuse and addictions

Chiropractic - manipulation of spinal column and other structures

Dermatology - skin disorders

Endocrinology - gland and hormone disorders

General practice (G.P.) - family medicine

Geriatrics - aging and senior citizen health

Gynecology - female health and reproduction

Internal medicine - (self-explanatory)

Nephrology - kidney disease

Obstetrics - pregnancy

Oncology - tumors and cancer

Ophthalmology - eye disorders

Orthopedics - muscles, joints, ligaments, and the skeletal system

Otolaryngology - ear, nose, and throat

Pediatrics - children's health

Podiatry - foot disorders

Psychiatry - mental/emotional disorders, psychoanalysis

Radiology - X-ray

Rheumatology - rheumatic disorders

Sports medicine - athletic injuries

Surgery - removal, replacement, or repair of diseased organs

Urology - urinary tract disorders

376. 4 LEADING CAUSES OF DEATH

The four leading causes of death in America are:

1. Cancer

2. Strokes

3. Heart Attacks

4. Accidents

The risk of all four of these major threats can be dramatically reduced through sensible living and a disciplined life style.

377. 8 SURE-FIRE WAYS TO LIVE LONGER

Every actuarial, medical, and longevity study published in recent years agrees on the following proven life-stretchers:

1. Get the sleep you need.

2. Fasten seat belts—every time you drive.

3. Quit smoking.

4. Cut down or cut out alcohol usage.

5. Protect your skin from the sun.

6. Eat as you know you should.

7. Get regular physical checkups.

8. Exercise regularly.

378. MORE HEALTH TIPS FOR BUSY PRINCIPALS

- Make friends with your doctor.
- If you're male, be sure to get a colon and prostate checkup every one to three years, depending on your age. If you're female, be sure to get a mammogram and Pap smear test every one to three years, depending on your age.
- Walk a lot.
- Guard your health—but don't become paranoid.
- Listen to your body.
- Don't lie or do other things that make you feel guilty.
- Schedule some escape into your life; have a place where you can go (physically or mentally) and find peace.
- Learn when to say "No."
- Take 1/4 to 1 tablet of aspirin daily.
- Cut back on night meetings. Don't work Saturdays.
- Break the habit of bringing work home.

379. SIGNS OF STRESS

Although everyone reacts to stress differently, the following are common symptoms of too much negative stress:

- Becoming argumentative and irritable
- Headaches
- Shouting
- Neck tension or pain
- Hostility
- Rapid pulse
- Indecisiveness
- Irregular breathing
- Poor judgment
- Chest pains
- Lack of concentration (inability to focus)
- Excessive perspiration
- Inconsistency
- Confusion
- Forgetfulness

379. SIGNS OF STRESS, CONTINUED

- Desire to escape
- Avoidance
- Insomnia
- Loss of appetite
- Frequent stomach acidity
- Fatigue
- Loss of sex drive
- Troubled relationships
- Skin rashes
- Nightmares
- Frequent accidents
- Increased smoking or drinking
- Diarrhea
- Blaming others

380. COMMON CAUSES OF UNHEALTHY STRESS

- Fear
- Uncertainty
- Self-doubt
- Lack of control
- Perfectionism
- People-pleasing (lack of assertiveness)
- Lack of direction

381. SPECIAL STRESSORS FOR PRINCIPALS

When the Principal is stressed, the whole school can be affected. As with most professionals, Principals have their own set of unique stress agents, which include:

- Relentless visibility
- Expectations of serving as problem solver for everyone else's problems
- Long hours (including nights and weekends)
- Lack of privacy
- Isolation
- Red tape/bureaucracy
- Responsibility for others' life and safety
- Pressure to do more, better, faster, and cheaper
- Pressures on family life
- Threats of physical harm
- Variety of audiences
- Too many bosses
- Paperwork
- Deadlines
- Negotiations
- Media treatment—lack of respect

382. 50 COPING MECHANISMS FOR RELIEVING STRESS

1. Develop rituals.
2. Change your routine.
3. Find a personal retreat.
4. Exercise at your desk.
5. Take brief "mental vacations" during each day.
6. Adopt a wait-and-see attitude.
7. Quit judging yourself and others.
8. Build your own support group.
9. Admit mistakes and ask for help when it's needed.
10. Don't hold grudges, and make amends when necessary.
11. Keep your sense of humor and use it often.
12. Learn to pace yourself.
13. Take one step at a time.
14. Do something for others.
15. Get advice or counseling.
16. Put more warmth in your relationships.
17. Get at the bottom of your stress and deal directly with the cause.
18. Simplify—get back to basics.
19. Remember why you became a professional educator.
20. Walk off tension.
21. Get a massage.
22. Delegate more.
23. Gain as much control over your job and your life as you can.
24. Get enough sleep.
25. Do something you really like for at least 30 minutes daily.
26. Cut down on nicotine, alcohol, caffeine, and sugar.
27. Do more with friends and loved ones.
28. Read to a child.
29. Take a shower or bubble bath.
30. Listen to music.
31. Try to remain positive and optimistic.

382. 50 COPING MECHANISMS FOR RELIEVING STRESS, CONTINUED

32. Get up earlier to avoid morning frenzy.

33. Always have a contingency plan.

34. Have something to do while you wait.

35. Allow extra time to get to appointments.

36. Plan ahead—practice preventive maintenance.

37. Say "No."

38. Lower your standards sometimes.

39. Keep a journal.

40. Get organized.

41. Unplug your phone if you need peace and quiet.

42. Avoid negative (destructive) self-talk.

43. Stay away from those who anger, threaten, frustrate, or intimidate you.

44. Practice relaxation techniques.

45. Associate with positive, supportive people.

46. Employ time-management techniques.

47. Practice deep breathing.

48. Break down big jobs into small, manageable parts.

49. Whistle.

50. Cry if you really feel like it.

383. WAYS TO REDUCE STRESS WHILE AT WORK

When tensions mount on the job, most Principals can't run away. Many successful administrators suggest the following tactics for breaking the cycle of tension and relieving stress while at work in the school:

- Take a brisk walk around the perimeter of the building and grounds. (Most people will think you're on some official errand.)
- Visit your favorite class and watch a master teacher at work.
- Read to a class of children.
- Listen to the choir practicing.
- Relax in the library (but stay away from the teachers' lounge).
- Have a cup of coffee with a custodian you like.
- Try some exercises at your desk.
- Shoot some hoops or work out with a physical education class.
- Read some stories the children have written.
- Seek out someone who makes you laugh.

384. 7 STEPS IN ANGER MANAGEMENT

Anger seldom solves problems. It does, however, add to stress overload. It pays to contain or control your anger. Many school administrators have found the seven steps below to be effective anger-management techniques:

1. Understand what makes you angry.
2. Know the symptoms of your anger.
3. Know your limits (tolerance levels).
4. Avoid anger-provoking situations where possible.
5. Whenever possible, express frankly what's bothering you—preferably to the source of your anger.
6. Do something physical and constructive to dissipate your anger (i.e., jogging, gardening, painting, etc.).
7. When necessary, act out your anger in harmless ways (i.e., punching pillows, writing an angry letter and then tearing it up, etc.).

385. RISK FACTORS FOR A STROKE

Following are personal medical history factors that may indicate high-risk potential for a stroke:

- hypertension
- smoking
- diabetes
- sedentary life style
- use of oral contraceptives
- sickle cell disorders
- coagulation disorders
- arthritis
- dehydration
- family history of phlebitis

386. STROKE SYMPTOMS

Following are common early warning signs or symptoms of a pending stroke or a stroke in progress:

1. Headaches (particularly sudden, violent pain)

2. Diminished consciousness (i.e., dizziness, confusion, or coma)

3. Difficulty with speech and/or swallowing

4. Paralysis (usually on one side)

5. Seizures

6. Coma

387. HOW TO SPOT CLINICAL DEPRESSION

Everyone gets depressed (sad, blue, etc.) at times. This is natural and normal, and not cause for concern. Serious, debilitating depression, however, is on the rise worldwide. Untreated, clinical depression can be fatal. One half of all suicides in America are caused by depression. Below are some of the most common, specific signals of the presence of serious (life-threatening) depression:

Loss of appetite

Difficulty in expressing feelings

Change in sleep patterns

Worrying

Pessimism

Withdrawal

Apathy

Crying spells

Sense of worthlessness

Loneliness

Nothing is fun anymore

Ongoing sense of hopelessness

Emotional exhaustion

Generalized dissatisfaction

Dropping activities

Suicidal thoughts

Irritability

Inertia (can't get started)

Reduced energy

Impaired concentration

Forgetfulness

Slow-down in psychomotor activity

In isolation, the symptoms above may be unimportant. If several of these behaviors are exhibited consistently over time, however, professional evaluation and help should be sought.

388. WHERE TO GET HELP FOR DEPRESSION

Sufferers from clinical depression can't just "snap out of it." They need help through counseling and drug therapy. For more information and help, contact:

American Psychiatric Association
1400 K Street W.
Washington, DC 20005

National Alliance for the Mentally Ill
2101 Wilson Blvd., Suite 202
Arlington, VA 22201

National Depression and Manic Depression Association
730 N. Franklin St., Suite 501
Chicago, IL 60610

National Foundation for Depression Illness, Inc.
P.O. Box 2257
N.Y., NY 10116

National Mental Health Association
1021 Prince St.
Arlington, VA 22314

389. OFFICE EXERCISES (7 MUSCLE GROUP EXERCISES YOU CAN DO AT YOUR DESK OR IN YOUR OFFICE)

Exercise is the exorcist of tension. You don't need a fully equipped gym or exercise spa to reduce stress through exercise. The seven exercises below are designed to relax major muscle groups and can be done almost anywhere:

1. Clench both fists as tightly as you can for five seconds, then relax for five seconds. Repeat until fingers, hands, and forearms feel completely exercised.

2. Wrinkle your forehead and raise your eyebrows for five seconds, then relax for five seconds.

3. Clench your jaws tightly for five seconds, then relax for five seconds.

4. Take a deep breath, and hold it for five seconds, then relax for five seconds. This can relax the entire chest area.

5. Tighten your abdomen and stomach muscles for five seconds, then relax for five seconds.

6. Arch your back. Hold it for five seconds, then relax for five seconds.

389. OFFICE EXERCISES (7 MUSCLE GROUP EXERCISES YOU CAN DO AT YOUR DESK OR IN YOUR OFFICE), CONTINUED

7. Extend both legs and point your toes away from your face for five seconds, then relax for five seconds. This exercise is good for easing tension in the calf muscles.

Note: These exercises may be done once or until the muscles involved feel relaxed. They can be used any time to induce relaxation for a specific purpose. They can also be done in any combination.

390. ERGONOMIC MEASURES FOR AVOIDING WORK-RELATED INJURIES

Repetitious tasks, poor work techniques, inappropriate office furniture and equipment, and dysfunctional work spaces can lead to needless wear and tear on joints and muscles called "cumulative stress trauma." The results can be painful and serious (e.g., carpal tunnel syndrome).

The science of ergonomics (applying common sense to the routine of the school or workplace) can help avoid or minimize such injury. Ergonomic experts suggest the following steps to make your office more user-friendly and injury-free.

- Organize the office to minimize stress and strain (e.g., put lightest items on highest shelves).
- Take breaks when needed.
- Vary activities (break up repetitious acts).
- Adjust office chairs to proper height.
- Don't wear high heels.
- Practice good posture at all times.
- Change positions and stretch often.
- Position work to avoid undue reaching or stretching.
- Check that work surfaces are at the proper height for those who use them.
- Always place computer terminals at eye level.
- Use office chairs that support the lumbar region of the back.
- Place computer keyboards at elbow level.
- Place feet flat on the floor when doing desk work for long periods.

391. COMMON TIME WASTERS FOR PRINCIPALS

Time is not only money; it is your life. What wastes your time, wastes your life. The most common time wasters for Principals include:

Procrastination

Waiting (on hold, e.g.)

Understaffing

Socializing

Correcting mistakes

Looking for lost items

Useless meetings

Interruptions

Poor organization

Confusion

Too many goals

Unnecessary paperwork

392. TIME MANAGEMENT TIPS FOR PRINCIPALS

Effective time management is a part of healthy living. The efficiencies and time-saving techniques below have worked for many Principals and can work for you as well:

- Set and enforce deadlines.
- Stress goal setting (for yourself and others).
- Model daily planning. (Have a plan for the day—every day.)
- Simplify paperwork (i.e., form letters, dictation, etc.).
- Attend only meetings where your presence makes a difference.
- Work on the big ticket items first.
- Match effort to the importance of the task.
- Block out time for planning.
- Use your secretary or assistant as a buffer.
- Delegate tasks that others can do better and faster than you can.
- Beat procrastination. Don't put off — "just do it!"

392. TIME MANAGEMENT TIPS FOR PRINCIPALS, CONTINUED

- Don't always have an open door policy. Sometimes, a door ajar policy is good enough.
- Use down time to read, plan, and so on.
- Set a specific time for responding to correspondence and returning calls.
- Make the best use of modern technology (e.g., voice mail, E-mail) to be more efficient.
- Refuse to do other people's work for them or to make their problems your own.
- Reward yourself for completing tough tasks.

393. 4-POINT PAPERWORK TEST

The way to gain control over paperwork is to analyze what's going on, why, and is it worth it? When paperwork piles up, use the following 4-point test to determine how best to handle it:

1. Who has the needed information?

2. Who has time to collect and organize the needed information?

3. Who has the staff to get the job done?

4. Who has the right technology for getting the work done in the prescribed manner, on time, and within budget?

394. 11 WAYS TO TELL IF YOU'RE A WORKAHOLIC

1. Yours is the only car in the school parking lot on Sunday.

2. You take more work home than the English composition teacher.

3. Sometimes, you redo paperwork because you don't have anything else to do.

4. You miss some of your kids' important activities because you "have" to work.

5. You haven't had a vacation in years.

6. You like to come in early and work before others arrive and stay late to work after others have left for the day.

7. You have no social life.

8. You forget your wife's birthday and your anniversary.

9. Your briefcase is worn out; your golf bag looks like new.

10. You know the kids in your school better than you do your own kids.

11. You actually look forward to Mondays.

395. POLITICAL SKILLS FOR PRINCIPALS

Every school and school system is a political entity. Savvy Principals use healthy politics to their advantage by:

- Developing negotiating skills.
- Making concessions when the results are worthwhile.
- Cultivating a variety of mentors.
- Respecting the rumor mill while not feeding it.
- Letting people become indebted to you and calling in markers when necessary.
- Avoiding being linked with factions.
- Concentrating on issues instead of personalities.
- Being bold when the risk is reasonable.
- Practicing heightened awareness. (Know what's going on in order to escape being blind-sided.)
- Practicing amnesty. (Don't hold grudges.)
- Practicing unrelenting honesty and authenticity.
- Refusing to break the rules for anyone.
- Avoiding the perception of favoritism.

396. 8 WAYS TO BOOST YOUR SELF-ESTEEM

1. Hang out with people who like you. They're most likely to give you positive feedback.
2. Review all you've accomplished in the past month/year.
3. Look at your school's most recent yearbook. It will make you proud.
4. Bring your resume up-to-date. It helps to document that you're still a well-qualified professional.
5. Believe it when your spouse and your kids say, "I love you."
6. List all of the people who are better off because of you.
7. Focus on all the things in your life that you feel good about.
8. Count your blessings. Most of us are better off than we think we are.

397. WAYS TO EAT RIGHT AT SCHOOL

School lunches are notoriously heavy on starchy carbohydrates and high-fat items. Teachers and administrators often complain about gaining weight by eating in the school cafeteria. It is possible, however, to eat at school and to eat right. Here's how:

- Bring your own healthy lunch from home.
- If you're tempted by others, eat alone.
- Stick to the soup and salad from the cafeteria line.
- Lobby for a special nutritious menu from your favorite cooks.
- Don't eat the whole lunch. Partial portions should be enough.
- Give away your dessert.
- Take the juice and skip the coffee.
- Stay away from the snack vending machines during the school day.

398. 16 REASONS TO STOP SMOKING

1. Reduce risk of lung cancer, emphysema, and heart disease.
2. Look better, feel better, and smell better.
3. Save money.
4. Reduce fire hazard.
5. Regain sense of taste.
6. Serve as a role model for children and others.
7. Regain energy and stamina.
8. Experience greater acceptance by others.
9. Have sweeter breath.
10. See an end to burn holes.
11. Have brighter teeth.
12. Lower blood pressure.
13. Reduce litter in your life (cleaner environment).
14. Reduce hassle.
15. Stop worrying about your "supply."
16. Have a sense of accomplishment and personal freedom.

399. 6 STEPS TO STOP SMOKING

1. Set a specific date for quitting. Don't equivocate. Don't back off. Don't extend the date.

2. Remove all tobacco products and smoking paraphernalia from your home, office, and car.

3. Spend your time in places that prohibit smoking.

4. Make public announcements of your commitment to quitting.

5. Have a plan for things to do instead of smoking.

6. Form a support group and call for help if you need it.

400. CHECK LIST FOR STOPPING SMOKING

_____ Identify personal reasons for wanting to quit.

_____ Switch to a lower nicotine brand of cigarettes.

_____ Admit your addiction to nicotine.

_____ Plan how to cope with withdrawal symptoms.

_____ Decide whether to use nicotine gum or nicotine patches.

_____ Arrange for a support system after you stop smoking.

_____ Practice frequent deep breathing exercises when you feel the urge to smoke.

_____ Reward yourself once you've stopped.

_____ Monitor and manage your weight after quitting.

_____ Practice other stress reduction techniques instead of smoking.

_____ Make and retain stopping smoking as your number-one priority.

401. SYMPTOMS OF RECOVERING FROM NICOTINE ADDICTION

Quitting smoking brings on a variety of physical and psychological symptoms. Most of these pass within two to four weeks. The most common reactions to smoking cessation include:

Irritability

Fatigue

Insomnia

Cough

Postnasal drip

Dizziness/lightheadedness

Constipation

Gas pains

Hunger

Lack of focus

Craving for nicotine or sweets

Anxiety

Tremors

Headaches

Mood swings

402. ALTERNATIVES TO SMOKING (THINGS TO DO WHEN CRAVING FOR NICOTINE OCCURS)

- Deep breathing. Change routine.
- Eat a low-cal snack.
- Suck on ice cubes.
- Exercise.
- Walk around.
- Drink cold water or juice.
- Get some fresh air.
- Listen to a relaxation tape.
- Practice positive self-talk.
- Chew gum.

402. ALTERNATIVES TO SMOKING (THINGS TO DO WHEN CRAVING FOR NICOTINE OCCURS), CONTINUED

- Suck on a cinnamon stick.
- Play with handgrips, hand toys, or other items.
- Suck on a straw.
- Talk to a fellow recovering smoker.
- Brush teeth.
- Take a shower.

403. QUIT-SMOKING PROGRAMS

There are many places you can go to for help in achieving freedom from smoking. Some of the most popular quit-smoking programs and resources include:

"Freedom from Smoking" (American Lung Association)

"Freshstart" Program (American Heart Association)

Nicotine Anonymous (a 12-step program similar to AA)

"Clearing the Air: A Guide to Quitting Smoking" (publication of the National Cancer Institute)

"Your Next Step" Program (residential cessation program at the Hazelden Clinic in Minnesota)

Mayo Clinic Nicotine Dependence Center, Rochester, MN

404. SIGNS YOU'RE DRINKING TOO MUCH . . . WHAT TO DO ABOUT IT

SIGNS YOU'RE DRINKING TOO MUCH

- Blackouts
- Tremors
- Gulping Drinks
- Drinking Alone
- Thinking About Drinking Frequently During the Day
- Concern over "Supply"
- Distancing Yourself from Nondrinkers
- Loss of Appetite
- Trouble Sleeping—Getting Up to Get a Drink to Go Back to Sleep
- Drinking Mixed Drinks You Don't Even Like
- Drinking Progressively Stronger Drinks (straight shots, boilermakers, etc.)
- Flushed Complexion
- Dislike for Sweets
- Denial—Lying About How Much You Drink
- Drinking Is the Best Part of Your Day
- Worrying About Your Breath Smelling Like Alcohol
- Refusing to Eat at Restaurants That Don't Serve Alcohol
- Needing a Drink to Get Started in the Morning
- Hiding Bottles
- Repeating Behavior Despite Negative Consequences
- Spending More Than You Can Afford on Alcohol
- Friends Tell You You're Drinking Too Much
- Drinking Becomes the Centerpiece of Your Life
- Feeling Drugged—Hard to Wake Up
- Drinking and Driving
- Drinking While Driving
- Open Bottle in the Car
- DWI
- Missing Work Because of Drinking

404. SIGNS YOU'RE DRINKING TOO MUCH . . . WHAT TO DO ABOUT IT, CONTINUED

WHAT TO DO ABOUT IT

- Try to cut down or quit on your own.
- Contact your EAP (Employee Assistance Program) or a counselor.
- Get a professional evaluation.
- Admit you have a problem.
- Go into treatment (inpatient or outpatient).
- Join AA.

405. THE 12 STEPS OF AA

The 12 steps of AA have become world famous. Many claim that these classic steps of recovery can serve as a guide for healthy living for everyone. The 12 steps are:

1. We admitted we were powerless over alcohol—that our lives had become unmanageable.

2. Came to believe that a Power greater than ourselves could restore us to sanity.

3. Made a decision to turn our will and our lives over to the care of God as we understood Him.

4. Made a searching and fearless moral inventory of ourselves.

5. Admitted to God, to ourselves, and to another human being the exact nature of our wrongs.

6. Were entirely ready to have God remove our shortcomings.

7. Humbly asked Him to remove our shortcomings.

8. Made a list of all persons we had harmed and became willing to make amends to them all.

9. Made direct amends to such people wherever possible, except when to do so would injure them or others.

10. Continued to take personal inventory and when we were wrong, promptly admitted it.

11. Sought through prayer and meditation to improve our conscious contact with God as we understood Him, praying only for knowledge of His will for us and the power to carry that out.

12. Having had a spiritual awakening as the result of these Steps, we tried to carry this message to others, and to practice these principles in all our affairs.

406. THE SERENITY PRAYER

This prayer is read or recited at most AA meetings around the world and is often analyzed in group discussions. It can also serve as inspiration to individuals in daily meditation. The prayer simply says:

God grant me
The serenity to accept the things I cannot change,
Courage to change the things I can,
And wisdom to know the difference.

407. 12-STEP AND OTHER SELF-HELP ORGANIZATIONS

You can now find 12-step, self-help groups for almost every known addiction, phobia, loss, or emotional problem. There's a reason for this proliferation of support groups. They work.

Following are the most common 12-step and other self-help organizations available in many parts of the country:

Adoptive Families of America

Adult Children of Sex Addicts

Alcoholics Anonymous (AA)

Al-Anon

Adults Recovering from Incest Anonymous (ARIA)

Bulimics and Anorexics Anonymous

Chronic Pain Outreach

Cocaine Anonymous (Coc-Anon)

Codependents Anonymous

Deaf Adult Children Anonymous

Debtors Anonymous

Emotions Anonymous

Families Anonymous

Gamblers Anonymous (Gam-Anon)

H.E.A.R.T. (Help Enable Alcoholics/Addicts Receive Treatment)

Jewish Recovery Network

Narcotics Anonymous

Obsessive-Compulsive Disorder Anonymous

Open Door (Agoraphobia and Panic Disorder Support)

Overeaters Anonymous

Parents Anonymous

Pills Anonymous

Recoveries Anonymous

Recovering Fundamentalists

Recovery, Inc. (nervous symptoms and fears)

RESOLVE: Infertility Education Support

Self-Abusers Anonymous (SABA)

407. 12-STEP AND OTHER SELF-HELP ORGANIZATIONS, CONTINUED

Sex Addicts Anonymous

Sex and Love Addicts Anonymous

Sexaholics Anonymous

Shoplifters Anonymous

Spenders Anonymous

TOUGHLOVE: Parent Support Groups

12 Steps for Christian Living Groups

12 Steps for Kids (upper elementary-senior high)

Women for Sobriety

Workaholics Anonymous

408. COMMERCIAL WEIGHT-REDUCTION PROGRAMS

Being overweight has become the norm and dieting has become a national pastime. Excess weight poses a serious health threat for many men and women. For those who want to lose pounds, there are a plethora of available commercial weight-loss programs. Some of the most popular include the following:

Weight Watchers

Jenny Craig

Ultra Slimfast

Dexatrim

Nestle's Sweet Success

Permathene 12

Quiletrim-Cybergenics

Easy Trim Diet Patch Program

Stop the Insanity (Susan Powter)

Note: No diet program (commercial or otherwise) should be undertaken without first consulting a qualified physician.

409. SAFE DRIVING TIPS—REDUCING YOUR CHANCES OF AN ACCIDENT

Driving is the most dangerous thing most people ever do. The simple safe driving tips below can help save your life and the lives of others:

- Drive defensively; be aware of the conditions around you and the actions of others.
- Fasten your seat belt—every time you ride or drive.
- Adjust your headrest properly to avoid whiplash.
- Minimize distractions (i.e., car phones, car faxes, radios and stereos, kids, food, pets, reading, and smoking.)
- Be sure everything about your car is in top-notch operating order. Keep up on inspections and maintenance.
- Know your car.
- Don't drink and drive.
- Avoid driving from midnight to 2:00 A.M. Saturday–Sunday. This is the most dangerous driving period.
- Obey speed limits.
- Pay attention to intersections. This is where most collisions occur.
- Be especially careful when passing. Do not pass in tunnels, on bridges, or in school zones.
- Obey railroad crossing signals. Never race a train or drive around gates.
- Know the law and how to recognize hazards.
- Always allow at least two seconds' stopping time between you and the vehicle immediately ahead of you.
- Be alert when driving in construction zones.
- Always pull over for all emergency vehicles.
- Remember that good driving is mostly a matter of attitude. Remain calm. Hold your temper.

410. 5 TIPS ON SKIN PROTECTION

Skin cancer is a serious threat to sun-worshipping Americans. It is a preventable affliction, however. Experts offer the following advice to reduce the risk of killer skin cancer:

1. Protect your skin from the sun year-round.

2. Practice self-examination and get a professional skin exam annually.

3. Use skin moisturizer regularly.

4. Humidify your home.

5. Take shorter baths or showers.

411. TIPS FOR FAMILIES WHERE BOTH SPOUSES WORK

Two-income families have more money, but less time and more stress. A fair division of household tasks can ease tension and avoid arguments. Efficiency experts offer the following advice for assuring domestic tranquillity:

- Hire someone to do as many of your mutually most-hated household tasks as possible.

- Negotiate the remaining disliked jobs.

- Don't alternate jobs. This just generates arguments about whose turn it is.

- Schedule quarterly or semiannual reviews for adjustments and trade-offs.

412. ADVANTAGES OF MALL WALKING (WHY IT MAY BE BETTER THAN GOING TO THE GYM)

Principals often have trouble finding time to get to a gym, club, or spa to work out. Consequently, they never stick to a sustained fitness program. Some Principals, however, have found a workable alternative in Mall Walking. It has these advantages:

- It is free.

- It is safe.

- It is all-season.

- It can be done on your time.

- It takes place in a controlled climate.

- It requires no special clothing or equipment.

- It is easily accessible (as close as your local mall or shopping mart).

- It encourages socializing. (In many places, mall walking is a "team sport.")

- It's fun.

- It is never boring. (There's always something new or exciting going on at the mall.)

413. MALL WALKING ETIQUETTE

If you take up Mall Walking as a form of fitness management, good manners require the following:

- Don't interfere with regular business or other visitors in the mall. Most walkers walk before the stores open (7:00–9:00 A.M.) or during lull periods (e.g., 4:00–9:30 P.M.).
- Use lockers to store coats and belongings.
- Abide by all temporary walking restrictions (i.e., construction zones, wet floors, etc.).
- Use designated parking areas.
- Avoid "dodge-em" walking.
- Keep to the right while walking.
- Always pass on the left.
- Don't turn suddenly.
- Leave room for other mall visitors to get around your walking group.
- Thank mall personnel for their support.
- Patronize supporting merchants.
- Be friendly to all those you meet while walking in the mall.

414. WHY PRINCIPALS NEED CONTINUOUS PROFESSIONAL IMPROVEMENT

Good Principals cannot afford not to keep learning, growing, and developing. The following are six compelling reasons why every Principal must continually pursue professional growth activities:

1. Continued learning shows you what is possible.

2. You can't expect teachers and other staff members to improve skills and knowledge unless you model lifelong learning.

3. Working at continuous renewal is the only way to build vitality for the long haul.

4. Without ongoing growth, you can't develop the organization; you can only maintain it.

5. You can't be innovative and renew the school unless you renew yourself.

6. Continuous growth gives you energy and helps keep you young.

415. PROFESSIONAL GROWTH OPPORTUNITIES FOR PRINCIPALS

Every Principal has easy access to a wide variety of opportunities for professional growth and improvement. There is no excuse for standing still. A partial list of professional development activities for Principals includes:

- Professional reading
- Listening to professional and self-help tapes
- University courses and seminars
- Workshops
- Conferences and conventions
- Sabbatical leaves
- Professional associations and organizations
- Teaching college courses
- Supervising interns (mentoring)
- Visiting schools
- Accessing consultants
- Professional writing
- Networking
- Viewing videotapes
- Watching how others work
- Professional journals and magazines
- Previewing learning materials and new textbooks
- Listening to sales reps
- Keeping up with technology (You can learn a lot from the internet.)

416. PROFESSIONAL ORGANIZATIONS OF INTEREST TO PRINCIPALS

The key professional organizations below can help good Principals get even better:

- American Association of School Administrators (AASA)
- National Association of Elementary School Principals (NAESP)
- National Association of Secondary School Principals (NASSP)
- Association of Supervision and Curriculum Development (ASCD)
- Phi Delta Kappa (PDK)
- National Council of Teachers of English (NCTE)
- American Association of School Librarians (AASL)
- National Council for the Social Studies (NCSS)
- National Council for Teachers of Mathematics (NCTM)
- International Reading Association (IRA)
- National Association for the Education of Young Children (NAEYC)
- Educational Research Service (ERS)
- National Education Association (NEA)
- American Federation of Teachers (AFT)

417. HOW TO JUMP-START A STALLED CAREER

Even Principals can feel burned out, in a rut, and bogged down in routine. It may be a temporary or a long-lasting feeling. Sometimes, the actions below can help get you and your work back on track:

- Take a sabbatical.
- Teach a class for one quarter or a semester.
- Become more active in a professional association.
- Spend time with one of the best, brightest, and most energetic Principals you know.
- Read the "hot" books in your field to see if the authors can get your juices going again.
- Transfer to another school.
- Take a long vacation.
- Turn your routine upside down. Do first things last and vice versa.
- Remember why you became an educator.
- Go back into the classroom full time.
- Switch places with your assistant for a period.
- Take a chance. Try some risky (but promising) innovation in your school.
- Ask the District Office to place you on special assignment for a period to complete a project of interest. Go on a one-person retreat to rediscover your values, priorities, and purpose in life.
- Rewrite your job description the way you'd like it to be and talk it over with your supervisor. Maybe it can become a reality.
- Take another job in the business.
- Walk away and follow your dream.

418. IF I HAD MY LIFE TO LIVE OVER . . .

If I had my life to live over, I'd try to

Make more mistakes;

Be sillier;

Be crazier;

Climb more mountains;

Swim more rivers;

Watch more sunsets;

Eat more ice cream;

418. IF I HAD MY LIFE TO LIVE OVER . . . ,
CONTINUED

Go places and do things;

Travel lighter;

Go barefooted more;

Play hooky more;

Ride more merry-go-rounds;

Pick more daisies.

—Author Unknown

419. WORDS ON WELLNESS (QUOTES)

"Health is better than wealth."—*Proverb*

"If I knew what I was anxious about, I wouldn't be so anxious."—*Mignon McLaughlin*

"I am a study of a man in chaos in search of frenzy."—*Oscar Levant*

"The winner is the one who knows when to drop out in order to get in touch."
—*Marshall McLuhan*

"If I had my way I'd make health catching, instead of disease."—*Robert G. Ingersoll*

"When I feel like exercise, I lie down until the feeling passes."—*Robert M. Hutchins*

"Start slow and taper off."—*Walt Stack*

"They intoxicate themselves with work so they won't see how they really are."
—*Aldous Huxley*

"To avoid sickness, eat less; to prolong life, worry less."—*Chu Hui Weng*

"Exercise is bunk. If you are healthy, you don't need it; if you are sick, you shouldn't
take it."—*Henry Ford*

"Exercise and temperance can preserve something of our early strength even in old
age."—*Cicero*

"Diet away your stress, tension, and anxiety. . ."—*Dr. J. Daniel Palm*

"The preservation of health is a duty."—*Hubert Spencer*

Section Eleven

MISCELLANY

420. GOALS 2000: EDUCATE AMERICA ACT

On March 31, 1994, President Clinton signed the <u>Goals 2000: Educate America Act</u>. For the first time in history, this act established a national mission statement for America's schools. The eight national goals in the act are to be achieved by the year 2000:

1. All children in America will start school ready to learn.

2. The high school graduation rate will increase to at least 90 percent.

3. All students will leave grades 4, 8, and 12 having demonstrated competency over challenging subject matter . . . and all students will be prepared for responsible citizenship, further learning, and productive employment. . . .

4. The nation's teaching force will have access to programs for the continued improvement of their professional skills. . . .

5. United States students will be the first in the world in mathematics and science achievement.

6. Every adult American will be literate.

7. Every school in America will be free of drugs and violence and will offer a disciplined environment conducive to learning.

8. Every school and home will engage in partnerships that will increase parental involvement and participation in promoting the social, emotional, and academic growth of children.

421. 4 THINGS ALL GOOD SCHOOLS HAVE TO DO

1. Agree on and teach a core of math, science, and language, and then measure results.

2. Create a sense of community, stressing discipline and caring for children, while reaching out to parents and local businesses.

3. Provide health, counseling, and other services for children, and find a way to provide resources such as books, maps, computers, and phone lines.

4. Teach children about ethics along with academics.

Source: Report from the Carnegie Foundation for the Advancement of Teaching and Learning, Princeton, NJ, 1995.

422. HELP FOR FAMILY LITERACY PROBLEMS

There is help for families in which there are members with literacy problems. The following organizations and agencies offer funding, volunteers, tutors, publications, videotapes, and other forms of assistance to combat adult illiteracy:

National Council for Family Literacy
Waterfront Plaza, Suite 200
325 West Main St.
Louisville, KY 40202-4251

Project Literacy U.S. (PLUS)
Box 2
4802 Fifth Ave.
Pittsburgh, PA 15213

Literacy Volunteers of America
5795 Widewaters Parkway
Syracuse, NY 13214

Barbara Bush Foundation for Family Literacy
1002 Wisconsin Ave. N.W.
Washington, DC 20007

National Clearinghouse on Literacy Education
1118 22nd St. N.W.
Washington, DC 20037

423. CELEBRITY DEATHS DUE TO ALLEGED DRUG OVERDOSE

Children and teenagers feel invincible. Sometimes, it helps for them to learn about real-world examples of the deadly consequences of drug abuse, which has killed the following celebrities:

John Belushi	—	comedian
John Bonham	—	"Led Zeppelin" musician
Lenny Bruce	—	comedian
Kurt Cobain	—	rock star
Brian Epstein	—	"Beatles" manager
Judy Garland	—	actress
Andy Gibb	—	singer
Jim Hendrix	—	rock star
Billie Holiday	—	singer
Janis Joplin	—	singer
Marilyn Monroe	—	actress
Elvis Presley	—	rock star
Sid Vicious	—	"Sex Pistols" musician
Dennis Wilson	—	"Beach Boys" musician

Source: The Social Studies Teacher's Book of Lists (Parlin), Prentice Hall, 1992.

424. RELIGIOUS HOLY DAYS OF DIFFERENT FAITHS

Awareness of the holy days and festivals of various faiths strengthens understanding and sensitivity to religious and ethnic diversity. Principals concerned with promoting multicultural experiences may find the list below a useful tool. The list is not exhaustive, but it does include both large and small religious communities. Exact dates may vary in different years:

SEPTEMBER

—Prophet Mohammed Birthday (Islamic)

—Rosh Hashanah (Jewish New Year)

—San Gennaro Day (Roman Catholic)

—Higan—First Day of Fall (Buddhist)

—Yom Kippur (Jewish)

OCTOBER

—Simchat Torah (Jewish)

—Dusseiah—Good over Evil (Hindu)

—Diwali—Festival of Lights (Hindu)

—Reformation Day (Protestant)

—Sukkot (Jewish)

NOVEMBER

—Guru Nanak Birthday (Sikh)

—First Sunday of Advent (Christian)

DECEMBER

—St. Nicholas Day (Christian)

—Bodhi Day—Enlightenment (Buddhist)

—Feast of Immaculate Conception (Roman Catholic)

—Hanukkah (Jewish Feast of Lights)

—Christmas (Christian)

424. RELIGIOUS HOLY DAYS OF DIFFERENT FAITHS, CONTINUED

JANUARY

—Feast of Basil (Eastern Orthodox Christian)

—Epiphany (Christian)

FEBRUARY

—Ramadan (Islamic)

—Death of Buddha (Buddhist)

—Ash Wednesday (Christian)

—Purim (Jewish)

MARCH

—St. Patrick's Day (Christian)

—Annunciation (Christian)

—Palm Sunday (Christian)

APRIL

—Good Friday (Christian)

—Easter (Christian — occasionally late March)

—Birth of Buddha (Buddhist)

—Baisakhi—Brotherhood (Sikh)

—Birth of Rama (Hindu)

—Palm Sunday (Eastern Orthodox Christian)

—Holy Friday (Eastern Orthodox Christian)

MAY

—Easter (Eastern Orthodox Christian)

—Ascension Day (Christian)

—Pentecost (Christian)

424. RELIGIOUS HOLY DAYS OF DIFFERENT FAITHS, CONTINUED

JUNE

—Pentecost (Eastern Orthodox Christian)
—Nativity of St. John the Baptist (Christian)

JULY

—Obon-e—Memorial Day (Buddhist)
—Pioneer Day (Mormon)

AUGUST

—Rakhi—Brotherhood/Sisterhood (Hindu)
—Transfiguration (Christian)
—Feast of the Blessed Virgin Mary (Roman Catholic, Eastern Orthodox Christian)

425. THE TAXPAYERS' BILL OF RIGHTS

In response to taxpayer complaints about unfair treatment, the United States Congress has passed into law the "Taxpayer Bill of Rights." Some of the rights include:

- Right to plain English statements
- Right to record audit conferences
- Right to know the specific basis for IRS decisions
- Right to installment payment of taxes
- Right to hardship relief
- Right to seek new audit locations
- Right to sue the IRS for damages

Source: *World Almanac*, 1992

426. FAMOUS PEOPLE WHO HAD LEARNING DISABILITIES OR DIFFICULTY IN SCHOOL

Hans Christian Anderson

Cher

Winston Churchill

Tom Cruise

Leonardo da Vinci

Walt Disney

Thomas Edison

Albert Einstein

Isaac Newton

Carl Sandburg

Albert Schweitzer

Woodrow Wilson

427. U. S. SECRETARIES OF EDUCATION 1979–1993

Secretary	Appointed
Shirley Hufstedler	1979
Terrell Bell	1981
William J. Bennett	1985
Lauro F. Cavazos	1988
Lamar Alexander	1991
Richard W. Riley	1993

428. TECHNOLOGY IN PUBLIC SCHOOLS, 1992-1994

Technology	% of Public Schools		
	1992	1993	1994
Schools with interactive videodisc players	8	14	21
Schools with modems	16	22	27
Schools with networks	5	14	21
Schools with CD-ROMS	7	13	25
Schools with Cable TV	0	57	69

World Almanac, 1995

429. IF YOU CAN'T SAY SOMETHING NICE . . .
(EUPHEMISMS FOR PRINCIPALS)

Honesty is always a good policy, but sometimes the whole truth or the blunt truth is not well received. In the interest of tact, Principals may want to use one of the euphemisms below in communicating with parents:

The Real Truth	*The Euphemism*
Your child . . .	Your child . . .
lies.	has difficulty distinguishing between fact and imagined material.
is a klutz.	has difficulty with motor skills and coordination.
fights.	uses physical means to get attention or make a point.
smells.	needs guidance in forming habits of good hygiene.
cheats.	needs to learn how to follow rules and ethical standards of fair play.
steals.	needs to learn to respect other people's property rights.
is lazy.	requires ongoing supervision to complete tasks.
is rude.	lacks an attitude of respect.
is gross.	needs guidance in developing appropriate social graces.
has a big mouth.	needs to develop quieter habits of communication.
bullies.	has leadership qualities, but needs to use them more constructively.
eats like a pig.	needs to develop more refined table manners.
acts like a baby.	lacks maturity in behavior and relationships.
is disliked.	needs help in developing positive peer relationships.
is often late.	needs to develop a better appreciation of time and habits of punctuality.
skips out.	needs to develop a greater sense of responsibility about regular attendance.

Source: Adapted from material in *The Reading Teacher's Book of Lists* (Fry, Kress, and Fountoukidis), Prentice Hall, 1993.

430. FINAL WORDS (QUOTES)

"The object of education is to prepare the young to educate themselves throughout their lives."—*Robert Maynard Hutchins*

"Education is what survives when what has been learnt has been forgotten."
—*B. F. Skinner*

"Try to be newer every day."—*Anon.*

"Just when you see light at the end of the tunnel, someone adds more tunnel."
—*Dr. Jim Benson*

"You never graduate from the school of life."—*David McNally*

"The secret of education is respecting the pupil."—*Ralph Waldo Emerson*

"Leadership is action, not position."—*Donald H. McGannon*

"Trying to find happiness and progress through computers and technological advancement is like trying to find butter by churning sand."—*Kumar*

"Change is the currency of leadership."—*Anon.*

"Failure is an event—not a person."—*Zig Ziglar*

"You can't make an omelette without breaking eggs."—*Proverb*

"What you live, you learn.
   What you learn, you practice.
   What you practice, you become.
   What you become has consequences."—*Earnie Larsen*

"Headmasters (Principals) have powers at their disposal with which Prime Ministers have never yet been invested."—*Winston Churchill*

431. THE LAST LIST (TOP 10 REASONS FOR
BECOMING A SCHOOL PRINCIPAL)

1. KIDS!!

2. Chance to shape tomorrow today.

3. Never grow old being around young people.

4. Name appears prominently in print (graffiti).

5. Get to keep teachers after school.

6. Neat office where you can read magazines and take naps.

7. Free tickets to games and plays.

8. Hot lunch every day.

9. Choice of parking spots.

10. Lots of cool keys.